BABY'S DAY OUT

IN

SOUTHERN CALIFORNIA:

FUN PLACES TO GO WITH BABIES AND TODDLERS

by
JoBea Holt

For Parents, Care Givers and Day Care/Nursery School Teachers

Gem Guides Book Co.

315 Cloverleaf Drive, Suite F
Baldwin Park, CA 91706

Published in the United States of America
Library of Congress Control Number: 2006928254
ISBN 10: 1-889786-36-5
ISBN 13: 978-1-889786-36-0

Cover design: Scott Roberts
Cover images from BigStockPhoto.com:
    Pumpkin Playground © Lisa Turay
    Vintage Baby Shoes © Anne Kitzman
    Father and Son © Glaina Barskaya
    Spring Baby © Edyta Linek
    Cute Tots on Beach © Cornelia Schaible
Cover image of tots holding hands, courtesy of Phyllis Fox

ACKNOWLEDGMENTS

This book is dedicated to Annie and Sammy

I would like to thank the many people who had ideas and came with me on these great adventures: the adults-my husband Ben; my sister Betsy Way; and my friends Susan Woolley, JoLynn Pollard, Adriana Lim, Leigh Chavez, Terry Meng, Peter Dreier, and Jean Pfaffinger; and the children-including: Annie, Sammy, Emily, MacKay, Michael, Brandon, Olivia, Sarah, Amelia, Ryan, Aiden, Kathaleen, Emily, Megan and Gwyn. I would like to thank those who encouraged me-my parents, Howard and Sally Way; my husband's parents, Ben and Virgina Holt; my friends, Bruce Murkoff, Suzanne Caporael, and Judy McCleese; my step-daughter, Janet Holt; the director of my favorite nursery school, Beverly Slocum; and those who reviewed early versions - Vickie Knight, Vita Simonian, and Jenina Quezada. For this second edition, I would like to thank those who made an extra effort to promote this book: Jenina Quezada, Jane Pipich, Suzanne Caporael, Jean Pfaffinger, Beverly Slocum, and Vroman's Bookstore. Finally, I would like to express my great appreciation to my publisher, Gem Guides Book Co., especially Kathy Mayerski, Janet Francisco, Ester Avetisian (currently www.paintedillusions.us), Michael Moran, Alfred Mayerski and Nancy Fox.

TABLE OF CONTENTS

INTRODUCTION

After twenty-five years of being immersed in the university and NASA communities, I found myself with two babies alone in a house with no idea what to do. I had been to Disneyland and a few museums as a childless adult, but where could I take my babies? Without knowing any better, we went to an IMAX movie about whales when my babies were six months old. We were all captivated. We wandered over to the Natural History Museum and discovered dioramas of elephants, musk ox and, my son's favorite, the kudu. We wandered into the museum's Discovery Center, found a corner full of shells and animal skins, and my babies proceeded to discover these things while I discovered how quickly I could wipe the spit-up off the carpet. It was a great day.

Soon I found a few friends who had discovered places for babies, including Green Meadows Farm and a particularly baby-friendly beach. I found myself breaking into conversations in the park to find out where other moms had been. My husband drove the babies by a school bus yard he had noticed on his way to work, and they loved all the yellow buses lined up just like in Donald Crew's book, *Buses*. My husband drove by over and over again. Now I tell everyone with a baby that the school bus yard is a must. Our resumé of adventures grew: while most of them were good, some were failures. These were the beginnings of this book. It turns out that it is wonderful to be a baby, and a new mom and dad, in Southern California.

Venturing out with young children not only makes a parent's quality of life better, but also may have a long-term benefit for your child. According to a report from the Carnegie Corporation of New York (2000), "children's early experiences affect not only the quality of their present lives, but also their later ability to learn and reason." Many recent articles on the development of children's brains emphasize the importance of early childhood experiences (e.g., Barbara Kantrowitz, *21st Century Babies, Newsweek* Special 2000 Edition, Fall/Winter, 2000, page 4-7). An article in the February 1996 issue of *Newsweek* states, "It is the experiences of childhood, determining which neurons are used, that wire the circuits of the brain as surely as a programmer at a keyboard reconfigures the circuits in a computer. Which keys are typed-which experiences a child has-determines whether the child grows up to be intelligent or dull, fearful or self-assured, articulate or tongue-tied. Early experiences are so powerful, says pediatric neurologist Harry Chugani of Wayne State University, that 'they can completely change the way a person turns out.'"

Baby's Day Out in Southern California is a travel guide for parents with babies or toddlers (six months to six years). The purposes of the book are to encourage parents to take their babies and toddlers to museums and public places around town, and to provide information about where to go in an easily accessible and simple format.

Baby's Day Out in Southern California describes more than two hundred places that are appropriate for babies and toddlers. Major categories include museums, our city, gardens and nature, zoos, aquariums, farms and ponies, water, flying, amusement, trains, and entertainment. Information on the location, hours, cost, web site, accommodations, other nearby places and related adventures are included. Within each chapter is a photograph of something a baby or toddler might recognize so that your toddler can be involved in selecting a destination. Throughout the book are "Picture Guides" for toddlers that include, in picture format, the kinds of things children will find at various locations, such as tide pool creatures, fire truck types, and pet store animals. At the end is a monthly calendar of events with things to look for each season (tadpoles, tulips, the peacock mating season, etc.).

The focus of the book is Los Angeles County, since I live in Pasadena and know the most about this area, and Orange County. There are also a few places in San Diego and Santa Barbara counties in case you are visiting the area. In addition, there are a few miscellaneous far away places, like the Temecula Balloon and Wine Festival and the Oak Glen Apple Farms, which are too good to pass up.

As you wander through these places, talk about not only the sights, but the sounds, smells, and feel of these places. Touch the tree bark on a nature walk or the sea hares in the tide pools. Smell the flamingos at the zoo and the peaches at the farmer's market. Listen to the birds at the beach and the trains at Union Station. These actions will help your child become a good observer of the world we live in.

As your children get older, there are many wonderful children's travel guides for Los Angeles and Southern California-these are listed at the end of this book. Some places that are not included here may be great for babies and toddlers-I would be happy to hear about places that I have missed.

Words of Advice
As you begin your adventures, here are a few words of advice:

1. Call ahead-hours and prices may change.
2. Have a map handy-preferably a *Thomas Guide*.
3. Be prepared for traffic delays (i.e. bring snacks and car toys).
4. Make sure you have plenty of time to enjoy your visit.
5. If you feel uncomfortable visiting a particular location alone with your child, wait until a friend or other parent can go with you.
6. If it turns out it is a bad day for your child, go home and try again another day.

BOOK FORMAT

Within each chapter is a picture of something that may remind your baby or toddler of a place. Allow your baby or toddler to look at these pictures and help choose a destination. You might consider identifying several possible places in advance and asking your child to choose one from this subset rather that offering the entire book of options.

ACCOMMODATIONS

Important accommodations to consider when visiting with a baby or toddler are included. I had twins so accommodations for a wide double stroller were particularly important. A playground to shake out the wiggles will often allow you to keep going a little longer. Gift shops are usually part of each establishment but remember to consider whether you want your toddler to know what a gift shop is!

Accommodations Key:

Stroller Access

Double-wide Strollers

Playground

Gift Shop

Snack Bar

Picnic Area

Pier

Tide Pools

ADDRESS

Included are the address, phone number (beware of constantly changing area codes), and website.

DIRECTIONS [GUIDE PAGE]

Directions are included from the nearest freeway. Also included in brackets is the guide page in *The Thomas Guide* (*Thomas Bros. California Road Atlas and Driver's Guide*).

LA	Los Angeles County
OC	Orange County
SB/V	Santa Barbara County and San Luis Obispo/Ventura Counties
SD	San Diego County
SB/R	San Bernardino/Riverside Counties

Thomas Guides are an excellent tool and are available in most bookstores. From printing to printing, the page numbers remain the same for each section of the city (thus the pages are not always consecutive).

Directions to return to your original destination may be different than those by which you arrived. Be sure to ask for directions back to the freeway, if it is not obvious.

GOOD THINGS TO SEE AND HEAR

This section includes comments on the best things to focus on for babies and toddlers at each location. Also included are comments that may make your visit easier and more enjoyable with your young child.

HOURS

Included are the hours of operation. If hours for summer and winter are different, both are included. Hours often change, and dates that summer and winter hours begin vary greatly so call in advance if there is a question. Also, note that many locations are closed for holidays, and others have extended hours for holidays. As Yogi Berra once said, "Nobody comes here anymore because it's too crowded." Try to avoid weekends and mid-mornings when school and summer field trips bring lots of children.

PARKING

Parking fees are noted. There are often options for free parking nearby. However, consider that the close parking lots are often safer and easier when toting babies or toddlers.

ADMISSION

Admission prices are included but often change from year to year. Children under the age of two or three are usually free. Many places also offer reduced admission prices for seniors and students, and some places have free days, however, these days are usually very crowded. You may also get a price break with AAA.

YEARLY MEMBERSHIP

For places that you really like (the zoo, your favorite museum, etc.) a yearly membership really pays. Also, with a membership, it is easier to justify a short visit, and easier to just go home and try again another day if you get there and your baby or toddler is having a bad day. You usually get a newsletter to keep you up-to-date on special events. Remember that babies and toddlers love repetition, so many repeat visits often make each trip better than the last. Family membership usually means two adults and children.

RELATED PLACES

If your baby or toddler really likes a place, here are some suggestions for other related places they might also like.

CLOSE-BY PLACES

For some areas it is easy to visit several places in one trip (like the Griffith Park Pony Rides and Train Ride). Also, you might want to drive by a close-by place when your baby or toddler falls asleep in the car to check it out for a potential future trip. Babies and toddlers are often happier with shorter more focused, unhurried visits. So don't try to see too many things in one outing.

BOOKS FOR YOUR CHILD

In many sections, either at the beginning of the section or for a specific site, books that relate to a place or a set of places are listed. These are also included in the "Library" section of Chapter 2 - Our City. Here are a few for the road:

- Crews, Donald-*Truck*
- Dorling Kindersley Publishing Co.-*What's Inside? Trucks*
- Fanelli, Sara-*My Map Book*
- Harrison, David L.-*Let's Go, Trucks!*

SPECIAL EVENTS

Many sites have special events that happen annually. These are included with each site and again in Chapter 12.

YOUR COMMENTS

This is a blank space for you and your child to add comments or to paste in your ticket stub or a photo.

PICTURE GUIDES

Picture Guides are included throughout the book. These guides are for your child's use. Show them to your child to help identify things you find at each location. Picture Guides will help your child learn to organize things into categories and may encourage collecting. Perhaps your child will want to color the pictures. The first Picture Guides are for vehicles found on the road to your destinations.

FIND SOMETHING NEW OR AN ERROR?

The number of places for young children to explore is increasing every year as more museums and parks set up interactive exhibits for young children. As you find new locations, or if you have opinions-good or bad-about the locations in this book, please write to me (see page 335). Your thoughts will be incorporated into future versions of this book.

CARS ON THE ROAD

LIMOUSINE   TAXI

POLICE CAR

MOTORCYCLE   CAMPER

TRUCKS ON THE ROAD

TRUCK   TANKER TRUCK

SCHOOL BUS

TOW TRUCK   CEMENT MIXER

Nursery School Outings

Many of the locations in this book make wonderful outings for Mommy and Me, Nursery School or Pre-school classes. The ones that are almost guaranteed are:

- Tide Pools
- Children's Nature Walks
- Your Local Nature Center
- Your Local Garden (Descanso or South Coast Botanical Gardens, etc.)
- Underwood Family Farms
- Santa Anita Race Track Morning Workout
- A Library Story Hour
- A Metrolink Train Ride

Safety Tips

1. Always use car seats. They let children see out the window better!

2. Always watch the road no matter how loud your child screams.

3. Plan your trip in advance and call ahead.

4. Take your cell phone.

5. Lock your car doors.

6. Bring a friend or another parent if you feel uncomfortable going to a certain location alone.

7. Restrain your child when visiting a dangerous location like the train station.

8. Avoid rush hour when possible.

9. Have water, snacks, and books handy to pass to the back seat.

10. Write your cell phone number on your child's arm with indelible ink.

11. Always wear sun block.

OUR FAVORITE PLACES

These are the places my family and I like the best.

MUSEUMS - CHAPTER 1
• Natural History Museum of Los Angeles County - Site 1
• Children's Museum at La Habra - Site 2
• Kidspace Museum - Site 4
• Petersen Automotive Museum - Site 5
• Discovery Science Center - Site 7
• Boone Children's Gallery, LACMA - Site 8

OUR CITY - CHAPTER 2
• Construction and Road Work Sites
• Your Local Library
• School Buses/Pasadena Unified School District - Site 19

GARDENS AND NATURE - CHAPTER 3
• Los Angeles County Arboretum and Botanical Garden - Site 37
• The Huntington - Site 39
• Children's Nature Institute - Site 43
• Eaton Canyon County Park and Nature Center - Site 44

THE ZOO -- CHAPTER 4
• Los Angeles Zoo - Site 63
• San Diego Wild Animal Park - Site 69
• Santa Ana Zoo - Site 64
• Santa Barbara Zoological Gardens - Site 70

AQUARIUMS - CHAPTER 5
• Long Beach Aquarium of the Pacific - Site 71
• Cabrillo Marine Aquarium - Site 72
• Little Corona Del Mar Tide Pools - Site 76
• Sea World - Site 87
• Birch Aquarium at Scripps - Site 88

OUR FAVORITE PLACES (CONTINUED)

FARMS AND PONIES - CHAPTER 6
- Green Meadows - Sites 90-91
- Santa Anita Race Track Morning Workout - Site 92
- Oak Glen Apple Farms - Site 93
- Underwood Family Farms - Site 99
- The Fair - Sites 106-111

AMUSEMENT - CHAPTER 7
- Adventure City - Site 113
- Legoland - Site 114
- Merry-Go-Rounds-Sites 115-123

WATER - CHAPTER 8
- Santa Catalina Island - Sites 126-131
- Snow in the Angeles Crest Forest - Site 133
- Manhattan Beach - Site 141

FLYING - CHAPTER 9
- Bob Hope Airport - Site 148
- Goodyear Blimp Airfield - Site 168
- Temecula Valley Balloon and Wine Festival - Site 169

TRAINS - CHAPTER 10
- Travel Town Museum - Site 170
- Union Station - Site 171
- Metrolink Regional Rail Trains - Site 194
- Griffith Park Train Ride - Site 198
- San Diego Model Railroad Museum - Site 202

ENTERTAINMENT - CHAPTER 11
- Bob Baker Marionette Theater - Site 204
- IMAX Theater at the California Science Center - Site 208
- Tournament of Roses® Parade - Site 216
- Ringling Bros. and Barnum & Bailey Circus - Site 217

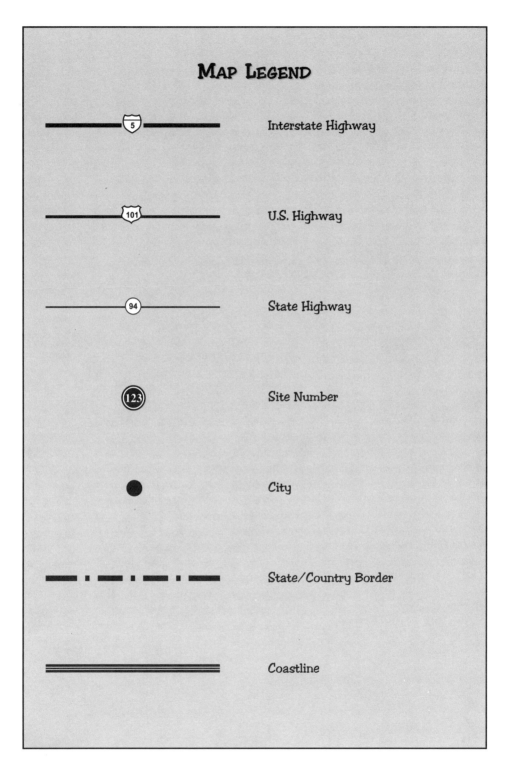

MAP LEGEND

Interstate Highway

U.S. Highway

State Highway

Site Number

City

State/Country Border

Coastline

SITE MAP ONE - LOS ANGELES COUNTY

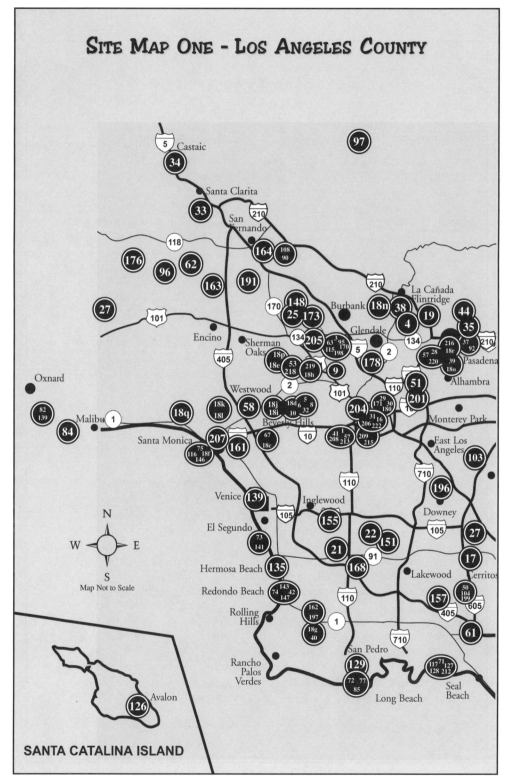

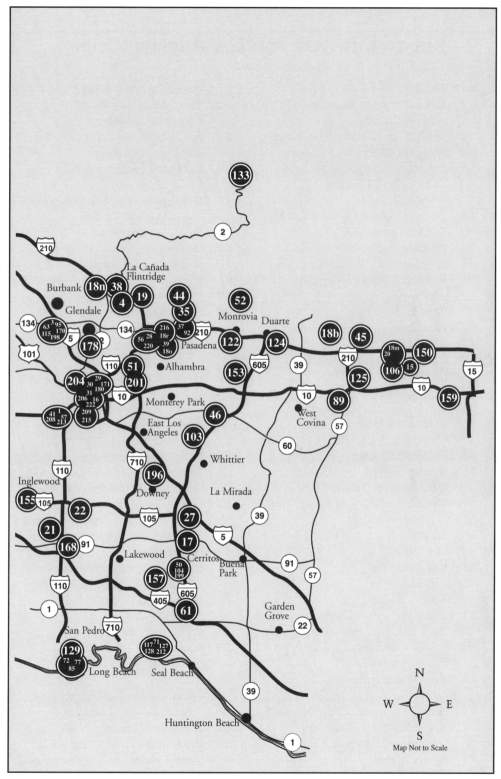

KEY TO SITE MAP FOR LOS ANGELES COUNTY

Site # Name

1 Natural History Museum of LA County
3 Museum of the American West
4 Kidspace Children's Museum
5 Petersen Automotive Museum
6 La Brea Tar Pits and Page Museum
8 Boone Children's Gallery-LACMA
9 Griffith Observatory
10 Zimmer Children's Museum
15 Raymond M. Alf Museum
16 Richard J. Riordan Central Library
17 Cerritos Library
18b Blue Chair Children's Books
18c Bookstar - Culver City
18d Bookstar - Los Angeles
18e Bookstar - Studio City
18f Bright Child
18g Catch Our Rainbow Books
18h Chevalier's Books
18i Children's Book World
18j Dutton's Beverly Hills Books
18k Dutton's Brentwood Bookstore
18l Every Picture Tells a Story
18m Mrs. Nelson's Toy & Book Shop
18n Once Upon a Time
18o San Marino Toy and Book Shoppe
18p Storyopolis
18q Village Books
18r Vroman's
19 School Buses/Pasadena Unified School District
20 Bonita Unified School Bus Yard
21 L.A. Unified School District Lot in Gardena
22 Carson and Rosewood School Bus Yard
25 North Hollywood School Bus Yard
27 Norwalk School Bus Yard
28 Doggie Day Camp at PETsMART
29 Olvera Street
30 Chinatown

31 Grand Central Market
32 The Original Los Angeles Farmer's Market
33 Sunshine Canyon Landfill
34 Big Rigs at Castaic
35 Pasadena Cruisin' Weekly Car Show
37 Los Angeles County Arboretum and Botanic Gardens
38 Descanso Gardens
39 The Huntington
40 South Coast Botanical Gardens
41 Exposition Park Rose Garden
42 Hopkins Wilderness Park
44 Eaton Canyon County Park and Nature Center
45 San Dimas Canyon Park and Nature Center
46 Whittier Narrows Nature Center
50 El Dorado East Regional Park and Nature Center
51 Audubon Center at Debs Park
52 Wilderness Park and Nature Center
53 Sooky Goldman Nature Center
56 California Institute of Technology
57 University of Southern California
58 University of CA, Los Angeles
61 Cal State University Long Beach
62 Cal State University Northridge
63 Los Angeles Zoo
67 STAR EcoStation Environmental Science and Wildlife Rescue Center
71 Long Beach Aquarium of the Pacific
72 Cabrillo Marine Aquarium
73 Roundhouse Marine Studies Lab and Aquarium
74 Sea Lab
75 Santa Monica Pier Aquarium
77 Cabrillo Beach Tide Pools
82 Leo Carrillo State Beach Tide Pools
84 Point Dume Beach Tide Pools
85 Marine Mammal Care Center at Fort MacArthur

Site #	Name
90	Green Meadows Farm/LA County
92	Santa Anita Race Track Morning Workout
95	Griffith Park Pony Rides
96	The Farm
97	Armours Orchard
103	Montebello Barnyard Zoo
104	Lakewood Pony Rides and Petting Farm
106	Los Angeles County Fair
108	San Fernando Valley Fair
115	Griffith Park Merry-Go-Round
116	Santa Monica Carousel
117	Shoreline Village Carousel
122	Westfield Santa Anita Fashion Park Carousel
124	Water Play Area/Santa Fe Dam Recreation Area
125	Puddingstone Reservoir Beach
126	Santa Catalina Island
127	Catalina Terminal/ Long Beach-Downtown
128	Catalina Terminal/ Long Beach-Queen Mary
129	Catalina Terminal/ San Pedro-Port of Los Angeles
133	Snow in the Angeles National Forest
135	Hermosa Beach
139	Leo Carrillo State Beach
141	Manhattan Beach
143	Redondo Beach
146	Santa Monica State Beach
147	Seaside Lagoon
148	Bob Hope Airport
149	Brackett Air Field
150	Cable Airport
151	Compton Airport
153	El Monte Airport
155	Hawthorne Municipal Airport/ Jack Northrop Field
157	Long Beach Airport
159	Ontario Airport
161	Santa Monica Municipal Airport
162	Torrance Municipal Airport/ Zamperini Field
163	Van Nuys Airport
164	Whiteman Airport
168	Goodyear Blimp Airfield
170	Travel Town Museum
171	Union Station
173	Burbank Train Station
176	Chatsworth Train Station
178	Glendale Train Station
180	Los Angeles/Union Station
191	Van Nuys Train Station
193	Amtrak Trains
196	Freight Trains
197	Lomita Railroad Museum
198	Griffith Park Train Ride
199	El Dorado East Regional Park Train Ride
201	Pasadena Model Railroad Club
204	Bob Baker Marionette Theater
205	Falcon Theater
206	KLOS Story Theater
207	Santa Monica Puppetry Center
208	IMAX Theater at the California Science Center
209	Los Angeles Convention Center
212	Long Beach Convention Center
213	Los Angeles Memorial Sports Arena
215	Staples Center
216	Tournament of Roses Parade®
218	Faery Hunt
219	Summer Sounds at the Hollywood Bowl
220	Musical Circus Pasadena Symphony
222	Walt Disney Music Concert Hall Toyota Symphonies for Youth

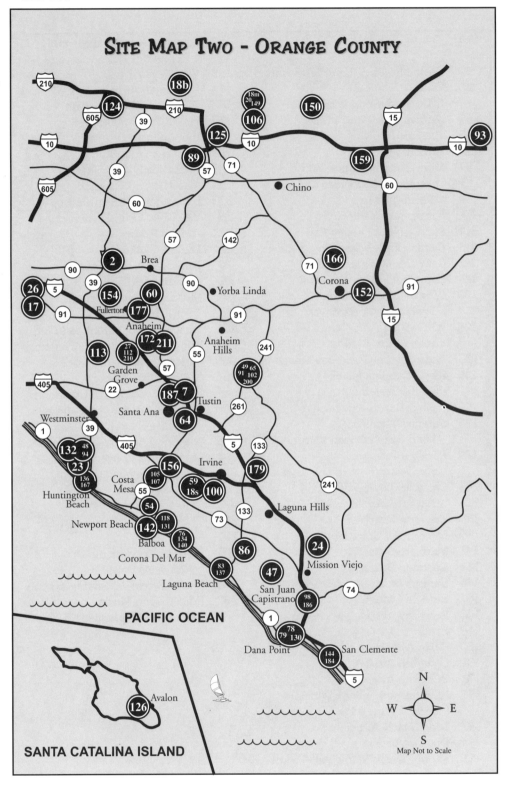

SITE MAP TWO - ORANGE COUNTY

KEY TO SITE MAP FOR ORANGE COUNTY

Site # Name

Site #	Name
2	Children's Museum at La Habra
7	Discovery Science Center
17	Cerritos Library
18m	Mrs. Nelson's Toy & Book Shop
18s	Whale of a Tale Bookstore
20	Bonita Unified School District
23	Huntington Beach School Bus Yard
24	Mission Viejo School Bus Yard
26	Norwalk School Bus Yard
27	Anaheim Union High School District Bus Yard
47	Aliso & Wood Canyons Wilderness Park and Orange County Natural History Museum
48	Shipley Nature Center at Huntington Central Park
49	Irvine Regional Park and Nature Center
54	ENC Native Butterfly House
59	University of California Irvine
60	California State University Fullerton
64	Santa Ana Zoo
65	Orange County Zoo
76	Little Corona Del Mar Tide Pools
78	Dana Point Tide Pools
79	Doheny State Beach Tide Pools
80	Diver's Cove Tide Pools/ North of Laguna Main Beach
83	Laguna Beach's Heisler Beach
86	PacificMarine Mammal Center & Laguna Koi Ponds
91	Green Meadows Farm/ Orange County
93	Oak Glen Apple Farms
94	Huntington Central Park Equestrian Center
98	Zoomars Petting Farm
100	Tanaka Farms
102	Irvine Regional Park Pony Rides
105	Centennial Farm
106	Los Angeles County Fair
107	Orange County Fair
112	Disneyland
113	Adventure City
118	Balboa Pavilion Carousel
124	Water Play Area/Santa Fe Dam Recreation Area
125	Puddingstone Reservoir Beach
126	Santa Catalina Island
130	Catalina Terminal/Dana Point
131	Catalina Terminal/Newport Beach
132	Bolsa Chica Ecological Reserve
134	Corona Del Mar State Beach
136	Huntington State Beach and Huntington City Beach
137	Laguna Main Beach
140	Little Corona Del Mar Beach
142	Newport Beach
144	San Clemente Beach
149	Bracket Air Field
150	Cable Airport
152	Corona Municipal Airport
154	Fullerton Municipal Airport
156	John Wayne Airport
159	Ontario International Airport
166	Chino Planes of Fame Air Museum
167	Kite Flying at the Beach
172	Anaheim Train Station
177	Fullerton Train Station
179	Irvine Train Station
184	San Clemente Train Station
186	San Juan Capistrano Train Station
187	Santa Ana Train Station
200	Irvine Park Railroad
210	Anaheim Convention Center
211	Arrowhead Pond of Anaheim

SITE MAP THREE - SAN DIEGO COUNTY

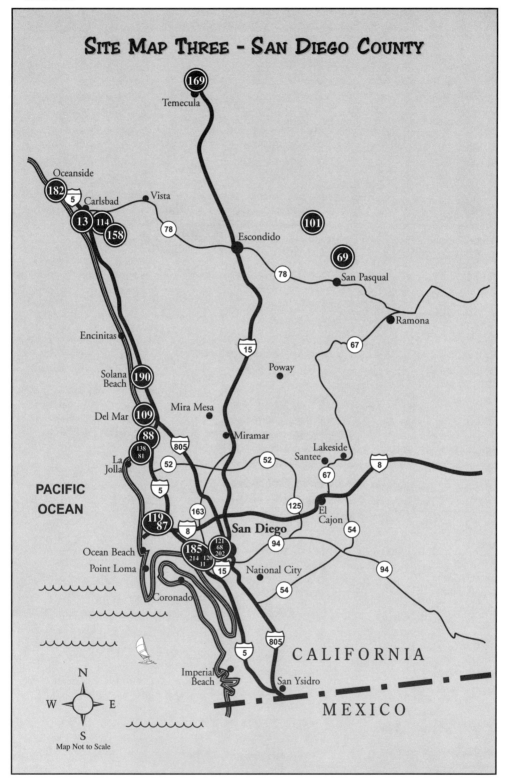

KEY TO SITE MAP FOR SAN DIEGO COUNTY

Site # Name

Site #	Name
12	The Children's Museum of San Diego/Museo de los Niños
13	Children's Discovery Museum of North County
68	San Diego Zoo
69	San Diego Wild Animal Park
81	La Jolla Shores Tide Pools
87	Sea World
88	Birch Aquarium at Scripps
101	Bates Nut Farm
109	Del Mar Fair
114	Legoland
119	Belmont Park Carousel
120	Seaport Village Carousel
121	Balboa Park Merry-Go-Round and Butterfly Rides
138	La Jolla Shores
158	McClellan-Palomar Airport
169	Temecula Valley Balloon and Wine Festival
182	Oceanside Train Station
185	San Diego Train Station
190	Solana Beach Train Station
202	San Diego Model Railroad Museum
214	San Diego Convention Center

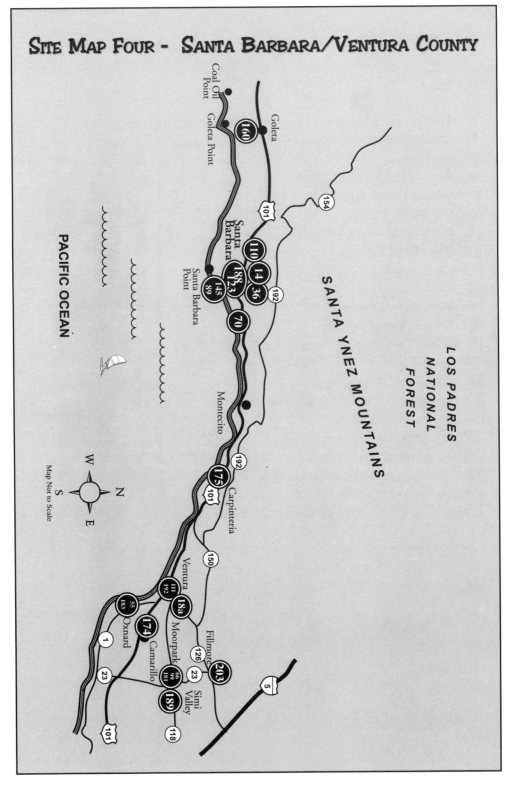

SITE MAP FOUR - SANTA BARBARA/VENTURA COUNTY

Coal Oil Point

Goleta Point

Goleta

160

154

101

Santa Barbara

110

188 3

14 36

145 89 123

192

Santa Barbara Point

70

SANTA YNEZ MOUNTAINS

LOS PADRES NATIONAL FOREST

PACIFIC OCEAN

Montecito

192

175

101

Carpinteria

N
W   E
S

Map Not to Scale

150

Ventura

111 192

55 183

18a

1

174

Oxnard

Moorpark

126

Fillmore

203

5

23

Camarillo

66 99 181

23

Simi Valley

189

101

118

KEY TO SITE MAP FOR SANTA BARBARA/VENTURA COUNTY

Site # Name

14	Santa Barbara Museum of Natural History
18a	Adventures for Kids
36	Kid's World
55	California Strawberry Festival
66	America's Teaching Zoo at Moorpark College
70	Santa Barbara Zoological Gardens
89	Ty Warner Sea Center
99	Underwood Family Farms
110	Santa Barbara County Fair and Exposition
111	Ventura County Fair
123	Chase Palm Park Carousel
145	Santa Barbara East Beach
160	Santa Barbara Airport
174	Camarillo Train Station
175	Carpenteria Train Station
181	Moorpark Train Station
183	Oxnard Train Station
188	Santa Barbara Train Station
189	Simi Valley Train Station
192	Ventura Train Station
203	Fillmore and Western Railway

The Discovery Center, Natural History Museum of Los Angeles County.

Photo by author: permission to use photo courtesy of Mary Baerg, Natural History Museum of Los Angeles County.

CHAPTER 1 - MUSEUMS

The number of museums that are interesting for young children grows every year in Southern California. This section describes a variety of hands-on museums including children's museums, museums with discovery centers, and museums that young children love even though they are not specifically designed for children.

During your visit, take your time. If you spend your entire visit in one room, that's okay. Follow your child's lead. After your visit to the museum, you may want to download a few pictures from the museum or other websites, and talk further about what you saw. Websites for each museum are listed with the address. Visit www.ed.gov/pubs/Museum/title.html for more about visiting museums with children. Also try www.EnchantedLearning.com for projects and more information about what you saw at each museum.

INSECTS, SPIDERS, AND SNAKES

Be calm and curious around bugs and snakes for the benefit of your child.
If you are calm and curious, your child will learn to be the same.

SITE 1 - NATURAL HISTORY MUSEUM OF LOS ANGELES COUNTY

ADDRESS
Exposition Park
900 Exposition Boulevard
Los Angeles, CA 90007
(213) 763-3466
www.nhm.org

DIRECTIONS [GUIDE PAGE 674 (LA)]
• Take Interstate Highway 110 south and exit Exposition Boulevard. Go through the traffic light to get onto Exposition Boulevard. Pass the airplanes and museums on left and turn left on Menlo Avenue. Park on the right hand side of the street.
• Take Interstate Highway 110 north and exit Martin Luther King Jr. Boulevard. Make a left from the exit. Make a right on Menlo Avenue and park on the left.

BOOKS FOR YOUR CHILD
• Boynton, Sandra-*Oh My Oh My Oh Dinosaurs!*
• Brett, Jan-*Annie and the Wild Animals*
• Carle, Eric-*The Very Hungry Caterpillar*
• Carrick, Carol-*Patrick's Dinosaurs*
• Himmelman, John-*A Pill Bug's Life*
• Walsh, Ellen Stoll-*Mouse Paint*
• Wild, Margaret-*My Dearest Dinosaur*

GOOD THINGS TO SEE AND HEAR
This is an extensive natural history museum with beautiful dioramas of North American and African mammals, and a hands-on, interactive Discovery Center with live animals, shells, bones, rocks, and an insect zoo. Watch for special exhibits. There is a live butterfly exhibit called "Pavilion of Wings" that has become a summer regular. There is also a dinosaur exhibit, and a Cenozoic fossil exhibit that includes some fossil from the La Brea Tar Pits.

There is easy stroller access on the north side of building. A pass for the Discovery Center is needed during the summer-get one free at the entrance desk.

There is a Members' Loan Service on the first floor that allows members to check out specimens to take home for two weeks for a very minimal fee.

HOURS
Monday-Friday	9:30 a.m. - 5:00 p.m.
Saturday-Sunday	10:00 a.m. - 5:00 p.m.

PARKING
$6.00
$3.00 on weekends for members

ADMISSION
Adult	$9.00
Child (Ages 5-18)	$2.00
Under 5	Free

YEARLY MEMBERSHIP
Family $60.00

RELATED PLACES
- Aliso & Wood Canyons Wilderness Park and
    Orange County Natural History Museum - Site 47
- Children's Museum at La Habra - Site 2
- Eaton Canyon County Park and Nature Center - Site 44
- El Dorado East Regional Park and Nature Center - Site 50
- Irvine Regional Park and Nature Center - Site 49
- La Brea Tar Pits and Page Museum - Site 6
- San Dimas Canyon Park and Nature Center - Site 45
- Santa Barbara Museum of Natural History - Site 14
- Shipley Nature Center at Huntington Central Park - Site 48
- STAR EcoStation Environmental Science and Wildlife Rescue Center-Site 67
- Whittier Narrows Nature Center - Site 46
- Wilderness Park and Nature Center - Site 52

CLOSE-BY PLACES
- Exposition Park Rose Garden - Site 41
- IMAX Theater at the California Science Center - Site 208
- Los Angeles Memorial Sports Arena - Site 213
- University of Southern California, USC - Site 57

SPECIAL EVENTS
- Insect Fair in May
- Pavilion of Wings exhibit in Summer

YOUR COMMENTS

_____

_____

_____

_____

SOMETHING TO DO - BONES
Explore bones further after your visit to the dinosaur skeletons and bones exhibit at the Natural History Museum. Find bones in your body and in your child's body. Feel them, talk about how hard they are, name them, and compare the size of your leg bone to your child's leg bone. Compare your body to that of a tree (backbone and leg bones are trunk, arms bones are branches, fingers are leaves, and feet are roots). Talk about what does and does not have bones (haves: dinosaurs, cats, dogs, people, and snakes; have-nots: plants, jellyfish, bugs (their support is from their outer skeleton - exoskeleton).

BUGS AND THEIR FRIENDS

SPIDER

SNAIL

BUTTERFLY

BEE

BEETLE

SITE 2 - CHILDREN'S MUSEUM AT LA HABRA

ADDRESS
Portola Park
301 South Euclid Street
La Habra, CA 90631
(562) 905-9693
www.lhcm.org

DIRECTIONS [GUIDE PAGE 708 (LA)]
Take Interstate Highway 605 to Highway 72/Whittier Boulevard. Go east for eight miles to Euclid Street and turn right.

GOOD THINGS TO SEE AND HEAR
An old Pacific Railroad Depot, complete with a caboose, a tank car, and several boxcars, houses this children's museum that focuses on hands-on interactive exhibits. Ride the small hand-painted Dentzel Carousel; shop at the Mini Market; pet wild animals in the Nature Walk Room (there are about a hundred stuffed real animals that children can touch); ride a real city bus; make the lights flash on a model Lionel train; pump gas with a real gas pump (no gas); dig for fossil in a giant sand box; and see yourself in a kaleidoscope mirror.

The Preschool Playpark is a large room with a tree house, garage, kitchen and many toys designed for children ages zero to five. It is a great room, but don't miss the rest of the museum.

HOURS
Monday	10:00 a.m. - 1:00 p.m.
Tuesday-Saturday	10:00 a.m. - 5:00 p.m.
Sunday	1:00 p.m. - 5:00 p.m.

PARKING
Free

ADMISSION
Adult, and Child	$5.00
Under 2	Free

YEARLY MEMBERSHIP
Family $50.00
• Includes grandparents

RELATED PLACES
• Fillmore and Western Railway - Site 203
• Freight Trains - Site 196
• Kidspace Children's Museum - Site 4
• Lomita Railroad Museum - Site 197
• Natural History Museum of Los Angeles County - Site 1
• San Diego Model Railroad Museum - Site 202
• Santa Barbara Museum of Natural History - Site 14
• Travel Town Museum - Site 170

YOUR COMMENTS

_____

_____

_____

_____

_____

SITE 3 - MUSEUM OF THE AMERICAN WEST

ADDRESS
Griffith Park (across from the Los Angeles Zoo)
4700 Western Heritage Way
Los Angeles, CA 90027
(323) 667-2000
www.museumoftheamericanwest.org

DIRECTIONS [GUIDE PAGE 564 (LA)]
• Take State Highway 134 west and exit Zoo Drive. Turn left on Crystal Springs Drive, and the museum is on your immediate left.
• Take State Highway 134 east and exit Victory Boulevard. Turn right at top of offramp and make a left on Zoo Drive. Drive onto Crystal Springs Drive, and the museum is on your immediate left.

GOOD THINGS TO SEE AND HEAR
The Museum of the American West (formerly the Autry Museum of Western Heritage) is a museum about cowboys and the American West. If your toddler likes cowboys, this is a good museum to visit. See the "Spirit of Imagination Galley" (see yourself in a TV western), all lower level galleries (look for the sheriffs' stars), and the Heritage Court Mural. Walk around the little outside trail.

Gene Autry was known as 'America's Favorite Singing Cowboy'. He has five stars on Hollywood's Walk of Fame for radio, records, film, television, and live theatrical performance.

The Children's Discovery Gallery was recently redone and is now geared for older children.

HOURS
Tuesday-Sunday,	10:00 a.m. - 5:00 p.m.
Thursday	10:00 a.m. - 8:00 p.m.

PARKING
Free

ADMISSION
Adult	$7.50
Child (Ages 2-12)	$3.00
Under 2	Free

YEARLY MEMBERSHIP
Family $65.00

RELATED PLACES
- The County Fair - Sites 106-111
- The Farm - Site 96
- Green Meadows Farm - Sites 90-91
- Griffith Park Pony Rides - Site 95
- Huntington Central Park Equestrian Center - Site 94
- Irvine Regional Park Pony Rides - Site 102
- Lakewood Pony Rides and Petting Farm - Site 104
- Montebello Barnyard Zoo - Site 103
- Santa Anita Race Track Morning Workout - Site 92
- Underwood Family Farms - Site 99
- Zoomars Petting Farm - Site 98

CLOSE-BY PLACES
- Bob Hope Airport - Site 148
- Burbank Train Station - Site 173
- Falcon Theater - Site 205
- North Hollywood School Bus Yard - Site 25
- Summer Sounds at the Hollywood Bowl - Site 219

YOUR COMMENTS

_____

_____

_____

_____

_____

GENE AUTRY'S COWBOY CODE
1. The Cowboy must never shoot first, hit a smaller man, or take unfair advantage.
2. He must never go back on his word, or a trust confided in him.
3. He must always tell the truth.
4. He must be gentle with children, the elderly, and animals.
5. He must not advocate or possess racially or religiously intolerant ideas.
6. He must help people in distress.
7. He must be a good worker.
8. He must keep himself clean in thought, speech, action, and personal habits.
9. He must respect women, parents, and his nation's laws.
10. The Cowboy is a patriot.

© 1994 Autry Qualified Interest Trust. Permission to reproduce Gene Autry's cowboy code granted by Karla Buhlman of Gene Autry Entertainment.

SITE 4 - KIDSPACE CHILDREN'S MUSEUM

ADDRESS
Brookside Park
480 North Arroyo Boulevard
Pasadena, CA 91103
(626) 449-9144
www.kidspacemuseum.org

DIRECTIONS [GUIDE PAGE 565 (LA)]
Take Interstate Highway 210 to the Seco Street Exit. Go west and then make a left on Arroyo Boulevard.

GOOD THINGS TO SEE AND HEAR:
The original Kidspace Museum closed on January 1, 2003. The spacious new museum opened in December 2004 in a new location near the Rose Bowl in Pasadena providing 3.4 acres of outdoor learning environments in addition to a brand new museum. Designed for hands-on and bodies-on, Kidspace is a busy place with many rooms focusing on different kinds of activities - all for kids. Spend some time in Kaleidoscope Hall, the Trike Trades, the Interpretive Arroyo and the Dig. The Ant, Wisteria and Raindrop climbers are a wonderful challenge for a toddler but watch your head!. The museum has nothing much to do with "space" (like the planets), but it is a lot of fun!

Children can bring in something they found in nature and exchange it for something else at the Nature Exchange.

HOURS
Daily	9:30 a.m. - 5:00 p.m.

PARKING
Free

ADMISSION
Adult or Child	$8.00
Under 1	Free

YEARLY MEMBERSHIP
Family (15 visits)	$100.00
Family (unlimited visits)	$100.00

RELATED PLACES
- Boone Children's Gallery, LACMA - Site 8
- Children's Discovery Museum of North Country - Site 13
- Children's Museum at La Habra - Site 2
- Discovery Science Center - Site 7
- Natural History Museum of Los Angeles County - Site 1
- Santa Barbara Museum of Natural History - Site 14
- STAR EcoStation Environmental Science and Wildlife Rescue Center - Site 67
- Zimmer Children's Museum - Site 10

CLOSE-BY PLACES
- California Institute of Technology, Caltech - Site 56
- Doggie Day Camp - Site 28
- Eaton Canyon County Park and Nature Center - Site 44
- The Huntington - Site 39
- Pasadena Civic Auditorium - Site 220
- Tournament of Roses® Float Viewing - Site 216
- Tournament of Roses® Parade - Site 216

SPECIAL EVENTS
- See Kaleidoscope Calendar
- Rosebud Parade During the Second Saturday in November

YOUR COMMENTS

_____

_____

_____

_____

_____

SITE 5 - PETERSEN AUTOMOTIVE MUSEUM

ADDRESS
Museum Row
6060 Wilshire Boulevard
Los Angeles, CA 90036
(323) 930-2277
www.petersen.org

DIRECTIONS [GUIDE PAGE 633 (LA)]
Take Interstate Highway 10 and exit Fairfax Avenue. Go north from the offramp. The museum is at southeast corner of Fairfax Avenue and Wilshire Boulevard.

GOOD THINGS TO SEE AND HEAR
The history of the automobile in America and Los Angeles is the focus of this car museum. If your toddler loves cars, this is an exciting museum to visit. Beautiful, shiny old cars fill the museum, including the cars of Hollywood, Model Ts, sedans, celebrity cars, hot rods, trucks, and motorcycles. Start with "Streetscape" on the first floor that has authentic scenes and vehicles that represent Los Angeles. The May Family Children's Discovery Center on the top floor has hands-on, interactive activities for all ages. Some include "May the Gears Be With You," "Off Balance," "Giant Engine," and "Battle of the Bubbles/Go with the Flow". You can climb in an old yellow Model T and there is a toddler lot with toy cars and trucks. Best of all is the Hot Wheels exhibit with hundreds of hot wheels cars on display. In addition, several cars that were made as only hot wheels cars have been built as full size cars and are quite spectacular.

HOURS
Tuesday-Sunday   10:00 a.m. - 6:00 p.m.

PARKING
$6.00

ADMISSION
Adult	$10.00
Child (Ages 5-12)	$3.00
Under 5	Free

YEARLY MEMBERSHIP
Family $65.00

RELATED PLACES
- Big Rigs at Castaic - Site 34
- Construction and Road Work Sites-Chapter 2
- Fire Stations-Chapter 2
- Los Angeles Convention Center-Auto Show - Site 209
- School Buses/Pasadena Unified School District - Site 19

CLOSE-BY PLACES
- Boone Children's Gallery, LACMA - Site 8
- Children's Book World - Site 18
- La Brea Tar Pits and Page Museum - Site 6
- The Original Los Angeles Farmer's Market - Site 32
- Storyopolis - Site 18
- Zimmer Children's Museum - Site 10

YOUR COMMENTS

_____

_____

_____

_____

_____

SITE 6 - LA BREA TAR PITS AND PAGE MUSEUM

ADDRESS
Museum Row
5801 Wilshire Boulevard
Los Angeles, CA 90036
(323) 934-7243
www.tarpits.org

DIRECTIONS [GUIDE PAGE 633 (LA)]
Take Interstate Highway 10 and exit La Brea Avenue. Go north from the offramp and make a left on Wilshire Boulevard. Make a right on Curson Avenue, and then a left into the parking lot.

GOOD THINGS TO SEE AND HEAR

The La Brea Tar Pits are in an area (now Hancock Park) that had pits of tar in which animals got stuck and died during the latter part of the last Ice Age (10,000 to 40,000 years ago). The animals thought the black pools of tar were water and got stuck. The black ooze preserved the bones that are being excavated today to discover what life was like then. The park includes an active paleontology excavation site in the summer, and a small lake with statues of mastodons stuck in the tar. You can smell the tar. The park also includes the Page Museum that houses animal skeletons from the La Brea Tar Pits, including mammoths, mastodons, dire wolves, saber-toothed cats, and a variety of birds. Note the color of the bones compared to fossil found in the desert.

There is a large mechanical woolly mammoth and a large saber-toothed cat attacking a sloth inside the museum that look very real and can be scary.

Note that the dinosaurs disappeared 65 million years before the tar pits formed.

You might also want to stroll through the Los Angeles County Museum of Art's sculpture garden to the west of the Page Museum.

HOURS

Monday-Friday	9:30 a.m. - 5:00 p.m.
Saturday-Sunday	10:00 a.m. - 5:00 p.m.

PARKING

$6.00 in lot behind Museum with validation

ADMISSION

Adult	$7.00
Child (Ages 5-12)	$2.00
Under 5	Free

YEARLY MEMBERSHIP

Adults (2 people)	$40.00
Family	$50.00

• Includes access to Natural History Museum

RELATED PLACES

• Children's Museum at La Habra - Site 2
• Natural History Museum of Los Angeles County - Site 1
• Santa Barbara Museum of Natural History - Site 14

CLOSE-BY PLACES

• Boone Children's Gallery, LACMA - Site 8
• Children's Book World - Site 18
• The Original Los Angeles Farmer's Market - Site 32
• Petersen Automotive Museum - Site 5
• Storyopolis - Site 18
• Zimmer Children's Museum - Site 10

YOUR COMMENTS

_____
_____
_____
_____
_____

SITE 7 - DISCOVERY SCIENCE CENTER

ADDRESS
2500 North Main Street
Santa Ana, CA 92705
(714) 542-2823
www.discoverycube.org

DIRECTIONS [GUIDE PAGE 799 (OC)]
Take Interstate Highway 5 south and exit Main Street. Follow the signs to Discovery Science Center (it is on North Main Street). It is the building with the huge cube on top.

GOOD THINGS TO SEE AND HEAR
This is a wonderful science center with all interactive (full body contact!) activities to help explain the way the world works. Your toddler and baby will enjoy walking into a tornado cloud; pushing pins in the Pin Wall; shaking in the Shake Shack (simulates an earthquake); and rolling, pulling, and throwing balls. There is an area upstairs called KidStation that is geared for toddlers, however, do not hesitate to let your toddlers and even your babies try some of the other exhibits. Your babies may also like watching the older kids maneuver the exhibits.

Do not hesitate to try an exhibit over and over (and over) again.

HOURS
Daily   10:00 a.m. - 5:00 p.m.

PARKING
$3.00

ADMISSION
Adult $11.00
Child (Ages 3-17) $8.50
Under 3   Free

YEARLY MEMBERSHIP
Adult plus guest $50.00
Family $75.00

RELATED PLACES
• Boone Children's Gallery, LACMA - Site 8
• Children's Discovery Museum of North Country - Site 13
• Griffith Observatory - Site 9
• Kidspace Children's Museum - Site 4
• Zimmer Children's Museum - Site 10

CLOSE-BY PLACES
- Adventure City - Site 113
- Anaheim Convention Center - Site 210
- Anaheim Train Station - Site 172
- Arrowhead Pond of Anaheim - Site 211
- Disneyland - Site 112
- Santa Ana Zoo - Site 64

YOUR COMMENTS

SITE 8 - BOONE CHILDREN'S GALLERY, LACMA

ADDRESS
Los Angeles County Museum of Art
LACMA West
5905 Wilshire Boulevard
Los Angeles, CA 90036
(323) 857-6000
www.lacma.org

DIRECTIONS [GUIDE PAGE 633 (LA)]
Take Interstate Highway 10 and exit La Brea Avenue. Go north for several miles and make a left on Wilshire Boulevard. Make a right on Ogden Avenue and then a left into the parking lot.

GOOD THINGS TO SEE AND HEAR
Every year or so the Los Angeles County Museum of Art, LACMA, invites about ten Southern California artists to create interactive art installations specifically for children in an effort to make art more accessible to all ages. These are on display in the Boone Children's Gallery in LACMA. In previous years, the exhibit included a white pillow room, a hilly AstroTurf-covered area with peeking holes, an entire quarter of a room piled with a clay hill, and a wooden musical sound area. Giant easels are available for all children to try their own hand at art.

The exhibit changes periodically so call to be sure the gallery is open.

HOURS
Monday,-Tuesday, Thursday 12:00 p.m. - 5:00 p.m.
Friday
Saturday-Sunday   11:00 a.m. - 5:00 p.m.

PARKING
$5.00

ADMISSION

Adult or Child	Free
Art Project	$2.00

YEARLY MEMBERSHIP
None (you can join the LACMA)

RELATED PLACES
- Children's Discovery Museum of North Country - Site 13
- Discovery Science Center - Site 7
- Kidspace Children's Museum - Site 4
- Zimmer Children's Museum - Site 10

CLOSE-BY PLACES
- Children's Book World - Site 18
- La Brea Tar Pits and Page Museum - Site 6
- The Original Los Angeles Farmer's Market - Site 32
- Petersen Automotive Museum - Site 5
- Storyopolis - Site 18
- Zimmer Children's Museum - Site 10

YOUR COMMENTS

_____

_____

_____

_____

_____

_____

SITE 9 - GRIFFITH OBSERVATORY

ADDRESS
Griffith Observatory
2800 East Observatory Road
Los Angeles, CA 90027
(323) 664-1181
www.griffithobs.org

DIRECTIONS [GUIDE PAGE 593 (LA)]
Take Interstate Highway 5 and exit Los Feliz Blvd. Go west on Los Feliz approximately three miles to Hillhurst Avenue. Turn right onto Hillhurst Avenue. Make a slight right onto N. Vermont Avenue. Turn left onto East Observatory Road.

GOOD THINGS TO SEE AND HEAR
The Griffith Observatory closed in 2002 for renovation and plans to open again in late 2006. The historical building and domes remain with additional space provided beneath the original building. The new observatory promises to provide fascinating exhibits of our solar system and universe. The planetarium will have innovative shows specifically designed for children and a telescope to view the moon and planets at night.

45

GOOD THINGS TO SEE AND HEAR (CONTINUED)

In the meantime, a satellite facility is available in the Los Angeles Zoo parking lot. The facility has a variety of hands-on exhibits to help your child begin her exploration of our solar system. Remember, planets are fun to draw and paint!

Check www.griffithobs.org/Skyinfo.html for information on current objects in the sky. It is difficult for babies and toddlers to look in a telescope but toddlers can usually see the moon with a little effort.

HOURS
Tuesday-Friday   1:30 p.m. - 10:00 p.m.
Saturday, Sunday   10:00 a.m. - 10:00 p.m.

PARKING
Free

ADMISSION
Free

YEARLY MEMBERSHIP
Family $50.00

RELATED PLACES
• Discovery Science Center - Site 7

CLOSE-BY PLACES
• Glendale Train Station - Site 178
• Griffith Park Pony Rides - Site 95
• Griffith Park Merry-Go-Round - Site 115
• Griffith Park Train Ride - Site 198
• Los Angeles Zoo - Site 63
• Travel Town Museum - Site 170

SITE 10 - ZIMMER CHILDREN'S MUSEUM

ADDRESS
Jewish Community Centers Association of Greater Los Angeles
Goldsmith Jewish Federation Center
6505 Wilshire Boulevard, Suite 100
Los Angeles, CA 90048
(323) 761-8989
www.zimmermuseum.org

DIRECTIONS [GUIDE PAGE: 633 (LA)]
Take Interstate Highway 10 and exit Fairfax Avenue. Go north, make a left on Wilshire Boulevard. The museum is on your right in the Goldsmith Jewish Federation Center. There is free parking on the west side of the building.

GOOD THINGS TO SEE AND HEAR
The Zimmer is a hands-on museum of discovery. The goal for the Zimmer Children's Museum is to provide a unique opportunity to share values, ethics, and culture while demonstrating community responsibility and sensitivity. The museum

has an area called Play Land just for toddlers, however, encourage your children to try any of the exhibits and projects. The museum encourages children starting at six months to participate and offers non-toxic paint for all art projects. Try the Discovery Airplane - a small real airplane that you can climb in and around. Also try Museum Main Street - especially the Corner Market and Bubbie's Bookstore. There is a giant two-story pinball machine-watch the pinwheels and lights as the discs fall.

The Slavin Children's Library is in the same building.

HOURS

Tuesday	10:00 a.m. - 5:00 p.m.
Wednesday-Thursday	10:00 a.m. - 5:00 p.m.
Friday	10:00 a.m. - 12:30 p.m.
Sunday	12:30 p.m. - 5:00 p.m.

PARKING
Free

ADMISSION

Adult	$5.00
Child (Ages 3-12)	$3.00
Under 3	Free

YEARLY MEMBERSHIP

Family	$65.00

RELATED PLACES
• Boone Children's Gallery, LACMA - Site 8
• Children's Discovery Museum of North Country - Site 13
• Children's Museum at La Habra - Site 2
• Discovery Science Center - Site 7
• Kidspace Children's Museum - Site 4

CLOSE-BY PLACES
• Boone Children's Gallery, LACMA - Site 8
• Children's Book World - Site 18
• La Brea Tar Pits and Page Museum - Site 6
• The Original Los Angeles Farmer's Market - Site 32
• Petersen Automotive Museum - Site 5
• Storyopolis - Site 18

YOUR COMMENTS

SITE 11 - CHILDREN'S MUSEUM OF LOS ANGELES

ADDRESS
Hansen Dam Recreation Park
Lake View Terrace, CA 91342
(818) 786-2656
www.childrensmuseumla.org

DIRECTIONS [GUIDE PAGE 502 (LA)]
Take Interstate Highway 210 to the Osborne Exit and follow signs to Hansen Dam Park.

GOOD THINGS TO SEE AND HEAR
The Children's Museum of Los Angeles closed its Civic Center location in 2000 to prepare a new campus located in northeast San Fernando Valley near the Hansen Dam Recreational Area. This location will be open in 2007. The new museum is located on an acre of land and promises to be a fully hands-on participatory children's museum incorporating the landscape into a "boundless playgound". The museum is being modeled after an ecosystem in which all parts are interrelated. A Big Fun Cool Thing conncts the parts of the system by incorporating interactive play with water, fire, earth and air. Elements of the museum include The Kitchen, where mising and measuring take place in the Gooey Kitchen, the Dinner for Tree area and the Dinner at My Place section; The Shop, which encourages building with sand and water, and large and small scale structures; and The Studio which allows children to create art, stories and performances. A weekly theme such as The Desert or The Pond is a centerpiece for children to decorate the space with paintings and create stories and performances. The Observatory invites children to observe their world in a Fun House, using See Me See You/Hear Me Hear You tools, and in a Light and Shadow area. And of course there is an Infact/Toddler area, but as usual, don't miss the rest of the museum with your young child.

RELATED PLACES
   • Boone Children's Gallery, LACMA - Site 8
   • Children's Discovery Museum of North Country - Site 13
   • Children's Museum at La Habra - Site 2
   • Discovery Science Center - Site 7
   • Natural History Museum of Los Angeles County - Site 1
   • Santa Barbara Museum of Natural History - Site 14
   • STAR EcoStation Environmental Science and Wildlife Rescue Center - Site 67
   • Zimmer Children's Museum - Site 10

CLOSE-BY PLACES
   • San Fernando Valley Fair - Site 108
   • Whiteman Airport - Site 164

YOUR COMMENTS

SITE 12 - THE CHILDREN'S MUSEUM OF SAN DIEGO/ MUSEO DE LOS NIÑOS

ADDRESS
Marina District
San Diego, CA 92101
(619) 233-8792
www.sdchildrensmuseum.org

COMMENTS
The Children's Museum is currently closed to build a new state-of-the-art facility with expanded programming. Stay Tuned!

CLOSE-BY PLACES
• Balboa Park Merry-Go-Round and Butterfly Ride - Site 121
• Bates Nut Farm - Site 101
• Belmont Park Carousel - Site 119
• San Diego Convention Center - Site 214
• San Diego Model Railroad Museum - Site 202
• San Diego Train Station - Site 185
• San Diego Zoo - Site 68
• Sea World - Site 87
• Seaport Village Carousel - Site 120

YOUR COMMENTS
_____
_____
_____
_____
_____

SITE 13 - CHILDREN'S DISCOVERY MUSEUM OF NORTH COUNTY

COMMENTS
As this edition of *Baby's Day Out in Southern California* was going to press, we learned that the Children's Discovery Museum of North County had closed its doors after eleven years of operation. If you are visiting this area, you may wish to consider visiting the following near-by locations: San Diego Wild Animal Park, Legoland, McClellan-Palomar Airport or the Oceanside Train Station.

YOUR COMMENTS

_____

_____

_____

_____

_____

_____

SITE 14 - SANTA BARBARA MUSEUM OF NATURAL HISTORY

ADDRESS
2559 Puesta del Sol Road
Santa Barbara, CA 93105
(805) 682-4711
www.sbnature.org

DIRECTIONS [GUIDE PAGE 995 (SB)]
Take U.S. Highway 101 and exit Mission Street. Go north (towards the mountains) at the offramp stop light. Make a left on Laguna Street and then a right on Los Olivos Street. From there, make a left on Mission Canyon Drive.

GOOD THINGS TO SEE AND HEAR
The Santa Barbara Museum of Natural History is full of interactive, rich exhibits, and is in a beautiful eleven-acre setting. Try Mammal Hall, Bird Diversity Hall, the Cartwright Hall of Plant and Insect Interaction, and Lizard Lounge. There is a small planetarium with shows geared for children ages five and under on Saturday at 11:00 a.m. There is a beautiful nature trail behind the museum. Check out a backpack with binoculars, a magnifying glass, and a field guide and take a hike. Let your child use the binoculars and magnifying glass even if they don't really see anything through them.

The Ty Warner Sea Center on Stearns Wharf (site 89) is part of the Santa Barbara Museum of Natural History.

HOURS
Daily   10:00 a.m. - 5:00 p.m.
Planetarium Show for Young Children:
Saturday-Sunday 11:00 a.m.

PARKING
Free

ADMISSION
Adult $8.00
Child (2-12) $5.00
Under 2   Free
• Free on the last Sunday of the month

YEARLY MEMBERSHIP
Adult $40.00
Family $60.00

RELATED PLACES
- Children's Museum at La Habra - Site 2
- Griffith Observatory - Site 9
- Natural History Museum of Los Angeles County - Site 1

CLOSE-BY PLACES
- Chase Palm Park Carousel - Site 123
- Kid's World - Site 36
- Santa Barbara Airport - Site 160
- Santa Barbara County Fair and Exposition - Site 110
- Santa Barbara East Beach - Site 145
- Santa Barbara Train Station - Site 188
- Santa Barbara Zoological Gardens - Site 70

YOUR COMMENTS

_____

_____

_____

_____

SITE 15 - RAYMOND M. ALF MUSEUM

ADDRESS
1175 West Baseline Road
Claremont, CA 91711
(909) 624-2798
www.alfmuseum.org

DIRECTIONS [GUIDE PAGE 571 (LA)]
Take Interstate Highway 1 and exit Towne Avenue. Go north to Baseline Road. Turn left on Baseline Road and make a right turn up the hill. The museum is located at Webb High School.

GOOD THINGS TO SEE AND HEAR
The Raymond M. Alf Museum is a small friendly dinosaur museum with fossil from all over the world and lots of hands-on activities. Included in the fossil collection are trilobites, casts or models of the dinosaurs Monoclonius, Allosaurus, Tyrannosaurus Rex and Velociraptor, dinosaur eggs from China and Mongolia, a giant fossil alligator skull from the Amazon and a large collection of fossil footprints.

HOURS
Daily   8:00 a.m. - 4:00 p.m.

PARKING
Free
ADMISSION
Adult, Child $1.00
Under 5   Free
- Free on the last Sunday of the month

RELATED PLACES
- Children's Museum at La Habra - Site 2
- La Brea Tar Pits and Page Museum - Site 6
- Natural History Museum of Los Angeles County - Site 1

CLOSE-BY PLACES
- Ontario International Airport - Site 159

YOUR COMMENTS

_____

_____

_____

_____

Laidlaw Buses in the Pasadena Unified School District School Bus Yard.
Photo by author; permission to use photo courtesy of Scott Walter and Trisha Kyles of
the Pasadena Unified School District.

CHAPTER 2 - OUR CITY

Your city, either the big cities of Los Angeles and San Diego, or your local city or town, provides a great variety of activities for very young children. This chapter includes some of these activities. Favorites are the school bus yard, construction sites, pet stores, farmer's markets, and libraries. Once you find a place your child likes that is close to your home, visit it over and over again.

For many of these locations, Internet and phone book categories are included rather than specific addresses and directions. In some cases, a list of local places is also included, however, these change frequently so call ahead.

If you want to take a walk around downtown Los Angeles with your stroller, take a look at the book, *Downtown Los Angeles-A Walking Guide*, by Robert D. Herman (published by Gem Guides Book Co., Baldwin Park, California).

Site 16 - Richard J. Riordan Central Library

Address
630 West 5th Street
Los Angeles, CA 90071
(213) 228-7272
www.lapl.org

Directions [Guide Page 634 (LA)]
• Take Interstate Highway 110 and exit 4th Street. Go east and then make a right on Grand Avenue. From there, make a right on 5th Street and then a right on Flower Street.
• Or take the Metro Rail Red Line - Site 195

Good Things to See and Hear
The Los Angeles Central Library is the third largest central library in the nation. The murals throughout are beautiful. The children's area is in a restored 1930s-era room. There is a separate young children's library with baskets of books next to cozy chairs. Be sure to note the chandelier representing the solar system. Puppet shows and story times occur frequently. The Children's Library also has a "Grandparents and Books" program when you can have a Library Grandparent read a story to your children. Go to the "Story Hours in Your Local Library" section in this chapter, visit their webpage, or call them for times.

Unless you live close-by, it may not be reasonable to check out books. Focus on spending some time reading in this library, and visit your local library to check out books for home. This chapter includes some ideas for books to read by subject, favorite author and main character (see "Ideas for Library Books" and "Resource for Children's Books".)

Hours
Library
Monday-Thursday   10:00 a.m. - 8:00 p.m.
Friday, Saturday   10:00 a.m. - 6:00 p.m.
Sunday   1:00 p.m. - 5:00 p.m.
Grandparents and Books
Wednesday   12:00 p.m. - 2:00 p.m.
Thursday   2:00 p.m. - 4:00 p.m.
Sunday   1:00 p.m. - 3:30 p.m.

Parking
$1.00 to $3.00 with library card

Admission
Free

Related Places
• Cerritos Library - Site 17
• Story Hours in Your Local Library-Chapter 2
• Your Local Library-Chapter 2

CLOSE-BY PLACES
- Bob Baker Marionette Theater - Site 204
- Chinatown - Site 30
- Grand Central Market - Site 31
- KLOS Story Theater - Site 206
- Olvera Street - Site 29
- Union Station - Site 171
- Walt Disney Music Concert Hall - Site 221

YOUR COMMENTS

_____

_____

_____

_____

_____

SITE 17 - CERRITOS LIBRARY

ADDRESS
18025 Bloomfield Avenue
Cerritos, CA 90703
(562) 916-1350
(562) 916-1343 Children's Reference
www.ci.cerritos.ca.us/library/library.html

DIRECTIONS [GUIDE PAGE 767 (LA)]
• Take Interstate Highway 605 to State Highway 91 east. Exit Bloomfield Avenue and go south. The library is located on the right hand side of the street before 183rd Street.

GOOD THINGS TO SEE AND HEAR
The Cerritos Library has made the world's first "Experience Library." The Children's Library includes a 15,000-gallon saltwater aquarium, a full-size model of a Tyrannosaurus Rex, a touchable globe of Earth, a model Space Shuttle, a rain forest tree, a lighthouse, and many cozy couches for reading. The ceiling is painted with titanium and changes colors with atmospheric conditions. The Little Theater offers a space for story times.

As with the Los Angeles Central Library, unless you live close-by, it may not be reasonable to check out books. Focus on spending some time reading in the library, and visit your local library to check out books for home. There are some ideas for books to read by subject, favorite author and main character in this chapter (see "Ideas for Library Books" and "Resources for Children's Books".)

HOURS

Monday-Friday   10:00 a.m. - 9:00 p.m.
Saturday   9:00 a.m. - 5:00 p.m.
Sunday   1:00 p.m. - 5:00 p.m.
Story Time:
Tuesday   10:30 a.m. & 3:30 p.m.
Wednesday   11:00 a.m.
Thursday-Saturday 10:30 a.m.

• Other story times are available for specific age groups including "Babies n Books," "Stories for 2's and 3's," and "Preschool Story Hour." Registration is required.

• Other story times are available for specific age groups including "Babies n Books," "Stories for 2's and 3's," and "Preschool Story Hour." Registration is required.

PARKING

Free

ADMISSION

Free

YEARLY MEMBERSHIP

Get a library card

RELATED PLACES

• Richard J. Riordan Central Library - Site 16
• Story Hours in Your Local Library-Chapter 2
• Your Local Library-Chapter 2

CLOSE-BY PLACES

• California State University Long Beach, CSULB - Site 61
• El Dorado East Regional Park and Nature Center - Site 50
• El Dorado East Regional Park Train Ride - Site 199
• Lakewood Pony Rides and Petting Farm - Site 104
• Long Beach Airport - Site 157
• Norwalk School Bus Yard - Site 26

YOUR COMMENTS

_____
_____
_____
_____
_____

BARKS AND BOOKS

The Pasadena Humane Society sponsors a program in which dogs are brought to local libraries to listen to children read or talk about their books. Look for similar opportunities at your local library.

YOUR LOCAL LIBRARY

INTERNET:
    All California Libraries   www.publiclibraries.com/california.htm

COUNTY LIBRARY BRANCHES:
    Los Angeles County   www.colapublib.org/libs
    Orange County   www.ocpl.org/
    San Diego County   www.sdcl.org/

CITY LIBRARY BRANCHES FOR MAIN CITIES:
    Los Angeles   www.lapl.org/branches
    San Diego   www.sannet.gov/public-library/locations
    Santa Barbara   www.ci.santa-barbara.ca.us/departments/library

PHONE BOOK:
    Yellow Pages   Libraries-Public
    White Pages   City Government Offices
                             (front of phone book, look under City then Library)
                             County Government Offices
                             (front of phone book, look under Library Public)

GOOD THINGS TO SEE AND HEAR

Your local library offers three basic things for babies and toddlers: a place to look at and read books; a place to check out books to bring home for reading; and a weekly story hour or two. Most libraries have a wide selection of picture books for babies and toddlers and often have magazines, records, tapes, and CDs that are appropriate for this age. Most also have a special children's book area and a regularly scheduled story hour-some have several for different age groups. Get a library card and find a regular library day in your week. There are some ideas for books to read and check out by subject, favorite author, and main character in this chapter. See "Ideas for Library Books" and "Resources for Children's Books".

If your child is fascinated with flowers or cars or trains, for example, look in the adult section of the library and check out a "coffee table" book with a lot of colorful pictures.

If there are a few libraries close to your house, try them all to see which one is most comfortable for you and your child. Keep a list of library story hours handy in your car in case you are desperate for something peaceful to do. A suggested format for your local set of library hours and their story times is included in this chapter. Exact story times may vary with season and year. Check your local library website or call for information.

RELATED PLACES
    • Cerritos Library - Site 17
    • Richard J. Riordan Central Library - Site 16

STORY HOURS IN YOUR LOCAL LIBRARY

PHONE BOOK:

Yellow Pages   • Books-New

White Pages   • City Government Offices
(front of phone book, look under city then "Library")
• County Government Offices
(front of phone book, look under "Library-Public")

GOOD THINGS TO SEE AND HEAR

Most libraries have a weekly story hour for children. A librarian usually reads a story or two. Sometimes there is also a simple craft, a little show, or a visiting character from the book that is read.

RELATED PLACES

• Cerritos Library - Site 17
• Richard J. Riordan Central Library - Site 16
• Your Local Library-Chapter 2

YOUR COMMENTS

_____
_____
_____
_____
_____

SITE 18 - CHILDREN'S BOOK STORES

Below are several independent children's bookstores and large bookstores with excellent children's book sections in the Southern California area that have story hours for children. Most bookstores encourage you to sit on the floor and look at books with your child. You can also check the phone book or online for your local Barnes & Noble (www.barnesandnoble.com) or Borders (www.bordersstores.com). These large chain stores often have special events and signings just for children.

18A ADVENTURES FOR KIDS

3457 Telegraph Road
Ventura, CA 93003
(805) 680-9688
www.adventuresforkids.com
[GUIDE PAGE 491 (SB/V)]
• Take Highway 101 north toward Ventura. Take the Main Street exit toward Ventura onto E Main Street. Turn right onto S. Mills Road. Turn left onto Telegraph Road.

18B BLUE CHAIR CHILDREN'S BOOKS

177 N. Glendora Avenue
Glendora, CA 91741
(626) 335-8630
www.bluechairbooks.com/
[GUIDE PAGE 569 (LA)]
• Take Interstate Highway 210 and exit Grand Avenue North. Continue north on Grand Avenue to Foothill Boulevard. Turn right onto W Foothill Boulevard, then left onto N Glendora Avenue.

18C BOOKSTAR - CULVER CITY

11000 W. Jefferson Boulevard
Culver City, CA 90230-3529
(310) 391-0818
[GUIDE PAGE 672 (LA)]
• Take Interstate Highway 405 and exit Jefferson Boulevard going east. Bear left on Sepulveda Boulevard which turns back into Jefferson Boulevard.

18D BOOKSTAR - LOS ANGELES

100 N. La Cienega Boulevard
Los Angeles, CA 90048-3527
(310) 289-1734
[GUIDE PAGE 632 (LA)]
• Take Interstate Highway 10 and exit La Cienega Boulevard heading north. The store is in the Beverly Connection shopping center.

18E BOOKSTAR - STUDIO CITY

12136 Ventura Boulevard
Studio City, CA 91604-3532
(818) 505-9528
[GUIDE PAGE 562 (LA)]
• Take Highway 101 and exit Laurel Canyon Boulevard going south. Turn left on Ventura Boulevard.

18F BRIGHT CHILD

1415 Fourth Street
Santa Monica, CA 90401
(626) 449-5320
[GUIDE PAGE 671 (LA)]
• Take Interstate Highway 10 and exit at the 4th Street/5th Street exit. Keep left at the fork in the ramp, turn right onto 4th Street.

18G CATCH OUR RAINBOW BOOKS

3132 Pacific Coast Highway
Torrance, CA 90505
(310) 325-1081
[GUIDE PAGE 793 (LA)]
• Take Interstate Highway 110 towards San Pedro. Exit at Highway 1 (Pacific Coast Highway) and go west.

18H CHEVALIER'S BOOKS

126 N. Larchmont Boulevard
Los Angeles, CA 90005
(323) 465-1334
[GUIDE PAGE 593 (LA)]
• Take Highway 101 and exit at Melrose Avenue going west past Paramount Studios to Larchmont Boulevard. Turn left onto Larchmont Boulevard.

18I CHILDREN'S BOOK WORLD

10580 ½ West Pico Boulevard
Los Angeles, CA 90064
(310) 559-2665
www.childrensbookworld.com
[GUIDE PAGE 632 (LA)]
• Take Interstate Highway 10 and exit Bundy Drive. Go north and make a right on Pico Boulevard.

18J DUTTON'S BEVERLY HILLS BOOKS

447 N. Canon Drive
Beverly Hills, CA 90219
(310) 281-0997
www.duttonsbeverlyhills.com
[GUIDE PAGE 632 (LA)]
• Take Interstate Highway 405, and exit onto California Highway 2/Santa Monica Boulevard heading east. Continue east on Santa Monica Boulevard for approximately three miles. Turn right onto Canon Drive.

18K DUTTON'S BRENTWOOD BOOKSTORE

11975 San Vicente Boulevard
Los Angeles, CA 90049
(310) 476-6263
www.duttonsbrentwood.com
[GUIDE PAGE 631 (LA)]
• Take Interstate Highway 405 and exit Wilshire Boulevard. Go west on Wilshire Boulevard. Turn right onto San Vicente Boulevard.

18L EVERY PICTURE TELLS A STORY

1311-C Montana Avenue
Santa Monica, CA 90403
(310) 451-2700
www.everypicture.com
[GUIDE PAGE 631 (LA)]
• Take Interstate Highway 10. Exit at Cloverfield Boulevard and go north onto Cloverfield Boulevard. Turn left onto Olympic Boulevard. Turn right onto 14th Street, then turn left onto Montana Avenue.

18M MRS. NELSON'S TOY AND BOOK SHOP

1030 Bonita Avenue
La Verne, CA 91750
(909) 599-4558
www.mrsnelsons.com
[GUIDE PAGE 600 (LA)]
• Take Interstate Highway 210 to State Highway 57 south. Exit Bonita Avenue and go east.

18N ONCE UPON A TIME

2284 Honolulu Avenue
Montrose, CA 91020
(818) 248-9668
www.onceupona.com
[GUIDE PAGE 534 (LA)]
• Take the 2 Freeway and exit Verdugo Boulevard heading west about two blocks. Verdugo Boulevard becomes Honolulu Avenue. Go straight on Honolulu Avenue.

18o SAN MARINO TOY AND BOOK SHOPPE

2424 Huntington Drive
San Marino, CA 91108
(626) 309-0222
www.toysandbooks.com
[GUIDE PAGE 566 (LA)]
• Take Interstate Highway 210 and exit at San Gabriel Boulevard. Go south to Huntington Drive. Turn right onto Huntington Drive.

18p STORYOPOLIS

12348 Ventura Blvd.
Studio City, CA 91604
(818) 509-5600
www.storyopolis.com
[Guide Page 562 (LA)]
• Take Highway 101 and exit onto Laurel Canyon Boulevard going south Turn right onto Ventura Boulevard.

18q VILLAGE BOOKS

1049 Swarthmore Avenue
Pacific Palisades, CA 90272
(310) 454-4063
[GUIDE PAGE 631 (LA)]
• Take Interstate Highway 10 west until it becomes Highway 1/Pacific Coast Highway. Continue north on Pacific Coast Highway to Chautauqua Boulevard. Turn right onto Chautauqua Boulevard. Turn left onto Sunset Boulevard, then turn right onto Swarthmore Avenue.

18r VROMAN'S

695 E Colorado Boulevard
Pasadena, CA 91101
(626) 449-5320
www.vromansbookstore.com/
[GUIDE PAGE 566 (LA)]
• Take Interstate Highway 210 and exit at Lake Avenue. Go south to Colorado Boulevard, and turn right. Bookstore is on the north side of Colorado Boulevard.

18s WHALE OF A TALE BOOKSTORE

4199 Campus Drive
Irvine, CA 92612
(949) 854-8288
www.awhaleofatale.com/mainpage.html
[GUIDE PAGE 889 (OC)]
• From California Highway 73 merge onto Macarthur Boulevard going towards John Wayne Airport. Take the University Drive ramp toward UC Irvine. Turn right onto University Drive S. Turn right onto Campus Drive.

STORY TIMES

Below is a list of library hours for the Los Angeles Central Library and the Cerritos Library. Contact your local libraries and bookstores to add those times as a handy reference.

Richard J. Riordan Central Library (323) 744-4052

	Mon.	Tues.	Wed.	Thurs.	Fri.	Sat.	Sun.
OPENS	10:00 a.m.	10:00 a.m.	10:00 a.m.	10:00 a.m.	10:00 a.m.	10:00 a.m.	1:00 p.m.
CLOSES	8:00 p.m.	8:00 p.m.	8:00 p.m.	8:00 p.m.	6:00 p.m.	6:00 p.m.	5:00 p.m.
STORY TIME		9:30 a.m-Babies*				10:00 a.m..	
STORY TIME		10:00 a.m.-Toddlers*					
STORY TIME		11:00 a.m.-Toddlers*					

* Registration required

Cerritos City Library   (562) 916-1350

	Mon.	Tues.	Wed.	Thurs.	Fri.	Sat.	Sun.
OPENS	10:00 a.m.	10:00 a.m.	10:00 a.m.	10:00 a.m.	10:00 a.m.	9:00 a.m.	1:00 a.m.
CLOSES	9:00 p.m.	9:00 p.m.	9:00 p.m.	9:00 p.m.	9:00 p.m.	5:00 p.m.	5:00 p.m.
STORY TIME		10:30 a.m.	11:00 a.m.	10:30 a.m.	10:30 a.m.	10:30 a.m.	10:30 a.m.
STORY TIME		3:30 p.m.					

Local Library _____

	Monday	Tuesday	Wednesday	Thursday	Friday	Saturday	Sunday
OPENS							
CLOSES							
STORY TIME							

Local Library _____

	Monday	Tuesday	Wednesday	Thursday	Friday	Saturday	Sunday
OPENS							
CLOSES							
STORY TIME							

Local Library _____

	Monday	Tuesday	Wednesday	Thursday	Friday	Saturday	Sunday
OPENS							
CLOSES							
STORY TIME							

INTERNET RESOURCES FOR CHILDREN'S BOOKS

For a list of good children's books, check these websites:

LOS ANGELES PUBLIC LIBRARY
www.lapl.org/kidspath/booklist/read2mela-0p.html

CALDECOTT MEDAL WINNERS AND HONOR BOOKS
www.ala.org/ala/alsc/awardscholarships/libraryawards/caldecottmedal/

THE CHILDREN'S LITERATURE WEB GUIDE
www.acs.ucalgary.ca/~dkbrown/index.html

100 PICTURE BOOKS-NEW YORK PUBLIC LIBRARY
kids.nypl.org

LIBRARY OF CONGRESS FAMILY WEBSITE
www.americaslibrary.gov

IDEAS FOR LIBRARY BOOKS

Below is a list of children's books by subject and with Caldecott Winners and Honors noted. Children's books are usually filed by author. If no book title is given, the author has written too many wonderful books to list. Check them out!

AUTHORS

Books

Aardema, Verna *Why Mosquitoes Buzz in People's Ears*	1976 Winner
Ackerman, Karen *Song and Dance Man*	1989 Winner
Adams Armer, Laura *The Forest Pool*	1939 Honor
Arnold McCully, Emily *Mirette on the High Wire*	1993 Winner
Artzybasheff, Boris *Seven Simeons: A Russian Tale*	1938 Honor
Awdry, Wilbert Vere *Thomas the Tank Engine* series	
Baker, Olaf *Where the Buffaloes Begin*	1982 Honor
Bang, Molly *When Sophie Gets Angry-Really, Really Angry*	2000 Honor
Bang, Molly *Ten, Nine, Eight*	1984 Honor
Bang, Molly *The Grey Lady and the Strawberry Snatcher*	1981 Honor
Bartone, Elisa *Pepe the Lamplighter*	1994 Honor
Baylor, Byrd *The Way to Start a Day*	1979 Honor
Baylor, Byrd *Hawk, I'm Your Brother*	1977 Honor
Baylor, Byrd *The Desert is Theirs*	1976 Honor
Baylor, Byrd *When Clay Sings*	1973 Honor
Belting, Natalia M. *The Sun is a Golden Earring*	1963 Honor
Bemelmans, Ludwig *Madeline*	1940 Honor
Bemelmans, Ludwig, *Madeline's Rescue*	1954 Winner
Birnbaum, A. *Green Eyes*	1954 Honor
Bond, Michael *Paddington Bear* (chapter books)	
Boynton, Sandra	
Brett, Jan	
Bridwell, Norman *Clifford* series	
Briggs Martin, Jacqueline *Snowflake Bentley*	1999 Winner
Brodsky McDermott, Beverly *The Golem: A Jewish Legend*	1977 Honor
Brown, Marcia *Dick Whittington and his Cat*	1951 Honor
Brown, Marcia *Henry Fisherman*	1950 Honor
Brown, Marcia *Once a Mouse*	1962 Winner
Brown, Marcia *Puss in Boots*	1953 Honor
Brown, Marcia *Shadow*	1983 Winner
Brown, Marcia *Skipper John's Cook*	1952 Honor
Brown, Marcia *Stone Soup*	1948 Honor
Brown, Marcia *Cinderella, or the Little Glass Slipper*	1955 Winner
Buff, Mary & Conrad *Dash and Dart*	1943 Honor
Bunting, Eve *Smoky Night*	1995 Winner
Carle, Eric	
Caudill, Rebecca *A Pocketful of Cricket*	1965 Honor
Chan, Chih-Yi *Good Luck Horse*	1944 Honor
Chodos-Irvine, Margaret *Ella Sarah Gets Dressed*	2004 Honor
Cooney, Barbara *Chanticleer and the Fox*	1959 Winner
Crews, Donald *Freight Train*	1979 Honor
Crews, Donald *Truck*	1981 Honor
Cronin, Doreen *Click, Clack, Moo: Cows that Type*	2001 Honor
Dagliesh, Alice *The Thanksgiving Story*	1955 Honor
Daugherty, James *Andy and the Lion*	1939 Honor
d'Aulaire, Ingri & Edgar Parin *Abraham Lincoln*	1940 Winner
Davis Pinkney, Andrea *Duke Ellington: The Piano Prince and the Orchestra*	1999 Honor

Books organized by author (continued)
- Davis, Lavinia R. *The Wild Birthday Cake*   1950 Honor
- Davis, Lavinia R. *Roger and the Fox*   1948 Honor
- Day, Alexandra *Good Dog, Carl* series
- Dayrell, Elphinstone *Why the Sun and the Moon Live
  in the Sky*   1969 Honor
- de Angeli, Marguerite *Book of Nursery and Mother Goose
  Rhymes*   1955 Honor
- de Angeli, Marguerite *Yonie Wondernose*   1945 Honor
- de Paola, Tomie *Bill and Peet* series
- de Paola, Tomie *Strega Nona*   1976 Honor
- Domanska, Janina *If All the Seas Were One Sea*   1972 Honor
- Durån Ryan, Cheli *Hildilid's Night*   1972 Honor
- Eastman, P. D.
- Ehlert, Lois *Color Zoo*   1990 Honor
- Eichenberg, Fritz *Ape in a Cape: An Alphabet of
  Odd Animals*   1953 Honor
- Elkin, Benjamin *Gillespie and the Guards*   1957 Honor
- Emberley, Barbara *Drummer Hoff*   1968 Winner
- Emberley, Barbara *One Wide River to Cross*   1967 Honor
- Falconer, Ian *Olivia*   2001 Honor
- Feelings, Muriel *Jambo Means Hello: A Swahili Alphabet
  Book*   1975 Honor
- Feelings, Muriel *Moja Means One: A Swahili Counting Book* 1972 Honor
- Field, Rachel *Prayer for a Child*   1945 Winner
- Fish, Helen Dean *Animals of the Bible, A Picture Book* 1938 Winner
- Fish, Helen Dean *Four and Twenty Blackbirds*   1938 Honor
- Flack, Marjorie *Boats on the River*   1947 Honor
- Fleming, Denise *In the Small, Small Pond*   1994 Honor
- Ford, Lauren *The Ageless Story*   1940 Honor
- Frasconi, Antonio *The House that Jack Built: La Maison
  Que Jacques A Batie*   1959 Honor
- Freeman, Don *Corduroy* series
- Freeman, Don *Fly High, Fly Low*   1958 Honor
- Gag, Wanda *Nothing at All*   1942 Honor
- Gag, Wanda *Snow White and the Seven Dwarfs*   1939 Honor
- Gerstein, Mordicai *The Man Who Walked Between
  the Towers*   2004 Winner
- Gibbons, Gail
- Goble, Paul *The Girl Who Loved Wild Horses*   1979 Winner
- Goffstein, M.B. *Fish for Supper*   1977 Honor
- Goudey, Alice E. *Houses from the Sea*   1960 Honor
- Goudey, Alice E. *The Day We Saw the Sun Come Up*   1962 Honor
- Graham, Al *Timothy Turtle*   1947 Honor
- Grifalconi, Ann *The Village of Round and Square Houses* 1987 Honor
- Gruelle, Johnny *Raggedy Ann* series
- Hader, Berta & Elmer *Cock-a-Doodle Doo*   1940 Honor
- Hader, Berta & Elmer *The Big Snow*   1949 Honor
- Hader, Berta & Elmer *The Mighty Hunter*   1944 Honor
- Haley, Gail E. *A Story A Story*   1971 Winner
- Hall Ets, Marie *In the Forest*   1945 Honor
- Hall Ets, Marie *Just Me*   1966 Honor
- Hall Ets, Marie *Mr. T.W. Anthony Woo*   1952 Honor
- Hall Ets, Marie *Play With Me*   1956 Honor
- Hall Ets, Marie *Mr. Penny's Race Horse*   1957 Honor
- Hall Ets, Marie & Aurora Labastida *Nine Days to Christmas* 1960 Winner
- Hall, Donald *Ox-Cart Man*   1980 Winner
- Handforth, Thomas *Mei Lei*   1939 Honor

Books organized by author (continued)

- Henkes, Kevin *Kitten's First Full Moon* — 2005 Winner
- Henkes, Kevin *Owen* — 1994 Honor
- Hill, Eric *Spot* series
- Hissey, Jane *Old Bear* series
- Ho, Mingfong *Hush! A Thai Lullaby* — 1997 Honor
- Hodges, Margaret *St. George and the Dragon* — 1985 Winner
- Hodges, Margaret *The Wave* — 1965 Honor
- Hogrogian, Nonny *One Fine Day* — 1972 Winner
- Hogrogian, Nonny *The Contest* — 1977 Honor
- Holabird, Katharine *Angelina* series
- Holbrook, Stewart *America's Ethan Allen* — 1950 Honor
- Holling, Holling C. *Paddle to the Sea* — 1942 Honor
- Hosea, Tobias & Lisa Baskin *Hosie's Alphabet* — 1973 Honor
- Howitt, Mary *The Spider and the Fly* — 2003 Honor
- Hurd, Thacher
- Isadora, Rachel *Ben's Trumpet* — 1980 Honor
- Issacs, Anne *Swamp Angel* — 1995 Honor
- Jackson, Richard *Yo! Yes* — 1994 Honor
- James, M.R. *The Steadfast Tin Soldier* — 1954 Honor
- Jarrell, Randall *Snow White and the Seven Dwarfs* — 1973 Honor
- Jeffers, Susan *Three Jovial Huntsmen* — 1974 Honor
- Jenkins, Steve and Robin Page *What Do You Do with a Tail Like This?* — 2004 Honor
- Johnson, Crockett *Harold and His Purple Crayon* series
- Johnson, Stephen T. *Alphabet City* — 1996 Honor
- Joslin, Sesyle *What Do You Say, Dear?* — 1959 Honor
- Keats, Ezra Jack *The Snowy Day* — 1963 Winner
- Keats, Ezra Jack *Goggles!* — 1970 Honor
- Kepes, Juliet *Five Little Monkeys* — 1953 Honor
- Kerley, Barbara *The Dinosaurs of Waterhouse Hawkins* — 2002 Honor
- Kimmel, Eric *Hershel and the Hanukkah Goblins* — 1990 Honor
- Kingman, Lee *Pierre Pidgeon* — 1944 Honor
- Krauss, Ruth *A Very Special House* — 1954 Honor
- Krauss, Ruth *The Happy Day* — 1950 Honor
- Langstaff, John *Frog Went-a-Courtin'* — 1956 Winner
- Lawson, Robert *They Were Strong and Good* — 1941 Winner
- Leaf, Munro *Wee Gillis* — 1939 Honor
- Lee Burton, Virginia *The Little House* — 1943 Winner
- Lehman, Barbara *The Red Book* — 2005 Honor
- Lesser, Rika *Hansel and Gretel* — 1985 Honor
- Lester, Julius *John Henry* — 1995 Honor
- Lionni, Leo *Inch by Inch* — 1961 Honor
- Lionni, Leo *Swimmy* — 1964 Honor
- Lionni, Leo *Alexander and the Wind-Up Mouse* — 1970 Honor
- Lionni, Leo *Frederick* — 1968 Honor
- Lipkind, William *Finders Keepers* — 1952 Winner
- Lipkind, William *The Two Reds* — 1951 Honor
- Lobel, Arnold *Fables* — 1981 Winner
- Lobel, Arnold *Frog and Toad are Friends* — 1971 Honor
- Lobel, Arnold *On Market Street* — 1982 Honor
- Low, Joseph *Mice Twice* — 1981 Honor
- Macaulay, David *Castle* — 1978 Honor
- Macaulay, David *Black and White* — 1991 Winner
- Macaulay, David *Cathedral* — 1974 Honor
- MacDonald, Suse *Alphabetics* — 1987 Honor
- Malcolmson, Anne *Song of Robin Hood* — 1948 Honor
- Marshall, James *George and Martha* series

Books organized by author (continued)

* Marshall, James *Goldilocks and the Three Bears*   1989 Honor
* Marzollo, Jean *I Spy* series
* Mayer, Mercer
* McCarty, Peter *Hondo & Fabian*   2003 Honor
* McCloskey, Robert *Blueberries for Sal*   1949 Honor
* McCloskey, Robert *Make Way for Ducklings*   1942 Winner
* McCloskey, Robert *Time of Wonder*   1958 Winner
* McCloskey, Robert *One Morning in Maine*   1953 Honor
* McDermott, Gerald *Raven: A Trickster Tale from the*
                          Pacific Northwest   1994 Honor
* McDermott, Gerald *Anansi the Spider: A Tale from*
                          the Ashanti   1973 Honor
* McDermott, Gerald *Arrow to the Sun*   1975 Winner
* McGinley, Phyllis *All Around the Town*   1949 Honor
* McGinley, Phyllis *The Most Wonderful Doll in the World*   1951 Honor
* McKissack, Patricia C. *Mirandy and Brother Wind*   1989 Honor
* McPhail, David
* Milhous, Katherine *The Egg Tree*   1951 Winner
* Minarik, Else Holmelund *Little Bear's Visit*   1962 Honor
* Mitchell Preston, Edna *Pop Corn & Ma Goodness*   1970 Honor
* Mosel, Arlene *The Funny Little Women*   1973 Winner
* Moss, Lloyd *Zin! Zin! Zin! a Violin*   1996 Honor
* Mother Goose
* Musgrove, Margaret *Ashanti to Zulu: African Traditions*   1977 Winner
* Myers, Walter Dean *Harlem*   1998 Honor
* Ness, Evaline *Tom Tit Tot*   1966 Honor
* Ness, Evaline *Sam, Bangs & Moonshine*   1967 Winner
* Nic Leodhas, Sorche *All in the Morning Early*   1964 Honor
* Nic Leodhas, Sorche *Always Room for One More*   1966 Winner
* Nolan Clark, Ann *In My Mother's House*   1942 Honor
* Olds, Elizabeth *Feather Mountain*   1952 Honor
* Orton Jones, Jessie *Small Rain: Verses from the Bible*   1944 Honor
* Oxenbury, Helen
* Peet, Bill *Bill Peet: An Autobiography*   1990 Honor
* Pelletier, David *The Graphic Alphabet*   1997 Honor
* Pene du Bois, William *Bear Party*   1952 Honor
* Pene du Bois, William *Lion*   1957 Honor
* Perrault, Charles *Puss in Boots*   1991 Honor
* Petersham, Maude & Miska *An American ABC*   1942 Honor
* Petersham, Maude & Miska *The Rooster Crows*   1946 Winner
* Pilkey, Dav *The Paperboy*   1997 Honor
* Pinkney, Jerry *Noah's Ark*   2003 Honor
* Pinkney, Jerry *The Ugly Duckling*   2000 Honor
* Plume, Ilse *The Bremen-Town Musicians*   1981 Honor
* Politi, Leo *Pedro, the Angel of Olvera Street*   1947 Honor
* Politi, Leo *Song of the Swallows*   1950 Winner
* Politi, Leo *Juanita*   1949 Honor
* Potter, Beatrix
* Provensen, Alice & Martin *The Glorious Flight: Across*
                          the Channel with Louis Bleriot   1984 Winner
* Raffi
* Ransome, Arthur *The Fool of the World and the Flying Ship*   1969 Winner
* Rappaport, Doreen *Martin's Big Words: the life of*
                          Dr. Martin Luther King, Jr.   2002 Honor
* Rathmann, Peggy *Officer Buckle and Gloria*   1996 Winner
* Reed, Philip *Mother Goose and Nursery Rhymes*   1964 Honor
* Rey, H. A. *Curious George* series

Books organized by author (continued)

- Reyher, Becky *My Mother is the Most Beautiful Woman in the World* — 1946 Honor
- Ringgold, Faith *Tar Beach* — 1992 Honor
- Robbins, Ruth *Baboushka and the Three Kings* — 1961 Winner
- Rohmann, Eric *My Friend Rabbit* — 2003 Winner
- Rohmann, Eric *Time Flies* — 1995 Honor
- Rylant, Cynthia *The Relatives Came* — 1986 Honor
- Rylant, Cynthia *When I Was Young in the Mountains* — 1983 Honor
- San Souci, Robert D. *The Faithful Friend* — 1996 Honor
- San Souci, Robert *The Talking Eggs: A Folktale from the American South* — 1990 Honor
- Sawyer, Ruth *Journey Cake, Ho!* — 1954 Honor
- Sawyer, Ruth *The Christmas Anna Angel* — 1945 Honor
- Say, Allen *Grandfather's Journey* — 1994 Honor
- Scarry, Richard
- Schart Hyman, Trina *Little Red Riding Hood* — 1984 Honor
- Scheer, Julian *Rain Makes Applesauce* — 1965 Winner
- Schenk de Regniers, Beatrice *May I Bring a Friend?* — 1965 Winner
- Schlein, Miriam *When Will the World Be Mine?* — 1954 Honor
- Schreiber, Georges *Bambino the Clown* — 1948 Honor
- Scieszka, Jon *The Stinky Cheese Man and Other Fairly Stupid Tales* — 1993 Honor
- Sendak, Maurice *Where the Wild Things Are* — 1964 Winner
- Sendak, Maurice *In the Night Kitchen* — 1971 Honor
- Sendak, Maurice *Outside Over There* — 1982 Honor
- Seuss, Dr. *Bartholomew and the Oobleck* — 1950 Honor
- Seuss, Dr. *If I Ran the Zoo* — 1951 Honor
- Seuss, Dr. *McElligot's Pool* — 1948 Honor
- Shannon, David *No, David!* — 1999 Honor
- Shulevitz, Uri *Snow* — 1999 Honor
- Shulevitz, Uri *The Treasure* — 1980 Honor
- Simont, Marc *The Stray Dog* — 2002 Honor
- Sis, Peter *Tibet Through the Red Box* — 1999 Honor
- Sis, Peter *Starry Messenger* — 1997 Honor
- Sleator, William *The Angry Moon* — 1971 Honor
- Snyder, Diane *The Boy of the Three-Year Nap* — 1989 Honor
- Spier, Peter *Fox Went out on a Chilly Night: An Old Song* — 1962 Honor
- Spier, Peter *Noah's Ark* — 1978 Winner
- St. George, Judith *So You Want to be President?* — 2001 Winner
- Steig, William *Sylvester and the Magic Pebble* — 1970 Winner
- Steig, William *The Amazing Bone* — 1977 Honor
- Steptoe, John *Muffaro's Beautiful Daughters: An African Tale* — 1988 Honor
- Steptoe, John *The Story of Jumping Mouse: A Native American Legend* — 1985 Honor
- Stevens, Janet *Tops & Bottoms* — 1996 Honor
- Stewart, Sarah *The Gardener* — 1998 Honor
- Taback, Simms *Joseph Had a Little Overcoat* — 2000 Winner
- Taback, Simms *There Was an Old Lady Who Swallowed a Fly* — 1998 Honor
- Tafuri, Nancy *Have You Seen My Duckling?* — 1985 Honor
- Thayer, Ernest *Casey at Bar* — 2001 Honor
- Thurber, James *Many Moons* — 1944 Winner
- Titus, Eve *Anatole* — 1957 Honor
- Titus, Eve *Anatole and the Cat* — 1958 Honor
- Torrey, Marjorie *Sing Mother Goose* — 1946 Honor
- Tresselt, Alvin *Hide and Seek Fog* — 1966 Honor

Books organized by author (continued)

- Tresselt, Alvin *Rain Drop Splash* — 1947 Honor
- Tresselt, Alvin *White Snow, Bright Snow* — 1948 Winner
- Tudor, Tasha *1 is One* — 1957 Honor
- Tudor, Tasha *Mother Goose* — 1945 Honor
- Turkle, Brinton *Thy Friend, Obadiah* — 1970 Honor
- Turlay Newberry, Clare *April's Kittens* — 1941 Honor
- Turlay Newberry, Clare *Barkis* — 1939 Honor
- Turlay Newberry, Clare *Marshmallow* — 1943 Honor
- Turlay Newberry, Clare *T-Bone, the Baby Sitter* — 1951 Honor
- Udry, Janice *A Tree is Nice* — 1957 Winner
- Udry, Janice May *The Moon Jumpers* — 1960 Honor
- Updike, John *A Child's Calendar* — 2000 Honor
- Van Allsburg, Chris *Jumanji* — 1982 Winner
- Van Allsburg, Chris *The Garden of Abdul Gasazi* — 1980 Honor
- Van Allsburg, Chris *The Polar Express* — 1986 Winner
- Ward, Lynd *The Biggest Bear* — 1953 Winner
- Wells, Rosemary
- Wheeler, Opal *Sing in Praise: A Collection of the Best Loved Hymns* — 1947 Honor
- Wiese, Kurt *Fish in the Air* — 1949 Honor
- Wiese, Kurt *You Can Write Chinese* — 1946 Honor
- Wiesner, David *Sector 7* — 2000 Honor
- Wiesner, David *The Three Pigs* — 2002 Winner
- Wiesner, David *Tuesday* — 1992 Winner
- Wiesner, David *Free Fall* — 1989 Honor
- Willard, Nancy *A Visit to William Blake's Inn* — 1982 Honor
- Willems, Mo *Knuffle Bunny: A Cautionary Tale* — 2005 Honor
- Willems, Mo *Don't Let the Pigeon Drive the Bus* — 2004 Honor
- Williams, Sherly Anne *Working Cotton* — 1993 Honor
- Williams, Vera B. *"More More More," Said the Baby: Three Love Stories* — 1991 Honor
- Williams, Vera B. *A Chair for My Mother* — 1983 Honor
- Wise Brown, Margaret *A Child's Good Night Book* — 1944 Honor
- Wise Brown, Margaret *Little Lost Lamb* — 1946 Honor
- Wise Brown, Margaret *The Little Island* — 1947 Winner
- Wise Brown, Margaret *Wheel on the Chimney* — 1955 Honor
- Wisniewski, David *Golem* — 1997 Winner
- Wood, Audrey *King Bidgood's in the Bathtub* — 1986 Honor
- Woodson, Jacqueline *Coming on Home Soon* — 2005 Honor
- Yashima, Taro *Crow Boy* — 1956 Honor
- Yashima, Taro *Seashore Story* — 1968 Honor
- Yashima, Taro *Umbrella* — 1959 Honor
- Yolen, Jane *Owl Moon* — 1988 Winner
- Yolen, Jane *The Emperor and the Kite* — 1968 Honor
- Yorinks, Arthur *Hey, Al* — 1987 Winner
- Young, Ed *Lon Po Po: A Red-Riding Hood Story from China* — 1990 Winner
- Young, Ed *Seven Blind Mice* — 1993 Honor
- Zelinsky, Paul O. *Rapunzel* — 1998 Winner
- Zelinsky, Paul O. *Rumpelstiltskin* — 1987 Honor
- Zemach, Harve *Duffy and the Devil* — 1974 Winner
- Zemach, Harve *The Judge: An Untrue Tale* — 1970 Honor
- Zemach, Margot *It Could Always Be Worse* — 1978 Honor
- Zion, Gene *All Falling Down* — 1952 Honor
- Zolotow, Charlotte *Mr. Rabbit and the Lovely Present* — 1963 Honor

Nursery Rhymes and Poems
Dyer, Jane-*Animal Crackers*
Grover, Eulalie Osgood-*Mother Goose: The Original Volland Edition*
Opie, Iona Archibald-*My Very First Mother Goose*
Wright, Blanche Fisher-*The Real Mother Goose*

BOOKS

BY FAVORITE CHARACTER
Angelina: Holabird, Katharine
Clifford: Bridwell, Norman
Corduroy: Freeman, Don
Curious George: Rey, H. A.
Frog and Toad: Lobel, Arnold
George and Martha: Marshall, James
Good Dog, Carl: Day, Alexandra
Harold and his Purple Crayon: Johnson, Crockett
Little Bear: Minarik, Else Holmelund
Madeline: Bemelmans, Ludwig
Old Bear: Hissey, Jane
Olivia: Falconer, Ian
Paddington Bear: Bond, Michael
Raggedy Ann: Gruelle, Johnny
Spot: Hill, Eric
Thomas the Tank Engine: Awdrey, Wilbert Vere

BY FAIRY TALE STORY
Beauty and the Beast
Bremen-Town Musicians
Cinderella
Gingerbread Man
Goldilocks and The Three Bears
Hansel and Gretel
Henny Penny
House that Jack Built
Jack and the Beanstalk
Little Red Hen
Little Red Riding Hood
Nutcracker
Old Woman and Her Pig
Peter and the Wolf
Peter Rabbit
Princess and the Pea
Puss in Boots
Rapunzel
Rumpelstiltskin
Saint George and the Dragon
Shoemaker and the Elves
Sleeping Beauty
Snow White and the Seven Dwarves
Snow White and Rose Red
Steadfast Tin Soldier
Teeny, Tiny Lady
Three Billy Goats Gruff
Three Little Kittens
Three Little Pigs
Tortoise and the Hare
Town Mouse and the Country Mouse
Ugly Duckling

BY TOPIC IN THE ADULT SECTION OF THE LIBRARY

Cars-Dewey Decimal Number 629.2
Fish-Dewey Decimal Number 597
Mammals-Dewey Decimal Number 599
Plants-Dewey Decimal Number 635, 582.1
Reptiles and Birds-Dewey Decimal Number 598
Worms and Insects-Dewey Decimal Number 595

BY SUBJECT

Amusement
Hill, Eric-*Spot Goes to the Circus*

Aquarium
Gunzi, Christiane-*Tide Pool* (Dorling Kindersley Publishing)
Jaques, Florence Page-*There Once Was a Puffin*
Lionni, Leo-*Swimmy*
Raffi-*Baby Beluga*
Rylant, Cynthia-*The Whale*
Seuss, Dr.-*McElligot's Pool*
Seuss, Dr.-*One Fish Two Fish Red Fish Blue Fish*

Buses
Crews, Donald-*School Bus*
Raffi-*The Wheels on the Bus*

Cars
Hurd, Thacher-*Zoom City*
Road and Track Magazine

Construction
Lee Burton, Virginia-*Mike Mulligan and His Steam Shovel*

Farms and Ponies
Brown, Margaret Wise-*Big Red Barn*
Flack, Marjorie-*Ask Mr. Bear*
Hill, Eric-*Spot Goes to the Farm*
Hobbie, Holly-*Toot and Puddle*
Kunhardt, Dorothy-*Pat the Bunny*
McPhail, David-*The Three Pigs*
Provensen, Alice and Martin-*Our Animal Friends*

Gardens and Nature
Bunting, Eve-*Sunflower House*
Carle, Eric-*The Very Hungry Caterpillar*
Day, Alexandra-*Carl's Afternoon in the Park*
Ehlert, Lois-*Planting a Rainbow*
Hill, Eric-*Spot Goes to the Park*
Himmelman, John-*An Earthworm's Life*
Kirk, David-*Miss Spider's Tea Party*
Kleven, Elisa-*The Puddle Pail*
Krauss, Ruth-*The Carrot Seed*
Mayer, Mercer-*A Boy, a Dog and a Frog*
McCloskey, Robert-*Make Way for Ducklings*
Morgan, Pierr-*The Turnip: An Old Russian Folk Tale*
Potter, Beatrix-*The Tale of Benjamin Bunny*
Potter, Beatrix-*The Tale of Peter Rabbit*
Rosen Michael-*We're Going on a Bear Hunt*
Yolen, Jane-*Owl Moon*

Museums
Boynton, Sandra-*Oh My Oh My Oh Dinosaurs!*
Brett, Jan-*Annie and the Wild Animals*
Carle, Eric-*The Very Hungry Caterpillar*
Carrick, Carol-*Patrick's Dinosaurs*
Himmelman, John-*A Pill Bug's Life*
Walsh, Ellen Stoll-*Mouse Paint*
Wild, Margaret-*My Dearest Dinosaur*

Music
Emerson, Sally, Moira MacLean, Colin MacLean-*The Kingfisher Nursery
    Rhyme Songbook: With Easy Music to Play for Piano and Guitar*
Kapp, Richard-*Metropolitan Museum of Art's Lullabies,
    An Illustrated Songbook*
Orozco, Jose-Luis-*De Colores and Other Latin American Folk Songs for Children*

Trains
Awdry, Wilbert Vere-*Thomas the Tank Engine*
Brown, Margaret Wise-*The Train to Timbuctoo*
Crews, Donald-*Freight Train*
Piper, Watty-*The Little Engine that Could*
Ziefert, Harriet-*Train Song*

Water
Brett, Jan-*The Mitten*
Gramatky, Hardie-*Little Toot*
Hill, Eric-*Spot Goes to the Beach*
Keats, Ezra Jack-*The Snowy Day*
Kleven, Elisa-*The Puddle Pail*
McPhail, David-*Snow Lion*
Raffi-*Down by the Bay*
Rey, H. A.-*Curious George Goes to the Beach*
Rockwell, Anne-*Boats*

Zoo
Christelow, Eileen-*Five Little Monkeys Sitting in a Tree*
Collard III, Sneed B.-*Animal Dads*
Daly, Kathleen N.-*Wild Animal Babies*
Hadithi, Mwenye-*Greedy Zebra*
Jackson, K.-*The Saggy Baggy Elephant*
Jackson, Kathryn-*Tawny Scrawny Lion*
Jorgensen, Gail-*Crocodile Beat*
Martin, Bill, Jr.,-*Brown Bear, Brown Bear, What Do You See?*
Priddy, Roger-*Baby's Book of Animals* (Dorling Kindersley Publishing)

SITE 19 - SCHOOL BUSES/PASADENA UNIFIED SCHOOL DISTRICT

ADDRESS
District Service Center
740 West Woodbury Road
Pasadena, CA 91001

• Or check with your local school district to find a closer school bus yard.

DIRECTIONS [GUIDE PAGE 535 (LA)]
Take Interstate Highway 210 north and exit Arroyo Boulevard/Windsor Avenue. Go north from the offramp and make a right on Woodbury Road. Then make a right on Cañada Avenue.

GOOD THINGS TO SEE AND HEAR
The District Service Center is the parking lot for the Pasadena District's buses. They are parked in several lots and along the street. The lot provides a unique opportunity to drive by real school buses of all shapes and sizes. These buses are parked for the night or weekend in their official parking lot and are waiting to take children to school in the mornings and pick them up in the afternoons. Your view will remind you of the buses in the book *Buses* by Donald Crews. The Pasadena Unified School District lot has very easy access, but most school districts have a lot somewhere.

Another place where you can often find many school buses is the Los Angeles Zoo parking lot weekday mornings during the school year.

HOURS
It is best to visit on weekends, or after school pick-up and drop-off times to see the most buses. Avoid times when the buses are coming or going as you may cause a traffic jam.

PARKING
Best to drive by

ADMISSION
Free

RELATED PLACES
• Big Rigs at Castaic - Site 34
• Children's Museum at La Habra - Site 2
• Construction and Road Work Sites-Chapter 2
• Fire Stations-Chapter 2
• Petersen Automotive Museum - Site 5
• Sunshine Canyon Landfill - Site 33

CLOSE-BY PLACES
• Descanso Gardens - Site 38
• The Snow in Angeles National Forest - Site 133

OTHER SCHOOL BUS PARKING LOTS

SITE 20 - BONITA UNIFIED SCHOOL DISTRICT BUS YARD

1000 San Dimas Boulevard
San Dimas, CA 91773
[GUIDE PAGE 570/600 (LA)]
• Take Interstate Highway 210 east (stay left on new 210), exit San Dimas Boulevard. Go south (right), lot will be on your right.

SITE 21 - L.A. UNIFIED SCHOOL DISTRICT LOT IN GARDENA

Transit Way
Gardena, CA 90248
[GUIDE PAGE 734/764 (LA)]
• Take Interstate Highway 110, then to State Highway 91 west. Exit and make immediate south turn on Vermont Avenue, then turn left on 182nd Street. Go into Home Depot parking lot and go straight to fence - buses are on other side of fence.

SITE 22 - CARSON AND ROSEWOOD SCHOOL BUS YARDS

14000-16000 South Avalon Boulevard
Rosewood, CA 90220
[GUIDE PAGE 734 (LA)]
• Take State Highway 91. Exit Avalon Boulevard and go north. The first lot is on left side of street just after Walnut Street. Second and third lots are on your right.

SITE 23 - HUNTINGTON BEACH SCHOOL BUS YARD

Goldenwest Street and Yorktown Avenue
Huntington Beach, CA 92648
[GUIDE PAGE 857 (OC)]
• Take Interstate Highway 405 south. Exit Goldenwest Street and go south. Make left on Yorktown Avenue.

SITE 24 - MISSION VIEJO SCHOOL BUS YARD

25631 Diseno Drive
Mission Viejo, CA 92691
[GUIDE PAGE 891 (OC)]
• Take Interstate Highway 5. Exit El Toro Road, and go northeast. Make a right turn on Jeronimo Road. Lot is just past Los Alisos Boulevard.

OTHER SCHOOL BUS PARKING LOTS (CONTINUED)

SITE 25 - NORTH HOLLYWOOD SCHOOL BUS YARD

11200 Sherman Way
North Hollywood, CA 91605
[GUIDE PAGE 532 (LA)]
• Take State Highway 170. Exit Sherman Way, go east. Lot is on left. Make a U-turn and park along street.

SITE 26 - NORWALK SCHOOL BUS YARD

12820 Pioneer Boulevard
Norwalk, CA 90650
[GUIDE PAGE 736 (LA)]
• Take Interstate Highway 5 north. Exit Imperial Boulevard, go west, then south on Pioneer Boulevard. Lot is on your left side. Make a U-turn, park along street and walk by gates.

SITE 27 - ANAHEIM UNION HIGH SCHOOL DISTRICT BUS YARD

Crescent Avenue, Anaheim, CA 92801
[GUIDE PAGE 768 (OC)]
• Take Interstate Highway 5. Exit, Euclid Street, go south. Make a right on Lincoln Avenue, then another right on Crescent Way. Follow to end and veer to left. Bus lot is to the left.

FIRE STATIONS

ADDRESS
Internet:
Los Angeles Fire Department   www.lafd.org, www.lafd.org/visit.htm
Orange County Fire Department   www.ocfa.org
San Diego Fire Department   www.sandiego.gov/fireandems/
Santa Barbara Fire Department   www.santabarbaraca.gov/government/
departments/fire/

Phone Book:
White Pages   County Government Offices
(look in front of phone book, under
"Fire Department")

GOOD THINGS TO SEE AND HEAR
Fire stations welcome children of all ages to visit. Call your local fire station in advance of your visit to arrange a time (even an hour in advance is o.k.). A brief, simple tour geared for your child's age and interest can be readily arranged. Ask a real fireman about his fire trucks, gear, and why there are no dalmatian dogs on fire trucks anymore. See the ladder trucks, the pumpers, and the ambulances, and where the firemen live when they are waiting for a fire.

Check the Los Angeles Fire Department's "Visit Your Neighborhood Fire Station" website at www.lafd.org/visit.htm for more information.

HOURS
Daily   9:00 a.m. - 5:00 p.m. (varies with station)

PARKING
Free

ADMISSION
Free

RELATED PLACES
• Big Rigs at Castaic - Site 34
• Construction and Road Work Sites-Chapter 2
• Sunshine Canyon Landfill - Site 33
• Kidspace Children's Museum - Site 4
• School Buses/Pasadena Unified School District - Site 19

YOUR COMMENTS
_____
_____
_____
_____

FIRE STATION

DALMATION

FIRE FIGHTER

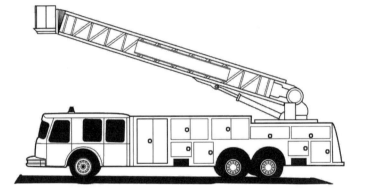

LADDER TRUCK

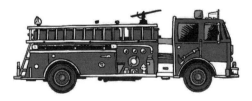

PUMPER TRUCK   AMBULANCE

SITE 28 - DOGGIE DAY CAMP AT PETSMART

ADDRESS
3347 East Foothill Boulevard
Pasadena, CA 91107
(626) 351-8434
www.petsmart.com/doggiedaycamp/

DIRECTIONS [GUIDE PAGE 566]
Take Interstate Highway 210 to the Madre Exit and go north. Make a right on Foothill Boulevard. PETsMART will be on your left.

GOOD THINGS TO SEE AND HEAR
Doggie Day Camp is a large area in the back of the store that boards dogs for the day to provide a place for them to play and interact with other dogs and people while their owners work. There is usually a wide assortment of breeds all playing happily (mostly) together. It is all quite comical.

A huge glass wall separates your child from the dogs so your child can watch all he wants without worrying about too many dog kisses.

Check the PETsMART web site for new Doggie-Day-Camps near you. They seem to be a big hit and will likely increase in number.

As owners come to retrieve or bring their dogs to camp, your child may want to pet the dogs. Be very careful to ask the owner first, let the dogs sniff your child's' hand first, and then pet carefully. Never let your child hug or be kissed by a strange dog no matter how cute. All dogs bite!

HOURS
Monday-Saturday 7:00 a.m. - 7:00 p.m.
Sunday 9:00 a.m. - 5:00 p.m.

PARKING
Free

ADMISSION
Free

RELATED PLACES
• Pet Stores-Chapter 2

CLOSE-BY PLACES
• California Institute of Technology, Caltech - Site 56
• Eaton Canyon County Park and Nature Center - Site 44
• The Huntington - Site 39
• Kidspace Museum - Site 4
• Pasadena Civic Auditorium - Site 220
• Tournament of Roses® Parade - Site 216
• Tournament of Roses® Float Viewing - Site 216

YOUR COMMENTS

_____

_____

_____

_____

_____

DOGS

SHEPHERD

RETRIEVER

COCKER SPANIEL

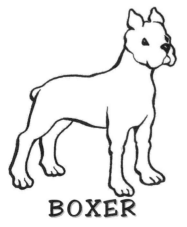

BOXER

TERRIER

PET STORES

ADDRESS
INTERNET:
Petco   www.petco.com
PETsMART   www.petsmart.com

PHONE BOOK:
Yellow Pages   Pet Supplies, Pets-Retail
White Pages   Petco, PETsMART

GOOD THINGS TO SEE AND HEAR
Most large pet stores have fish, birds, and small animals like rabbits, guinea pigs, mice, and rats. Some have reptiles. Go in just to look and let your child become familiar with these small animals - it may make them better pet owners in the future. If you want to buy something, the small rubber balls for dogs are great for babies and toddlers. They are colorful, and easy to pick up.

Pet stores provide a good opportunity to teach your children not to touch the animals and birds for the safety of both your child and the animals.

HOURS
Monday-Saturday   9:00 a.m. - 9:00 p.m.
Sunday   10:00 a.m. - 6:00 p.m. (hours vary with store location)

PARKING
Free

ADMISSION
Free

RELATED PLACES
• Birch Aquarium at Scripps - Site 88
• Cabrillo Marine Aquarium - Site 72
• Doggie Day Camp at PETsMART - Site 28
• Long Beach Aquarium of the Pacific - Site 71
• Roundhouse Marine Studies Lab and Aquarium - Site 73
• STAR EcoStation Environmental Science and Wildlife Rescue Center-Site 67

YOUR COMMENTS

_____

_____

_____

_____

PETS

MOUSE

CAT

PARROT

GOLDFISH

RABBIT

SITE 29 - OLVERA STREET

ADDRESS
El Pueblo de Los Angeles State Historic Park
845 North Alameda Street
Los Angeles, CA 90012
(213) 680-2525
olvera-street.com

DIRECTIONS [GUIDE PAGE 634 (LA)]
• Take Interstate Highway 110 to the Hill Street Exit and go south. Make a left on Cesar Chavez Avenue East and then a right on Alameda Street. Park at Union Station.
• Or take the Metro Rail Gold Line- Site 195
• or Metrolink to Union Station - Site 194

GOOD THINGS TO SEE AND HEAR
Visit the oldest street in Los Angeles where Spanish Governor Felipe de Neve founded the pueblo of Los Angeles in 1781. Since 1930, Olvera Street has been a Mexican marketplace lined with shops and stalls filled with piñatas, tortillas, and mariachis. Children love the Mexican musical instruments like tambourines or maracas. Tortillas and desserts are great finger foods while strolling through the colorful booths. Weekends include mariachi bands and dancers in the plaza.

This is a good place for a stroller, as it is often very crowded.

HOURS
Daily   10:00 a.m. - 7:00 p.m. (store hours may vary)

PARKING
$6.00 on weekends on North Main Street (between Caesar Chavez and Arcadia Street) or park at Union Station

ADMISSION
Free

RELATED PLACES
• Chinatown - Site 30
• Grand Central Market - Site 31
• Local Farmer's Markets-Chapter 2
• The Original Los Angeles Farmer's Market - Site 32

CLOSE-BY PLACES
• Bob Baker Marionette Theater - Site 204
• Chinatown - Site 30
• Walt Disney Music Concert Hall - Site 221
• Grand Central Market - Site 31
• KLOS Story Theater - Site 206
• Richard J. Riordan Central Library - Site 16
• Union Station - Site 171

OTHER SPECIAL EVENTS ON OLVERA STREET

LOS TRES REYES / Early January
Celebration of the visit of the Three Kings with music and a procession.

MARDI GRAS / Mid-February
Celebration of "Fat Tuesday" with Brazilian singing and dancing, and a parade.

BLESSING OF THE ANIMALS / Saturday Before Easter
Celebration of the animal world with a procession of house pets and exotic animals.

CINCO DE MAYO / Weekend Closest to May 5
Celebration of Mexico's victory over the French in Puebla, Mexico, 1862.

FOURTH OF JULY
Celebration of Independence Day with a musket salute, dance, and entertainment.

LOS ANGELES CITY BIRTHDAY CELEBRATION / Early September
Celebration of the anniversary of the founding of Los Angeles.

MEXICAN INDEPENDENCE DAY CELEBRATION / Early September
Celebration of Mexican Independence from Spain.

DIA DE LOS MUERTOS / Early November
Colorful ancient ceremony in memory of departed loved ones.

LAS POSADAS / Mid-December Evenings
Presentation of the nine-day journey of Mary and Joseph to Bethlehem.

YOUR COMMENTS

_____
_____
_____
_____
_____

SITE 30 - CHINATOWN

ADDRESS
Old Chinatown Plaza
930 North Broadway
Los Angeles, CA 90012
(213) 617-0396 Chinese Chamber of Commerce
(213) 626-4028 Los Angeles Old Chinatown Merchants Association
oldchinatownla.com

DIRECTIONS [GUIDE PAGE 634 (LA)]
• Take Interstate Highway 110 exit Hill Street Exit and go south. Park in a lot along Hill Street or Broadway. Old Chinatown is between Hill Street and Broadway, and College Street and Bernard Street. The famous arches leading to Gin Ling Way (a walking street) are along Broadway between College Street and Bernard Street, and along Hill Street between College Street and Bernard Street. Many of the shops are along Broadway near Alpine Street.
• Or take the Metro Rail Gold Line-Site 195 or Metrolink to Union Station-Site 194.

GOOD THINGS TO SEE AND HEAR
The second largest Chinatown in the United States is in Los Angeles. Chinatown was dedicated in June 1938. It is a unique place in Southern California, although a bit old and faded. Visit the plaza at Broadway and Gin Ling Way with its fancy neon gate and exotic roofs. Talk about the Foo Dogs that guard against evil spirits and the dragons that are symbols of power; and about the color red which means happiness. Here you will find shops with toy cars, tea sets, little purses, fans, and bamboo whistles. Bring a lot of pennies for the Seven Star Cavern Wishing Well. Buy some lotus leaves in the food market and paint on them (paint on the light side). Also visit the fish, herb, and poultry shops (with live fish and poultry) along Broadway to smell the smells and talk about where our food comes from.

Try taking the Dash Bus ($.25 for adults, children are free) to the Richard J. Riordan Central Library.

The Chinese New Years Parade is something to see, but is crowded and very loud with firecrackers.

HOURS
Daytime is best
Stores   10:00 a.m. - 6:00 p.m.

PARKING
$12.00   Fee for all day
$1.00 per hour   Metered spaces

ADMISSION
Free
• But bring a little money to buy a souvenir from the gift shops

RELATED PLACES
- Grand Central Market - Site 31
- Local Farmer's Markets-Chapter 2
- Olvera Street - Site 29
- The Original Los Angeles Farmer's Market - Site 32

CLOSE-BY PLACES
- Bob Baker Marionette Theater - Site 204
- Grand Central Market - Site 31
- KLOS Story Theater - Site 206
- Olvera Street - Site 29
- Richard J. Riordan Central Library - Site 16
- Union Station - Site 170
- Walt Disney Music Concert Hall - Site 221

SPECIAL EVENTS
- Chinese New Year Celebrations in December, January or February
  (Varies Each Year) www.ladragonparade.com

YOUR COMMENTS

SITE 31 - GRAND CENTRAL MARKET

ADDRESS
317 South Broadway
Los Angeles, CA 90013
(213) 624-2378
www.grandcentralsquare.com

DIRECTIONS [GUIDE PAGE 634 (LA)]
- Take Interstate Highway 110 to the 4th Street Exit and go east. Turn left on Broadway and then left on 3rd Street. From there, make a left on Hill Street. Parking is off 3rd and Hill Street.
- Or take the Metro Rail Red Line - Site 195.

GOOD THINGS TO SEE AND HEAR
Grand Central Market is a bustling, noisy open market (in a large warehouse) built in 1917. The aisles are full of places to see, smell, and buy produce, fish, breads, meats (including pig and lamb heads), flowers, and special foods. There are plenty of places to eat - try a tortilla from the giant tortilla-making machine, or some fruit.

This is a very busy place - use a backpack.

HOURS
Monday-Sunday   9:00 a.m. - 6:00 p.m.

PARKING
Validated parking with $10.00 purchase at 308 South Hill street

ADMISSION
Free

RELATED PLACES
- Chinatown - Site 30
- Local Farmer's Markets-Chapter 2
- Olvera Street - Site 29
- The Original Los Angeles Farmer's Market - Site 32

CLOSE-BY PLACES
- Bob Baker Marionette Theater - Site 204
- Chinatown - Site 30
- KLOS Story Theater - Site 206
- Olvera Street - Site 29
- Richard J. Riordan Central Library - Site 16
- Union Station - Site 171
- Walt Disney Music Concert Hall - Site 221

YOUR COMMENTS

_____

_____

_____

_____

_____

SITE 32 - THE ORIGINAL LOS ANGELES FARMER'S MARKET

ADDRESS
6333 West 3rd Street
Los Angeles, CA 90036
(323) 933-9211
www.farmersmarketla.com

DIRECTIONS [GUIDE PAGE 633 (LA)]
Take Interstate Highway 10 to the Fairfax Avenue Exit and go north. Pass 3rd Street and make a right on Farmer's Market Place.

GOOD THINGS TO SEE AND HEAR
The Original Los Angeles Farmer's Market began in 1934 when farmers displayed their produce on the tailgates of their trucks-probably much like your local farmer's market. The Original Farmer's Market has been the home to circus acts, parades, and petting zoos. The Farmer's Market today is a collection of open-air stores with a great variety of food, flowers, and gifts from around the world. Eat outdoors in the original turquoise metal tables and chairs. Try the fruits, breads, or ice cream. Smell the different international foods. Plan to buy some fruits, vegetables, or meats. Also, let your child help select by touching, smelling, and perhaps tasting - if the vendor is willing to give you a sample.

There are often special family events (see below).

Big stores, including FAO Schwartz, are rapidly surrounding the Original Farmer's Market.

HOURS
Monday-Friday	9:00 a.m. - 9:00 p.m.
Saturday	9:00 a.m. - 8:00 p.m.
Sunday	10:00 a.m. - 7:00 p.m.

PARKING
Free for first 3 hours with validation

ADMISSION
Free

RELATED PLACES
- Chinatown - Site 30
- Grand Central Market - Site 31
- Local Farmer's Markets-Chapter 2
- Olvera Street - Site 29

CLOSE-BY PLACES
- Boone Children's Gallery, LACMA - Site 8
- Children's Book World - Site 18
- La Brea Tar Pits and Page Museum - Site 6
- Petersen Automotive Museum - Site 5
- Storyopolis - Site 18
- Zimmer Children's Museum - Site 10

SPECIAL EVENTS AT THE FARMER'S MARKET

Mardi Gras / Mid-February
Feast on delicious New Orleans beignets, jambalaya, and gumbo while dancing to live Cajun music or strolling with the Dixieland Band.

St. Patrick's Day / March
Enjoy the tastiest traditional Irish corned beef, cabbage and potatoes. See live Irish bands and strolling Celtic entertainment.

Easter Celebration / March or April
Celebrate the day before Easter at a petting zoo complete with sheep, pigs, rabbits, goats, and llamas. There is also egg decorating and breakfast with the Easter Bunny.

Cinco de Mayo / Early May
Enjoy the superb foods of Mexico along with Mariachi bands and folklorico dancing with a true fiesta atmosphere.

Annual Gilmore Heritage Auto Show
The Gilmore Family Auto Show celebrates antique cars, classics, hot rods, and race cars.

Twilight Summer Music Festival / Friday Evenings-Late May through Labor Day
Great food from around the world is offered, along with music ranging from the blues to the sounds of the Caribbean, Scottish pipes, Cajun zydeco, swing, and Brazilian jazz.

Fall Festival / Late October
Enjoy live country music, square dancing, hay rides, a Harvest Moon Ball, pumpkin patch, Oktoberfest, and the Skirball Cultural Center's Sukkot.

Holiday Festivities / December
Entertainment throughout the month includes klezmer bands and yuletide carolers; Celtic flutes, harps, and tin whistles; holiday swing; and violin and banjo carols.

YOUR COMMENTS

_____

_____

_____

_____

_____

LOCAL FARMER'S MARKETS

Many cities have regular farmer's markets with open air stands selling fruits and vegetables that are in season, as well as breads, fresh flowers, and honey. Most items can be tasted as you stroll around. Some markets have music, petting zoos, pony rides, and more. Some farmer's markets are seasonal.

Let your child help choose the fruits and vegetables, and try getting a strange fruit or vegetable that your child has not yet tried.

To find your local farmer's market, try these options.

INTERNET:

www.cafarmersmarkets.com

PHONE BOOK:

White Pages   City Government Offices (front of phone book, look under "City" and call City Hall or the Chamber of Commerce)

FRUITS AND VEGETABLES

APPLE

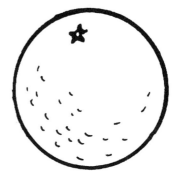

ORANGE

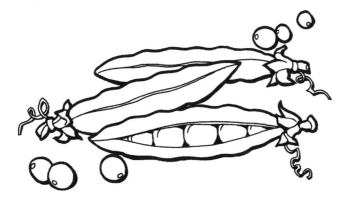

PEAS

CARROT

BROCOLLI

HARDWARE STORES

PHONE BOOK:
Yellow Pages   Hardware-Retail

GOOD THINGS TO SEE AND HEAR

In the first part of the 1900s, hardware stores often carried model trains and toys. Some still do. All hardware stores carry items that make great toys. Try the hardware store near you and involve your toddler or baby in buying a funnel, a cheap paintbrush or a small paint roller (use them with water to decorate your driveway), some white PVC pipe and pipe joints (better than Tinker Toys), or a plastic bucket. If your hardware store also carries kitchen items, try some cookie cutters, Jello molds, measuring cups and spoons, cake pans and wooden spoons. Get a big bag of flour from your grocery store and have a great time outside with your baby or toddler. These items are also handy for homemade play dough (1 cup salt, 1 cup water, 2 cups flour and a bag of Kool-aid mix for color and flavor). The bigger hardware stores also carry plants. A six-pack of colorful flowers may keep your toddler busy in the garden all afternoon.

Be sure the items you select are safe for your child.

HOURS

Monday-Saturday   9:00 a.m. - 5:00 p.m.
          (larger hardware stores like Orchard Supply Hardware (OSH) have longer hours)

RELATED PLACES

• Petersen Automotive Museum - Site 5
• San Diego Model Railroad Museum - Site 202
• School Buses/Pasadena Unified School District - Site 19
• Travel Town Museum - Site 170

HARDWARE TOOLS FOR CHILDREN

FUNNEL

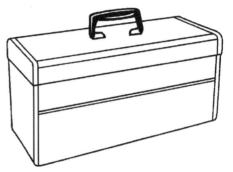

TOOL BOX

PAINT BRUSH

PVC PIPE

PAINT ROLLER

CONSTRUCTION AND ROAD WORK

CEMENT MIXER   BULLDOZER

STEAM ROLLER

EXCAVATOR   DUMP TRUCK

CONSTRUCTION AND ROAD WORK SITES

ADDRESS

There is no information on construction or roadwork sites for the viewing pleasure of little children. This is not information that Departments of Public Works has on hand. However, there are usually several active projects in your city at any given time-watch for them and they may become regular stops.

GOOD THINGS TO SEE AND HEAR

Every city has construction or road work somewhere. Watch for it when you drive around town. Look for a good place to stop and watch, either from your car or in your stroller. Once you find a site with an easy parking place, this can be a regular stop to watch the ongoing progress. See and hear the cement mixers, dump trucks, and back hoes in action.

Be sure you are watching from a safe location and are not interfering with the ongoing work.

HOURS
Weekdays   7:00 a.m. - 4:00 p.m.

PARKING
Usually free

ADMISSION
Free

RELATED PLACES
- Big Rigs at Castaic - Site 34
- Sunshine Canyon Landfill - Site 33
- Fire Stations-Chapter 2
- School Buses/Pasadena Unified School District - Site 19

BOOKS FOR YOUR CHILD
- Lee Burton, Virginia-*Mike Mulligan and His Steam Shovel*

YOUR COMMENTS

_____

_____

_____

_____

SITE 33 - SUNSHINE CANYON LANDFILL

ADDRESS
Sunshine Canyon Landfill
14747 San Fernando Road
Sylmar, CA 91342
(818) 833-6500
www.sunshinecanyonlandfill.com

DIRECTIONS [GUIDE PAGE 481 (LA)]
Take Interstate Highway 5 north (past the State Highway 118 junction) to the Roxford Street Exit. At the stop sign, turn left onto Roxford Street then a right onto Sepulveda Boulevard for about two miles to San Fernando Road. Turn left on San Fernando Road and go about two miles to Sunshine Canyon Road. Turn left at the signal and follow the paved road to the front of the building, park in front, go into the office, and ask for Larry Cubit.

GOOD THINGS TO SEE AND HEAR
Sunshine Canyon Landfill is an amazingly tidy and large area where Browning Ferris Industries-(BFI) garbage trucks come to dump their garbage. On weekdays there are mostly garbage trucks, and it is very busy. On Saturday, it is less busy and the trucks are mostly smaller and filled with waste from backyard projects. Watch for big caterpillar trucks grooming the hillsides. Sunshine Canyon Landfill also has the largest oak tree nursery in California.

Although it is possible to visit the landfill with your family in your car, it is best to arrange a tour. The tour can be very short and geared for babies and toddlers. Call (818) 833-6507 to arrange a tour. At the end of the tour, you can plant a tree.

HOURS
Monday-Friday	6:00 a.m. - 6:00 p.m.
Saturday	7:00 a.m. - 2:00 p.m.

PARKING
Free

ADMISSION
Free, if you are not dumping

RELATED PLACES
• Big Rigs at Castaic - Site 34
• Construction and Road Work Sites-Chapter 2
• Fire Stations-Chapter 2
• School Buses/Pasadena Unified School District - Site 19

CLOSE-BY PLACES
• Big Rigs at Castaic - Site 34

YOUR COMMENTS

_____

_____

_____

_____

_____

SITE 34 - BIG RIGS AT CASTAIC

ADDRESS
Castaic Road and Lake Hughes Road
Castaic, CA 91384

DIRECTIONS [GUIDE PAGE 4369 (LA)]
Take Interstate Highway 5 north to the Lake Hughes Road Exit. Drive around Castaic to see trucks.

GOOD THINGS TO SEE AND HEAR
The town of Castaic off Interstate Highway 5 provides an easy stop for trucks before or after they tackle the steep grades of the Grapevine. The Castaic Truck Stop is a clean, organized, and safe truck stop where you can see many big rigs parked for a rest or a burger at one of the many fast food restaurants. Talk about the parts of the big rigs, including the sleeper cabs and the large number of wheels. Ask your children what might be inside the trucks.

It is best to see the trucks from your car. If you get out and walk to the trucks, stay clear of any moving trucks and do not bother the truck drivers.

HOURS
All

PARKING
Free

ADMISSION
None

RELATED PLACES
• Construction and Road Work Sites-Chapter 2
• Sunshine Canyon Landfill - Site 33
• Fire Stations-Chapter 2
• School Buses-Pasadena Unified School District - Site 19

YOUR COMMENTS

_____
_____
_____
_____
_____

SITE 35 - PASADENA CRUISIN' WEEKLY CAR SHOW

ADDRESS
Robin's Restaurant
395 N. Rosemead Boulevard
Pasadena, CA 91107
(626) 351-8885

DIRECTIONS [GUIDE PAGE 566 (LA)]
(*Robin's Restaurant*) Take Interstate Highway 210 and exit on Rosemead Boulevard. Go north on Rosemead Boulevard.

GOOD THINGS TO SEE AND HEAR
A variety of old fixed-up very cool looking cars show up in Robin's Restaurant parking lot on Saturday evenings.

HOURS
Saturday   4:00 p.m. - 8:00 p.m.

PARKING
Free

ADMISSION
Free

RELATED PLACES
• Peterson Automotive Museum-Site 5

CLOSE-BY PLACES
• Santa Anita Race Track Morning Workout - Site 92
• Water Play Area-Santa Fe Dam Recreation Area - Site 124
• Wilderness Park and Nature Center - Site 52

YOUR COMMENTS

_____
_____
_____
_____
_____

SITE 36 - KID'S WORLD

ADDRESS
Alameda Park
1400 Santa Barbara Street
Santa Barbara, CA 93101
(805) 564-5418

DIRECTIONS [GUIDE PAGE 996 (SB)]
Take U.S. Highway 101 to the State Street Exit and go northwest. Make a right on Micheltorena Street.

GOOD THINGS TO SEE AND HEAR
The best park for young children, in my opinion, is your neighborhood park so you can visit it over and over again. However, there is one very special park in Santa Barbara that is not to be missed. Kid's World in Alameda Park was designed by architect Bob Leathers and is based on the wishes of children. This is a huge, beautifully made wooden play structure with sections that are right for every age.

There is a very young children's section that is nicely sectioned off from the area for the bigger kids, however, two-year-olds will have no problem climbing all over the whole structure. Some of the wood sections are close together making it hard to visually follow your child up the structure.

HOURS
Daily   Sunrise-10:00 p.m.

PARKING
Free

ADMISSION
None

RELATED PLACES
• Legoland - Site 114

CLOSE-BY PLACES
• Chase Palm Park Carousel - Site 123
• Santa Barbara Airport - Site 160
• Santa Barbara East Beach - Site 145
• Santa Barbara County Fair and Exposition - Site 110
• Santa Barbara Museum of Natural History - Site 14
• Santa Barbara Train Station - Site 188
• Santa Barbara Zoological Gardens - Site 70

YOUR COMMENTS

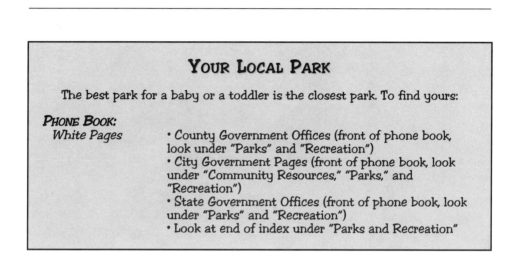

YOUR LOCAL PARK

The best park for a baby or a toddler is the closest park. To find yours:

PHONE BOOK:
White Pages
• County Government Offices (front of phone book, look under "Parks" and "Recreation")
• City Government Pages (front of phone book, look under "Community Resources," "Parks," and "Recreation")
• State Government Offices (front of phone book, look under "Parks" and "Recreation")
• Look at end of index under "Parks and Recreation"

Canada Geese Wait Patiently for Bread Crumbs.

Photo by author; permission to use photo courtesy of Peter Atkins of The Arboretum of Los Angeles County,

CHAPTER 3 - GARDENS AND NATURE

The gardens and nature centers around Southern California provide excellent opportunities to observe, explore, and discover. As you walk along, talk about the smells, the textures (leaves, bark), the sounds (birds, water), and the colors (leaves, flowers). Bring along a magnifying glass. Your child may not use it correctly at first, but they are a lot of fun.

Try collecting something. Start by collecting one thing (leaves, rocks, pine cones, feathers, flowers, or bottle caps). Bring an empty egg carton or plastic bag for your collection. At home, start a "nature drawer" where you can put all the things you collect. Later, egg cartons can be used to sort the collections. Sort them by color, size, and shape. Talk about your own collections and the collections you have seen in museums (cars, animals, bones, and trains). When you visit the library, you can check out a book on the things your child is interested in collecting.

When you visit a nature center, ask a docent to bring out a snake or a lizard. Pet the snake with your child and be calm and curious so your child will learn to be calm and curious.

POISON OAK
"Leaves of three, let them be."

Poison oak is recognized by its triple leaf. The leaves are usually shiny but may not be in the late summer. All parts of the plant contain a substance that irritates the skin. Some people are bothered more than others. You can get poison oak from the plant itself or from things that have touched the plant including dogs, parent's pants, etc. If you think you have touched poison oak, wash immediately with cold water and soap.

ADDITIONAL PLACES TO HIKE
Visit the website tchester.org/sgm/places/index.html for additional places to hike in the San Gabriel Mountains.

BOOKS FOR YOUR CHILD
- Bunting, Eve-*Sunflower House*
- Carle, Eric-*The Very Hungry Caterpillar*
- Day, Alexandra-*Carl's Afternoon in the Park*
- Ehlert, Lois-*Planting a Rainbow*
- Hill, Eric-*Spot Goes to the Park*
- Himmelman, John-*An Earthworm's Life*
- Kirk, David-*Miss Spider's Tea Party*
- Kleven, Elisa-*The Puddle Pail*
- Krauss, Ruth-*The Carrot Seed*
- Mayer, Mercer-*A Boy, A Dog and A Frog*
- McCloskey, Robert-*Make Way for Ducklings*
- Morgan, Pierr-*The Turnip: An Old Russian Folk Tale*
- Potter, Beatrix-*The Tale of Benjamin Bunny*
- Potter, Beatrix-*The Tale of Peter Rabbit*
- Rosen Michael-*We're Going on a Bear Hunt*
- Yolen, Jane-*Owl Moon*

SOMETHING TO DO - BRING SOME LADYBUGS HOME
On your walk, you may find a ladybug. If your child is interested in ladybugs, you may buy a box of one thousand ladybugs from your local nursery in the spring or summer. Ladybugs are harmless, friendly, and fascinating to children. Let them all out-they are very helpful to your plants as they eat aphids. Let them crawl on you and your child. Talk about the colors, the spots, where the head, antenna, eyes and wings are, and see what happens if the ladybug is turned gently on its back. Are the spots on each wing the same? You may also find ladybug eggs (groups of little yellow eggs on leaves), larvae (they look like little black alligators), or pupae (they look like sleeping yellowish ladybugs) on your hike or in your yard.

SOMETHING TO DO - BUILD A NEST
Using play dough you have bought or made (one cup of water, one cup of salt, and two cups flour), help your child mold a nest shape. Ask your child to gather things a bird would use for a nest (sticks, hair, grass, and leaves) and poke them into the play dough. Use additional play dough to make eggs for your nest. (Add a little food color or a package of Kool-Aid for color to your play dough.

SITE 37 - LOS ANGELES COUNTY ARBORETUM AND BOTANIC GARDENS

ADDRESS
301 North Baldwin Avenue
Arcadia, CA 91007
(626) 821-3222
www.arboretum.org

DIRECTIONS [GUIDE PAGE 567 (LA)]
Take Interstate Highway 210 to the Baldwin Avenue Exit and go south. The arboretum is on right.

GOOD THINGS TO SEE AND HEAR
The Los Angeles County Arboretum and Botanic Garden (formerly the Arboretum of Los Angeles County) is home to a great variety of plants of all sorts. At first you may not think your child would be interested in an arboretum, however, for young children, it is not about the trees, it is about the birds. Baldwin Lake is home to ducks, Canada Geese, and migratory birds. The Los Angeles area in general is rich in bird life since birds migrate from the north (the site is along the Pacific Flyway) and the interior to the warmer coastal regions in the winter. The Arboretum also probably has more peacocks than visitors on any given day. They will happily join you for lunch at the Peacock Café. During the mating season (February to August), look for peacocks fanning their feathers for the peahens. It is okay to feed the birds-fresh bread is best.

With the arrival of the Spanish, the area where the arboretum is today became Rancho Santa Anita, an outpost of the San Gabriel Mission. It was later purchased by Lucky Baldwin and became the site of Hollywood films like *Tarzan*.

Most of the birds are harmless, however, the Canada Geese and the peacocks can get aggressive during mating season.

Check the arboretum website to see what is currently blooming.

HOURS
Daily   9:00 a.m. - 4:30 p.m.

PARKING
Free

ADMISSION
Adult $7.00
    Child (Ages 5-12) $2.50
    Under 5   Free

YEARLY MEMBERSHIP
Adult $40.00
    Family $60.00

RELATED PLACES
- Descanso Gardens - Site 38
- Eaton Canyon County Park and Nature Center - Site 44
- El Dorado East Regional Park and Nature Center - Site 50
- The Huntington - Site 39
- Irvine Regional Park and Nature Center - Site 49
- San Dimas Canyon Park and Nature Center - Site 45
- South Coast Botanical Gardens - Site 40
- Whittier Narrows Nature Center - Site 46

CLOSE-BY PLACES
- Pasadena Cruisin' Weekly Car Show - Site 35
- Santa Anita Race Track Morning Workout - Site 92
- Water Play Area-Santa Fe Dam Recreation Area - Site 124
- Wilderness Park and Nature Center - Site 52

SPECIAL EVENTS
- Arcadia Insect Fair in March
- Festival on the Green Summer Concert Series from July to September

GUIDE BOOKS

To augment what you find on your walks and in nature centers, try a guidebook. Here are some suggestions:

Audubon First Field Guide Series Scholastic Inc., 1999.

Birds: A Guide to Familiar Birds of North America (Golden Guide), Herbert Spencer Zim, Ira Noel Gabrielson, St. Martin's Press, 2001.

Butterflies and Moths: A Guide to the More Common American Species (Golden Guide), Robert T. Mitchell, Martin's Press, 2001.

Insects: A Guide to Familiar American Insects (Golden Guide), Herbert Spencer Zim, Clarence Cottam, Jonathan P. Latimer, David Wagner, Martin's Press, 2001.

Pond Life: A Guide to Common Plants and Animals of North American Ponds and Lakes (Golden Guide), George Kell Reid, Herbert S. Zim (Editor), George S. Fichter (Editor), Martin's Press, 2001.

Seashore Life: A Guide to Animals and Plants Along the Beach (Golden Field Guide Series.), Herbert Spencer Zim, Lester, Ingle, Martin's Press, 2001.

Trees: A Guide to Familiar American Trees (Golden Guides), Herbert Spencer Zim, Alexander C. Martin, Martin's Press, 2001.

Weeds, Alexander C. Martin, Martin's Press, 2001.
Peterson First Guide to Birds of North America, Roger Tory Peterson, Houghton Mifflin Co, 1998.

Peterson First Guide to Insects of North America, Roger Tory Peterson, Houghton Mifflin Co, 1998.

First Guide to Trees (Peterson Field Guides), George A. Petrides and Roger Tory Peterson, Houghton Mifflin Co, 1998.

See also field guides by:
National Geographic, Reader's Digest, Stokes (Little, Brown), Sibley (Knopf), Simon and Schuster, or check with your favorite natural history museum.

POND LIFE

FROG

TURTLE

FISH

WATER STRIDER

DUCK

SITE 38 - DESCANSO GARDENS

ADDRESS
1418 Descanso Drive
La Cañada, CA 91011
(818) 949-4200
www.DescansoGardens.org

DIRECTIONS [GUIDE PAGE 535 (LA)]
Take Interstate Highway 210 to the Angeles Crest Highway Exit and go south. Make a right on Foothill Boulevard and then a left on Verdugo Boulevard. From there, turn left on Descanso Drive.

GOOD THINGS TO SEE AND HEAR
Descanso Gardens is one hundred and sixty acres of beautiful roses, camellias, native plants and trees, and seasonal flowers. A stream runs near the West Camellia Forest - look for bugs and tadpoles. Try the Enchanted Railway (although times of operation vary greatly), the Bird Observation Station, the Secret Garden in the International Rosarium, and the Japanese Teahouse. In the spring, be sure to visit the tulip gardens. The big white goose is named Henry.

Beware that the tram ride (not the train) is to introduce people to the gardens, and may be too long for babies and toddlers. Ducks and geese at the Bird Observation Station cannot be fed.

There is a series of classes called Acorn Bears for children ages two to four and their parents. Call for current class information.

Check the website for plants that are currently in bloom.

HOURS
Daily	9:00 a.m. - 4:30 p.m.
Train:	
Saturday-Sunday	10:00 a.m. - 4:00 p.m.

PARKING
Free

ADMISSION
Adult	$7.00
Child (Ages 5-12)	$2.00
Under 5	Free
Train:	
Adult or Child	$1.50
Under 34 inches	Free

YEARLY MEMBERSHIP
Adult	$45.00
Family	$65.00

RELATED PLACES
- Exposition Park Rose Garden - Site 41
- The Huntington - Site 39
- Los Angeles County Arboretum and Botanic Gardens - Site 37
- South Coast Botanical Gardens - Site 40
- University Campuses-Chapter 3

CLOSE-BY PLACES
- School Buses/Pasadena Unified School District - Site 19
- The Snow in Angeles National Forest - Site 133

SPECIAL EVENTS
- Annual Christmas Festival in December
- Pasadena Pops Children's Concert in the Summer
- Tulip Mania and Easter Egg Hunt in March-April

YOUR COMMENTS

_____

_____

_____

_____

_____

FLOWERS

ROSE

LILY

CAMELIA

TULIP

POPPY

CACTI

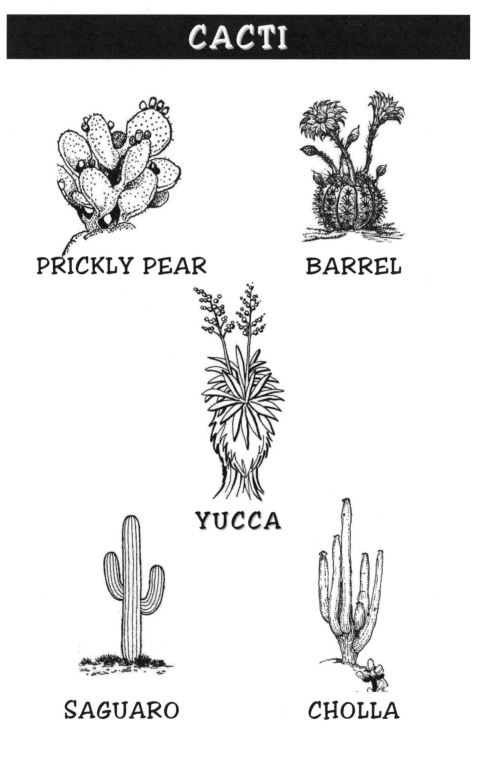

PRICKLY PEAR   BARREL

YUCCA

SAGUARO   CHOLLA

SITE 39 - THE HUNTINGTON

ADDRESS
1151 Oxford Road
San Marino, CA 91108
(626) 405-2100
www.huntington.org

DIRECTIONS [GUIDE PAGE 566 (LA)]
Take Interstate Highway 210 to the Hill Street Exit and go south. From there, make a left on California Boulevard, then a right on Allen Avenue and go south to end of Allen Avenue.

GOOD THINGS TO SEE AND HEAR
The Huntington Library and art collections are in the buildings that once made up the estate of Henry Huntington. Henry Edwards Huntington was the nephew of one of the original owners of the Central Pacific Railroad and managed the Southern Pacific Railroad. Surrounding the beautiful buildings are extensive botanical gardens. Visit the Japanese Garden (huge koi and bamboo trails) via a path of rose trellises, the Jungle Gardens, and the Lily Pond (look for the turtles). Walk through the grand cactus, camellia, and rose gardens when flowers are in bloom. Also try the new Conservatory-especially the Carnivorous Plant Bog and the interactive learning stations

A new children's garden, the Helen and Peter Bing Children's Garden, opened in 2004. The one-acre space is filled with nine kinetic sculptures set in whimsically landscaped gardens. Children can interact with mist, rainbows, sound waves, and magnetic sand. This is a magical experience! However, don't forget to see the rest of the gardens.

Do not feed the fish anything except food you get from a docent.

HOURS
Winter:
Tuesday-Friday   12:00 p.m. - 4:30 p.m.
Saturday-Sunday   10:30 a.m. - 4:30 p.m.
Summer:
Tuesday-Sunday   10:30 a.m. - 4:30 p.m.

PARKING
Free

ADMISSION
Adult $15.00
Child (Ages 5-11) $6.00
Under 5   Free
• Free admission the first Thursday of the month

YEARLY MEMBERSHIP
Family $100.00

RELATED PLACES
- Descanso Gardens - Site 38
- Exposition Park Rose Garden - Site 41
- Los Angeles County Arboretum and Botanic Garden - Site 37
- South Coast Botanical Gardens - Site 40
- University Campuses-Chapter 3

CLOSE-BY PLACES
- California Institute of Technology, Caltech - Site 56
- Doggie Day Camp at PETsMART - Site 28
- Eaton Canyon County Park and Nature Center - Site 44
- Kidspace Museum - Site 4
- Pasadena Civic Auditorium - Site 220
- Tournament of Roses Parade® - Site 216
- Tournament of Roses® Float Viewing - Site 216

YOUR COMMENTS

_____
_____
_____
_____
_____

SITE 40 - SOUTH COAST BOTANICAL GARDENS

ADDRESS
26300 Crenshaw Boulevard
Palos Verdes Peninsula-Rolling Hills Estates
Rancho Palos Verdes, CA 90274
(310) 544-6815
parks.co.la.ca.us/south_coast_botanic.html

DIRECTIONS [GUIDE PAGE 793 (LA)]
Take Interstate Highway 110 and go west on Pacific Coast Highway 1. From there, go south (left) on Crenshaw Boulevard and make a left into the gardens.

GOOD THINGS TO SEE AND HEAR
The South Coast Botanical Gardens are quite extensive and include all the favorites including roses, fruit trees, cactus gardens, and vegetable gardens. Best of all, there is a lake with ducks, geese, and other birds that you may feed. As you walk toward the lake, you may discover two favorite stops - a Children's Garden with miniature houses and figures from various nursery rhymes; and a Garden for the Senses with plants you can enjoy by their smell.

This eighty-seven-acre botanical garden was once a landfill. There are some wide paths that are easy for strollers, and other winding narrow paths that are challenging.

HOURS

Daily   9:00 a.m. - 5:00 p.m.

PARKING

Free

ADMISSION

Adult $7.00
Child (Ages 5-12) $2.50
Under 5   Free

YEARLY MEMBERSHIP

Adult $25.00
Family $40.00

RELATED PLACES

- Descanso Gardens - Site 38
- Los Angeles County Arboretum and Botanic Gardens- Site 37
- Sunshine Canyon Landfill - Site 33
- Exposition Park Rose Garden - Site 41
- The Huntington - Site 39

CLOSE-BY PLACES

- Goodyear Blimp Airfield - Site 168
- Lomita Railroad Museum - Site 197
- Santa Ana Train Station - Site 187
- Torrance Municipal Airport/Zamperini Field - Site 162

YOUR COMMENTS

_____

_____

_____

_____

SITE 41 - EXPOSITION PARK ROSE GARDEN

ADDRESS

701 State Drive
Los Angeles, CA 90007
(213) 763-0114
www.laparks.org/exporosegarden/rosegarden.htm

DIRECTIONS [GUIDE PAGE 674 (LA)]

- Take Interstate Highway 110 south to the Exposition Boulevard Exit. From there, make a left on Flower Street (first light) and park on right.
- Take Interstate Highway 110 north to the Martin Luther King Jr. Boulevard Exit. and go left. Make a right on Flower Street and park on left.

GOOD THINGS TO SEE AND HEAR

Sixteen thousand roses cover the seven-acre Rose Garden next to the Natural History Museum. Roses of all colors, shapes, and smells are there for touching, smelling and running around and around. This is a great place for a picnic after a trip to the Natural History Museum.

Blooms are at their peak April through May and September through October. The roses should not be picked and beware of the thorns.

HOURS

Daily	9:00 a.m. - Sunset
Closed	January 1 - March 15 for maintenance

PARKING
$6.00

ADMISSION
Free

RELATED PLACES
• Descanso Gardens - Site 38
• The Huntington - Site 39
• South Coast Botanical Gardens - Site 40

CLOSE-BY PLACES
• IMAX Theater at the California Science Center - Site 208
• Los Angeles Memorial Sports Arena - Site 213
• Natural History Museum of Los Angeles County - Site 1
• University of Southern California, USC - Site 57

YOUR COMMENTS

_____

_____

_____

_____

_____

SITE 42 - HOPKINS WILDERNESS PARK

ADDRESS
1102 Camino Real
Redondo Beach, CA 90277
(310) 318-0668
www.redondo.org/depts/public_works/parks/hopkins.asp

DIRECTIONS [GUIDE PAGE 763 (LA)]
• Take Interstate Highway 110 Sepulveda Boulevard. Go west to the top of the hill, and turn right into the parking lot (Sepulveda turns into Camino Real).

GOOD THINGS TO SEE AND HEAR

Hopkins Wilderness Park is overgrown with trails, streams, and ponds. There are lots of wild animals to spot if you are quiet-rabbits, frogs, butterflies and lizards.

Sometimes the Audubon Society hosts a children's program on Saturdays. Call (310) 318-0610 for more information.

HOURS

Thursday-Tuesday   10:00 a.m. - 4:00 p.m.

PARKING

Free

ADMISSION

Free

RELATED PLACES

- Aliso & Wood Canyons Wilderness Park and the Orange County Natural History Museum - Site 47
- Children's Nature Institute - Site 43
- Eaton Canyon County Park and Nature Center - Site 44
- El Dorado East Regional Park and Nature Center - Site 50
- Irvine Regional Park and Nature Center - Site 49
- San Dimas Canyon Park and Nature Center - Site 45
- Shipley Nature Center at Huntington Central Park - Site 48
- Whittier Narrows Nature Center - Site 46
- Wilderness Park and Nature Center - Site 52

CLOSE-BY PLACES

- Hermosa Beach - Site 135
- Redondo Beach - Site 143
- Seaside Lagoon - Site 147

YOUR COMMENTS

_____

_____

_____

_____

SITE 43 - CHILDREN'S NATURE INSTITUTE

ADDRESS
www.childrensnatureinstitute.org
(310) 860-9484

DIRECTIONS
Each location is different. Your walk leader will provide directions when he or she confirms your walk by phone. You can also check the website for directions to each location.

GOOD THINGS TO SEE AND HEAR
The Children's Nature Institute organizes wonderful nature walks geared for young children with the goal of helping them discover natural science and their environment. The walks are led by volunteers and are scheduled at eighty-five different sites in Los Angeles and Ventura Counties seven days a week. The sites are specifically selected for very young children and stroller access if possible. Call or check the website for a three-month calendar to find walks that are in your area.

Formerly Nursery Nature Walks. One adult per each mobile child under three years is required. Bring sun block, water, and a snack. Wear long pants, long-sleeve shirts, and shoes.

BOOK ON NATURE WALKS:
Trails, Tails & Tidepools in Pails by the Docents of Nursery Nature Walks, Nursery Nature Walks (Santa Monica, California).

HOURS
Walks start 10:00 a.m. unless otherwise noted

PARKING
Some parks have parking fees

ADMISSION
Suggested Donation:
Family $7.00
Member (Family) $5.00

YEARLY MEMBERSHIP
Family $35.00

RELATED PLACES
• Aliso & Wood Canyons Wilderness Park and
    Orange County Natural History Museum - Site 47
• Eaton Canyon County Park and Nature Center - Site 44
• El Dorado East Regional Park and Nature Center - Site 50
• Irvine Regional Park and Nature Center - Site 49
• San Dimas Canyon Park and Nature Center - Site 45
• Shipley Nature Center at Huntington Central Park - Site 48
• Whittier Narrows Nature Center - Site 46
• Wilderness Park and Nature Center - Site 52

SPECIAL EVENTS
• Kid's Nature Festival   May

YOUR COMMENTS

_____
_____
_____
_____

SUGGESTED HIKES FROM THE CHILDREN'S NATURE INSTITUTE

The following hikes are part of a collection of walk sites offered by the Children's Nature Institute. Included here are some of those in Los Angeles County (The Children's Nature Institute offers hikes in both Los Angeles and Ventura Counties). For the best hike with your child, contact the Institute and join a Family Nature Walk with a walk leader. The walks are held at specific kid-friendly trails at these sites.

Chantry Flats in Arcadia. [GUIDE PAGE 567/537 (LA)]. Take Interstate Highway 210 to the Santa Anita Boulevard Exit and go north. Drive to the mountain road gate. Continue up the mountain for two miles until the road ends. Most strollers are okay.

Cobb Estate in Altadena. [GUIDE PAGE 536/566 (LA)] see also Millard Canyon in Angeles National Forest on the Nature Institute web site]. Take Interstate Highway 210 to Lake Avenue Exit. Go north all the way to the end. Park at curb on the right. Rugged strollers are okay.

Franklin Canyon in Beverly Hills. [GUIDE PAGE 562/592 (LA)]. See also Fryman Canyon Park, Iredale Trail, Tree People, and Wilacre Estate Park on their website. Take U.S. Highway 101 to the Coldwater Canyon Exit. Go south and drive through Studio City. Go up the hill until you reach the intersection of Coldwater and Mulholland Drive. Turn right onto Franklin Canyon Drive, which is at the intersection. It is not marked. Continue past the residential area to the Outdoor Classroom sign and turn left into the parking lot.

George F. Canyon in Rolling Hills Estates. [GUIDE PAGE 794/793 (LA)]. Take Interstate Highway 110 to the Anaheim Street Exit and go west. Drive one mile and bear left up the hill onto Palos Verdes Drive. Go east on Palos Verdes Drive and the entrance to the canyon is immediately on the right. Park along the street or in the turnout beyond the canyon sign. Rugged strollers are okay.

Griffith Park Bird Sanctuary in Los Angeles. [GUIDE PAGE 594 (LA)]. Take U.S. Highway 101 to the Vermont Avenue Exit and go north. Stay on Vermont Avenue and drive past Los Feliz Boulevard. Pass the Greek Theater and go to the Bird Sanctuary parking lot. No stroller access.

Kenneth Hahn in Baldwin Hills. [GUIDE PAGE 633/673 (LA)]. Take Interstate Highway 10 to the Fairfax Avenue Exit and go south. This street turns into La Cienega Boulevard. Take La Cienega Boulevard up the hill, past Rodeo Road. Stay to the right (look for signs). Enter the park and park in the lot to your right. All strollers are okay.

Lime Kiln Canyon Park in Northridge. [GUIDE PAGE 500 (LA)]. Take Interstate Highway 405 to State Highway 118 west. Take the Tampa Avenue Exit and go north. After half a block, turn left on Rinaldi Street and drive approximately one hundred yards to the end of the condominium complex. Park on the right side of the street near the park gate. If you pass the white church on the left, you have gone too far. Some strollers may be able to make it.

Madrona Marsh in Torrance. [GUIDE PAGE 763 (LA)]. Take Interstate Highway 405 to the Crenshaw Exit and go south. Pass the refinery and go over the railroad tracks. Make a right on Plaza Del Amo and pass the townhouses. You will see Madrona Marsh on the left side of the street. Park in the lot on the right. Most strollers are okay.

Runyon Canyon Park in Hollywood Hills. [GUIDE PAGE 593 (LA)]. Take U.S. Highway 101 to the Hollywood Boulevard Exit and go west to Fuller Avenue where you will turn north. Continue past Franklin Avenue to its end. Park at the end of the cul-de-sac. All strollers are okay.

Santa Ynez Canyon Park in Pacific Palisades. [GUIDE PAGE 631/630 (LA)]. See also Temescal Canyon and Sullivan Canyon on their website. Take Interstate Highway 405 to the Sunset Boulevard Exit and go west. Continue to Palisade Drive and go north. Proceed about two miles to the divided highway and park on the left side of the street in front of the brick wall. Look for the sign for the Santa Ynez Canyon Park. All strollers are okay.

Topanga State Park in Topanga. [GUIDE PAGE 560/590 (LA)]. Take U.S. Highway 101 to the Topanga Canyon Boulevard Exit and go south towards the ocean. Continue past Mulholland Drive to Entrada Road of your left. If you pass Old Topanga Canyon Road, you have gone too far. Make a left on Entrada and make two left turns to stay on Entrada. Follow the signs to the park entrance on your left and the drive through to the large parking lot. There is a parking fee or you can park outside and walk in. No strollers access.

Wattles Park in Hollywood Hills. [GUIDE PAGE 593 (LA)]. Take U.S. Highway 101 to the Hollywood Boulevard Exit and go west. Pass La Brea Avenue to Curson Avenue. Turn north on Curson Avenue and park in front of the gate, just before the junction of Curson Place and Curson Terrace. Most strollers are okay.

Wilderness Park in Redondo Beach. [GUIDE PAGE 733/763 (LA)]. Take Interstate Highway 405 to the Hawthorne Boulevard Exit and go south. Continue to Sepulveda Boulevard and turn right. Go to Knob Hill Avenue and turn right into the parking lot. Most strollers are okay.

Wildwood Canyon Park in Burbank. [GUIDE PAGE 533 (LA)]. Take Interstate Highway 5 to the Olive Avenue Exit and turn right. Proceed north. Turn left on Sunset Canyon Drive and then make a right on Harvard Road. Continue to Wildwood Canyon Road. The mountain gate is located at the junction of Wildwood Canyon Road and Harvard Road. Proceed on Wildwood Canyon, past the stone kiosk to the parking lot. All strollers are okay.

Will Rogers in Pacific Palisades. [GUIDE PAGE 631 (LA)]. Take Interstate Highway 405 to the Sunset Boulevard Exit and go west. Continue about four and a half miles to the park entrance on your right. There is a parking fee. The path is bumpy, but most strollers are okay.

Permission to reproduce Children's Nature Institute Walks courtesy of Lizette Castaño of the Docents of The Children's Nature Institute.

SITE 44 - EATON CANYON COUNTY PARK AND NATURE CENTER

ADDRESS

1750 North Altadena Drive
Pasadena, CA 91107
(626) 398-5420 Nature Center
(626) 794-6773 County Park
ecnca.org

DIRECTIONS [GUIDE PAGE 566 (LA)]

Take Interstate Highway 210 to the Rosemead Boulevard Exit and go north. From there, turn right on New York Drive and right onto Altadena Drive. The entrance is on right.

GOOD THINGS TO SEE AND HEAR

Eaton Canyon County Park is located at the base of Mt. Wilson and surrounds Eaton Creek. Eaton Creek flows to various degrees depending on the season. Near the entrance off Altadena Drive is the Nature Center with terrariums full of live local snakes, lizards, and toads. There are drawers to pull out that contain butterflies, seeds, feathers, etc., and a reading area with nature books of all sorts. A special trail for small children encourages you and your children to look, listen, and smell the plants and wildlife of Eaton Canyon. Pick up a map in the Nature Center. Talk about what might live in the many holes in the ground, but teach your children to avoid reaching in these holes.

The Nature Center and its surrounding paths present a full outing; but also try the nature trails near Eaton Creek - especially exciting during tadpole and bug season. Do not try to take the tadpoles home - they never live more than a day in captivity.

HOURS

Daily	9:00 a.m. - 5:00 p.m.
Nature Walks:	
Saturday	9:00 a.m.
Friday*	7:30 p.m.
* nearest full moon	

PARKING

Free

ADMISSION

Free

YEARLY MEMBERSHIP

Adult	$30.00
Family	$45.00

RELATED PLACES

- Aliso & Wood Canyons Wilderness Park and
   Orange County Natural History Museum - Site 47
- Children's Nature Institute - Site 43
- El Dorado East Regional Park and Nature Center - Site 50
- Hopkins Wilderness Park - Site 42
- Irvine Regional Park and Nature Center - Site 49
- San Dimas Canyon Park and Nature Center - Site 45
- Shipley Nature Center at Huntington Central Park - Site 48
- Whittier Narrows Nature Center - Site 46
- Wilderness Park and Nature Center - Site 52

CLOSE-BY PLACES

- California Institute of Technology, Caltech - Site 56
- Doggie Day Camp at PETsMART - Site 28
- The Huntington - Site 39
- Kidspace Museum - Site 4
- Pasadena Civic Auditorium - Site 220
- Tournament of Roses® Parade - Site 216
- Tournament of Roses® Float Viewing - Site 216

SPECIAL EVENTS

- Family Nature Walks   Saturday Mornings

YOUR COMMENTS

_____

_____

_____

_____

_____

SITE 45 - SAN DIMAS CANYON PARK AND NATURE CENTER

ADDRESS

1628 North Sycamore Canyon Road
San Dimas, CA 91773
(909) 599-7512
parks.co.la.ca.us/san_dimas_narea.html

DIRECTIONS [GUIDE PAGE 570 (LA)]

Take Interstate Highway 210 continue west along new section. Exit San Dimas Avenue and go north. Go right on Foothill Boulevard and left on San Dimas Canyon Road. Left onto Sycamore Canyon Drive and go north.

GOOD THINGS TO SEE AND HEAR

San Dimas Canyon Park is located between San Dimas and Sycamore Canyons. The nature center is a wildlife sanctuary for injured or non-releasable native animals. Most of these birds and mammals are in cages for children to see and hear. A one-mile nature trail loop is a perfect length for little legs (but bring a back pack anyway or be prepared to carry). An adjacent park provides a playground and large picnic area.

As always, be aware of poison oak.

HOURS

Monday-Friday   9:00 a.m. - 3:00 p.m.
Saturday-Sunday   9:00 a.m. - 5:00 p.m.

PARKING

Free

ADMISSION

Free

RELATED PLACES

- Aliso & Wood Canyons Wilderness Park and
     Orange County Natural History Museum - Site 47
- Children's Nature Institute - Site 43
- Eaton Canyon County Park and Nature Center - Site 44
- El Dorado East Regional Park and Nature Center - Site 50
- Hopkins Wilderness Park - Site 42
- Irvine Regional Park and Nature Center - Site 49
- Shipley Nature Center at Huntington Central Park - Site 48
- Whittier Narrows Nature Center - Site 46
- Wilderness Park and Nature Center - Site 52

CLOSE-BY PLACES

- Brackett Air Field - Site 149
- Los Angeles County Fair - Site 106
- Mrs. Nelson's Toy and Book Shop - Site 18
- Puddingstone Reservoir Beach - Site 125

YOUR COMMENTS

_____
_____
_____
_____
_____

WILD MAMMALS

SQUIRREL

SKUNK

OPOSSUM

RACCOON

COYOTE

BIRDS

HUMMINGBIRD

SPARROW

CROW

HAWK

WOODPECKER

SITE 46 - WHITTIER NARROWS NATURE CENTER

ADDRESS
1000 North Durfee Avenue
South El Monte, CA 91733
(626) 575-5523
parks.co.la.ca.us/whittier_narea.html

DIRECTIONS [GUIDE PAGE 637 (LA)]
Take Interstate Highway 605 to State Highway 60 west. Exit Peck Road and go south. Make a quick right on Durfee Avenue and the Nature Center is on the left.

GOOD THINGS TO SEE AND HEAR
The Whittier Narrows Nature Center includes a main building with several terrariums containing snakes and lizards; a variety of stuffed birds and local animals; and a wonderful touching table with bones, feathers, plants, and seeds. In another section of the complex is a great horned owl - a little hard to see at first but worth the effort. He likes to watch you as you watch him. There is a nature trail where you can find a variety of local plants and perhaps a lizard or two.

Whittier Narrows Park borders the San Gabriel River. The park is large and the Nature Center is not near the main park areas. There is poison oak along the nature trail, so be sure you know how to recognize it.

HOURS
Daily   9:30 a.m. - 5:00 p.m.
Nature Center:
Tuesday-Saturday   9:30 a.m. - 5:00 p.m.

PARKING
Free

ADMISSION
Free

RELATED PLACES
• Aliso & Wood Canyons Wilderness Park and
    Orange County Natural History Museum - Site 47
• Children's Nature Institute - Site 43
• Eaton Canyon County Park and Nature Center - Site 44
• El Dorado East Regional Park and Nature Center - Site 50
• Hopkins Wilderness Park - Site 42
• Irvine Regional Park and Nature Center - Site 49
• San Dimas Canyon Park and Nature Center - Site 45
• Shipley Nature Center at Huntington Central Park - Site 48
• Wilderness Park and Nature Center - Site 52

CLOSE-BY PLACES
• El Monte Airport - Site 153
• Freight Trains - Site 196
• Montebello Barnyard Zoo - Site 103

YOUR COMMENTS

_____

_____

_____

_____

SITE 47 - ALISO & WOOD CANYONS WILDERNESS PARK AND ORANGE COUNTY NATURAL HISTORY MUSEUM

ADDRESS
28373 Alicia Parkway
Laguna Niguel, CA 92677
(949) 831-3287
www.ocnhm.org

DIRECTIONS [GUIDE PAGE 921/951 (OC)]
Take Interstate Highway 5 to the Alicia Parkway Exit and go south. Look to the right for the Aliso and Wood Canyons Wilderness Park.

GOOD THINGS TO SEE AND HEAR
The Orange County Natural History Museum is actually a small nature center with nice displays of local mammals, birds, footprints, marine fossil, and a mammoth bone from the Irvine area. It is at the beginning of a series of trails through Aliso and Wood Canyons. Walk along the Aliso Creek Trail and then, if you have the energy, take the Wood Canyon Trail.

The building you see from the road is actually a church - the museum is in a trailer a little farther down the road.

HOURS
Trails:
Daily   7:00 a.m. - Sunset
Museum:
Wednesday-Sunday 11:00 a.m. - 5:00 p.m.

PARKING
$3.00

ADMISSION
Adult $2.00
Child $1.00

YEARLY MEMBERSHIP
Adult $25.00
Family $35.00

RELATED PLACES
- Children's Nature Institute - Site 43
- Eaton Canyon County Park and Nature Center - Site 44
- El Dorado East Regional Park and Nature Center - Site 50
- Hopkins Wilderness Park - Site 42
- Irvine Regional Park and Nature Center - Site 49
- San Dimas Canyon Park and Nature Center - Site 45
- Shipley Nature Center at Huntington Central Park - Site 48
- Whittier Narrows Nature Center - Site 46
- Wilderness Park and Nature Center - Site 52

CLOSE-BY PLACES
- Diver's Cove Tide Pools - Site 80
- Pacific Marine Mammal Center and Laguna Koi Ponds -Site 86
- Laguna Main Beach - Site 137

YOUR COMMENTS

SITE 48 - SHIPLEY NATURE CENTER AT HUNTINGTON CENTRAL PARK

ADDRESS
Central Park Drive
Huntington Beach, CA 92648
(714) 960-8847
www.stockteam.com/shipley.html

DIRECTIONS [GUIDE PAGE 857 (OC)]
Take Interstate Highway 405 to the Brookhurst Street Exit and go south. Turn right on Talbert Avenue, pass the library, and make a right on Goldenwest Street. Then turn left on Slater Avenue, left on Edwards, and left on Central Park Drive into the parking lot.

GOOD THINGS TO SEE AND HEAR
Shipley Nature Center includes an eighteen-acre area of forest, grasslands, and freshwater marshes. It has self-guided walking trails, and an interpretive center with animals you can touch with the help of the docent, and many hands-on exhibits including a stuffed coyote that you can pet.

Donald Shipley, after whom the Nature Center is named, said, "We sleepwalk through our environment. Most of us are totally unaware of how little of our natural environment now remains in coastal Southern California. I submit that man may need some natural areas in his human environment much more than does our depleted wildlife."

HOURS
Nature Center Area:
Daily   9:00 a.m. - 5:00 p.m.
Interpretive Center:
Daily   Hours vary

PARKING
Free

ADMISSION
Free

RELATED PLACES
• Aliso & Wood Canyons Wilderness Park and
    Orange County Natural History Museum - Site 47
• Eaton Canyon County Park and Nature Center - Site 44
• El Dorado East Regional Park and Nature Center - Site 50
• Irvine Regional Park and Nature Center - Site 49
• San Dimas Canyon Park and Nature Center - Site 45
• Whittier Narrows Nature Center - Site 46
• Wilderness Park and Nature Center - Site 52

CLOSE-BY PLACES
• Bolsa Chica Ecological Reserve - Site 132
• Kite Flying at the Beach - Site 167
• Huntington Beach School Bus Yard - Site 23
• Huntington Central Park Equestrian Center - Site 94
• Huntington State Beach and Huntington City Beach - Site 136

YOUR COMMENTS

SITE 49 - IRVINE REGIONAL PARK AND NATURE CENTER

ADDRESS
Santiago Canyon
1 Irvine Park Road
Orange, CA 92862
(714) 973-6835 Park
www.ocparks.com/irvinepark/

DIRECTIONS [GUIDE PAGE 800/801 (OC)]
Take Interstate Highway 5 to the Jamboree Road Exit and go north. Jamboree Road ends at Irvine Regional Park. The Nature Center is across from the zoo.

GOOD THINGS TO SEE AND HEAR

Irvine Regional Park is a large park with extensive grassy areas and a Nature Center in the middle. The Orange County Zoo (see Site 65) is across the street and the park also has pony rides (see Site 102) and a train ride (see Site 200). The Nature Center has a variety of displays of local animals, ecosystems, and a grass house.

The Nature Center is small - combine your visit with the zoo or a train or pony ride, and a picnic. You can also rent a surrey and ride around the park. Get a map at the park entrance to find your way to all these places.

HOURS

Park:
Summer:
Daily   7:00 a.m. - 9:00 p.m.
Winter:
Daily   7:00 a.m. - 6:00 p.m.
Nature Center:
Saturday-Sunday   11:30 a.m. - 3:30 p.m.

PARKING

Park Entrance:
Weekdays $3.00
Weekends $5.00

ADMISSION

Free

RELATED PLACES

• Aliso & Wood Canyons Wilderness Park and
    Orange County Natural History Museum - Site 47
• Eaton Canyon County Park and Nature Center - Site 44
• El Dorado East Regional Park and Nature Center - Site 50
• Hopkins Wilderness Park - Site 42
• San Dimas Canyon Park and Nature Center - Site 45
• Shipley Nature Center at Huntington Central Park - Site 48
• Whittier Narrows Nature Center - Site 46
• Wilderness Park and Nature Center - Site 52

CLOSE-BY PLACES

• Green Meadows Farm-Orange - Site 91
• Irvine Regional Park Pony Rides - Site 102
• Irvine Park Railroad - Site 200
• Orange County Zoo - Site 65

YOUR COMMENTS

_____
_____
_____
_____

SITE 50 - EL DORADO EAST REGIONAL PARK AND NATURE CENTER

ADDRESS
7550 East Spring Street
Long Beach, CA 90815
(562) 570-1745 Nature Center
(562) 570-1771 Park
www.longbeach.gov/park/facilities/parks/el_dorado_nature_center.asp

DIRECTIONS [GUIDE PAGE 766/796 (LA)]
Take Interstate Highway 605 south to the Spring Street/Cerritos Exit. From there go west to the park entrance.

GOOD THINGS TO SEE AND HEAR
To the south of Spring Street in El Dorado Regional Park is the one hundred-acre El Dorado Nature Center. The interpretive building is on an island in the middle of a lake. The center has some touchable items including skulls, antlers, pine cones, and insects. The best part is the trail around the lake - get a trail map from the interpretive building and look for turtles and ducks.

El Dorado Park has several sections - ask for a map when you enter the park. El Dorado East Regional Park is north of Spring Street and east of the San Gabriel River and has lakes and a train (see Site 199). To the south of Spring Street is the one hundred-acre El Dorado Nature Center.

HOURS
Park:
Daily   7:00 a.m. - Dusk
Nature Center Trails:
Tuesday-Sunday   8:00 a.m. - 5:00 p.m.
Nature Center Building:
Tuesday-Friday   10:00 a.m. - 4:00 p.m.
Saturday-Sunday   8:30 a.m. - 4:00 p.m.

PARKING
Park Entrance Per Vehicle:
Weekdays $3.00
Weekends $5.00

ADMISSION
Free

YEARLY MEMBERSHIP
$35.00   Annual Vehicle Pass

RELATED PLACES

- Aliso & Wood Canyons Wilderness Park and
    Orange County Natural History Museum - Site 47
- Eaton Canyon County Park and Nature Center - Site 44
- Irvine Regional Park and Nature Center - Site 49
- San Dimas Canyon Park and Nature Center - Site 45
- Shipley Nature Center at Huntington Central Park - Site 48
- Whittier Narrows Nature Center - Site 46
- Wilderness Park and Nature Center - Site 52

CLOSE-BY PLACES

- California State University, Long Beach, CSULB - Site 61
- Cerritos Library - Site 17
- El Dorado East Regional Park Train Ride - Site 199
- Hopkins Wilderness Park - Site 42
- Lakewood Pony Rides and Petting Farm - Site 104
- Long Beach Airport - Site 157
- Norwalk School Bus Yard - Site 26

SPECIAL EVENTS

- Evening Campfires (reservations required)   Summer

YOUR COMMENTS

_____
_____
_____
_____
_____

SITE 51 - AUDUBON CENTER AT DEBS PARK

ADDRESS

4700 North Griffin Avenue
Los Angeles, CA 90031
(323) 221-2255
www.audubon-ca.org/debs_park.htm

DIRECTIONS [GUIDE PAGE 595 (LA)]

Take Highway 110 to the Avenue 60 Exit and go south. Make a right on Monterey Road. The park is on the right.

GOOD THINGS TO SEE AND HEAR

The National Audubon Society is setting up nature centers in parks across the United States. One of their recent is at Debs Park in Los Angeles. A brand new nature center is now open where children can pet Fluffy the gopher snake or check out a backpack filled with a magnifying glass for inspecting bugs, an insect net to catch bugs (and preferably let them go), and watercolor paints. There are many paths through the native California woodland. Look for a Sycamore Tree, a Desert

Cottontail Rabbit or a Western Toad. In the trees, look for birds, including meadowlarks, sparrows, kingbirds, hawks or a White-Tailed Kites. Birding is best in spring, especially late April, but also good in winter and fall. You will also find a little pond that is home to dragonflies and fish.

HOURS
Wednesday-Saturday   9:00 a.m. - 5:00 p.m.

PARKING
Free

ADMISSION
Free

RELATED PLACES
- Aliso & Wood Canyons Wilderness Park and
    Orange County Natural History Museum - Site 47
- Eaton Canyon County Park and Nature Center - Site 44
- El Dorado East Regional Park and Nature Center - Site 50
- Hopkins Wilderness Park - Site 42
- Irvine Regional Park and Nature Center - Site 49
- San Dimas Canyon Park and Nature Center - Site 45
- Shipley Nature Center at Huntington Central Park - Site 48
- Whittier Narrows Nature Center - Site 46

CLOSE-BY PLACES
- Los Angeles County Arboretum and Botanic Gardens - Site 37
- Pasadena Cruisin' Weekly Car Show - Site 35
- Pasadena Model Railroad Museum - Site 201

YOUR COMMENTS

_____
_____
_____
_____
_____

SITE 52 - WILDERNESS PARK AND NATURE CENTER

ADDRESS
2240 Highland Oaks Drive
Sierra Madre, CA 91006
(626) 355-5309 Nature Center
(626) 574-5113 Recreation Department

DIRECTIONS [GUIDE PAGE 537 (LA)]
Take Interstate Highway 210 to the Santa Anita Exit and go north. Make a right on Elkins Avenue and a left on Highland Oaks Drive. The park is behind a chain link fence, and the Nature Center is just off the parking lot.

GOOD THINGS TO SEE AND HEAR

Wilderness Park is a small park that includes a nature center and a short hiking trail. The nature center has a great variety of local stuffed animals on display. There are several live animals in the back education room, but you must ask the park ranger to bring them out. As you hike along the trail, watch for wild cucumbers.

Beware of snakes. The trail is steep on the east side - start on this side as it is easier to go up steep hills with a baby or toddler than down. The steps offer a great climbing opportunity for a toddler with a lot of help from mom and dad.

HOURS

Winter:
Monday-Friday   8:30 a.m. - 4:30 p.m.
Summer:
Monday-Friday   8:30 a.m. - 7:00 p.m.

PARKING
Free

ADMISSION
Free

RELATED PLACES
• Aliso & Wood Canyons Wilderness Park and
    Orange County Natural History Museum - Site 47
• Eaton Canyon County Park and Nature Center - Site 44
• El Dorado East Regional Park and Nature Center - Site 50
• Hopkins Wilderness Park - Site 42
• Irvine Regional Park and Nature Center - Site 49
• San Dimas Canyon Park and Nature Center - Site 45
• Shipley Nature Center at Huntington Central Park - Site 48
• Whittier Narrows Nature Center - Site 46

CLOSE-BY PLACES
• Los Angeles County Arboretum and Botanic Gardens - Site 37
• Pasadena Cruisin' Weekly Car Show - Site 35
• Santa Anita Race Track Morning Workout - Site 92
• Water Play Area-Santa Fe Dam Recreation Area - Site 124

YOUR COMMENTS

_____
_____
_____
_____
_____
_____

SITE 53 - SOOKY GOLDMAN NATURE CENTER

ADDRESS
2600 Franklin Canyon Drive
Beverly Hills, CA 90210
(310) 858-7272
www.lamountains.com/programs_natureCenters.html

DIRECTIONS [GUIDE PAGE 592 (LA)]
Take Highway 101 to the Coldwater Canyon Boulevard Exit and go south. At the intersection of Coldwater Canyon and Mulholland Drive make a 90 degree turn right onto Franklin Canyon Drive. Road signs read "Road Closed 800 Feet" "Sunset to Sunrise"; this is the park entrance. Stay on the paved surface to reach the Sooky Goldman Nature Center.

GOOD THINGS TO SEE AND HEAR
The Sooky Goldman Nature Center is in Franklin Canyon Park, where you will find a variety of trails for children. Take a stroll around Franklin Canyon Lake, for example. In addition to the regular exhibits in the Nature Center, children may create nature-inspired art.

HOURS
Daily   Sunrise to Sunset (park hours)

PARKING
Free

ADMISSION
Free

RELATED PLACES
• California Strawberry Festival - Site 55
• Underwood Family Farms - Site 99

SPECIAL EVENTS
• Faery Hunt   Saturday mornings ($10 suggested donation)

YOUR COMMENTS

_____
_____
_____
_____
_____

SITE 54 - ENC NATIVE BUTTERFLY HOUSE

ADDRESS
Environmental Nature Center
1601 16th Street
Newport Beach, CA 92663
(949) 645-8489
www.ENCenter.org

DIRECTIONS [GUIDE PAGE 889 (OC)]
• Take Pacific Coast Highway 1 to the north of Newport Bay, turn inland on Dover Drive to 16th Street. Turn left, the center is on the left side of the road.

GOOD THINGS TO SEE AND HEAR
The ENC Native Butterfly House is part of the Environmental Nature Center which includes a variety of native California habitats, including Chaparral, Cone Forest, Coastal Sage Scrub, Desert, Foothill Woodland, Fresh Water Marsh, Northern Oak Woodland, and Redwood Forest, plus a Discovery Center with many native plants, seeds and fossil to touch and smell. There are Toddler Time programs featuring stories and hands-on activities. The Enc Native Butterfly House is a greenhouse filled with native plants and hundreds of native butterflies, including Mourning Cloak, Painted Lady, and Lorquin's Admiral butterflies, all in full color.

HOURS
Environmental Nature Center:
Monday-Friday   8:00 a.m. - 5:00 p.m.
Saturday   8:00 a.m. - 4:00 p.m.

Butterfly House April 15 - October 15:
Monday-Saturday   9:00 a.m. - 3:00 p.m.

PARKING
Free

ADMISSION
Free

RELATED PLACES
• Aliso & Wood Canyons Wilderness Park and Orange County Natural History Museum - Site 47
• Children's Nature Institute - Site 43
• Eaton Canyon County Park and Nature Center - Site 44
• El Dorado East Regional Park and Nature Center - Site 50
• Hopkins Wilderness Park - Site 42
• Irvine Regional Park and Nature Center - Site 49
• Natural History Museum of Los Angeles County - Butterfly Pavilion - Site 1
• San Dimas Canyon Park and Nature Center - Site 45
• Shipley Nature Center at Huntington Central Park - Site 48
• Whittier Narrows Nature Center - Site 46
• Wilderness Park and Nature Center - Site 52

CLOSE-BY PLACES
- Balboa Pavilion Carousel - Site 118
- Catalina Terminal/Newport Beach - Site 131
- Newport Beach - Site 142

YOUR COMMENTS

_____
_____
_____
_____
_____

SITE 55 - CALIFORNIA STRAWBERRY FESTIVAL

ADDRESS
Strawberry Meadows of College Park
3250 South Rose Avenue
Oxnard, CA 93033
(805) 385-4739
www.strawberry-fest.org

DIRECTIONS [GUIDE PAGE 522 (SB/V)]
- Take U.S. Highway 101 to the Las Posas Road Exit and turn left (south). Proceed to Pleasant Valley by turning right and follow Pleasant Valley to Rice Avenue. From there, go over the overpass at Pacific Coast Highway 1 heading west.
- Or take Amtrak - Site 193 or Metrolink-Site 194

GOOD THINGS TO SEE AND HEAR
The Strawberry Festival offers an amazing variety of food full of strawberries, strawberry juices, and, of course, bushels of strawberries. This festival also has a Strawberryland for children that includes puppet shows, a Berry-Go-Round, a Jungle Train, and a petting area with llamas, pigs, and ducks.

You can take Amtrak directly to the Strawberry Festival, however, this may be too big of a day for small children. The festival is in May. Call for exact dates.

HOURS
Weekends in May:
Saturday-Sunday   10:00 a.m. - 6:30 p.m.

PARKING
Free

ADMISSION
Adult	$12.00
Child (Ages 5-12)	$5.00
Under 5	Free

RELATED PLACES

- Oak Glen Apple Farms - Site 93
- Underwood Family Farms - Site 99

CLOSE-BY PLACES

- Leo Carrillo State Beach - Site 139
- Leo Carrillo State Beach Tide Pools - Site 82
- Oxnard Train Station - Site 183
- Ventura County Fair - Site 111
- Ventura Train Station - Site 192

YOUR COMMENTS

_____

_____

_____

_____

_____

UNIVERSITY CAMPUSES

ADDRESS

Addresses for favorite universities are listed, however, one that is close to you is the best.

GOOD THINGS TO SEE AND HEAR

Take your stroller or tricycle to your nearest university campus. Ride around and have a picnic. The campuses are beautifully maintained and provide a pleasant and safe place to stroll or ride. You will often find fountains, gardens, and koi ponds. The students will never notice you.

Bring a children's book to read under the shade of a tree and a little bag of Cheerios (or two) in case there are ducks in the ponds. Please do not feed the koi, however.

HOURS

All

PARKING

Usually challenging

ADMISSION

Free

RELATED PLACES

- Descanso Gardens - Site 38
- The Huntington - Site 39
- Los Angeles County Arboretum and Botanic Gardens - Site 37
- South Coast Botanical Gardens - Site 40

YOUR COMMENTS

_____

_____

_____

_____

_____

FAVORITE UNIVERSITIES

SITE 56 - CALIFORNIA INSTITUTE OF TECHNOLOGY, CALTECH

1200 East California Boulevard
Pasadena, CA 91125
(626) 395-6811
www.caltech.edu
[GUIDE PAGE 566 (LA)]
• Take Interstate Highway 210 to the Hill Street Exit and go south. Make a right on Del Mar Boulevard. From there, make a left on Holliston Avenue and enter a parking structure on your left. There you will register your car and receive instructions on where to park.
• Wander along the paths in the center of campus near the very tall Millikan Library.

SITE 57 - UNIVERSITY OF SOUTHERN CALIFORNIA, USC

3551 University Avenue
Los Angeles, CA 90089
(213) 740-2311
www.usc.edu
[GUIDE PAGE 674 (LA)]
• Take Interstate Highway 110 north to the Martin Luther King Jr. Boulevard Exit and go west. Make a right on Figueroa Street and then a left on 35th Street. From there, enter campus at Gate #3.
• Take Interstate Highway 110 south to the Exposition Boulevard Exit. Make a right on Figueroa Street and then a left on 35th Street. Enter campus at Gate #3.
• USC is across from Exposition Park (Natural History Museum, the IMAX Theater, and the Rose Garden.

SITE 58 - UNIVERSITY OF CALIFORNIA LOS ANGELES, UCLA

405 Hilgard Avenue
Box 951361
Los Angeles, CA 90095
(310) 825-4321
www.ucla.edu
[GUIDE PAGE 632 (LA)]
• Take Interstate Highway 405 to the Wilshire Boulevard Exit and go east towards Westwood. Turn left on Westwood Boulevard and follow Westwood Boulevard into campus. Stop at any of the parking kiosks once you enter the UCLA campus for instructions on what parking structure to park in and to get a campus map.
• Visit the UCLA Botanical Gardens in the southeast corner of the campus.

SITE 59 - UNIVERSITY OF CALIFORNIA IRVINE, UCI

University Drive
Irvine, CA 92612
(949) 824-5011
www.uci.edu
[GUIDE PAGE 859/889/890 (OC)]
• Take Interstate Highway 405 south to the Jamboree Road Exit and go south. Make a left on Campus Drive and then a right on Peltason Drive.
Take Interstate Highway 405 north to the University Drive Exit and go left (south). Make a left on Campus Drive and then a right on Peltason Drive.
• Visit Aldrich Park, a botanical garden, in the center of the campus.

SITE 60 - CALIFORNIA STATE UNIVERSITY FULLERTON, CSUF

800 North State College Boulevard
Fullerton, CA 92831-3547
(714) 278-2011
www.fullerton.edu
[GUIDE PAGE 739 (OC)]
• Take Interstate Highway 5 to State Highway 91 east and then to State Highway 57 north. Exit Yorba Linda Boulevard and go west. From there, make a left at Associated Road. The arboretum parking lot is on the left.
• Visit the Fullerton Arboretum which has a duck pond.

SITE 61 - CALIFORNIA STATE UNIVERSITY LONG BEACH, CSULB

1250 North Bellflower Boulevard
Long Beach, CA 90840
(562) 985-4111
www.csulb.edu
[GUIDE PAGE 796 (LA)]
• Take Interstate Highway 405 to the Bellflower Boulevard Exit and go south. Left on Atherton Street. Make a right on Earl Warren Drive. The gardens are on your right.
• Visit the Japanese Gardens.

SITE 62 - CALIFORNIA STATE UNIVERSITY NORTHRIDGE, CSUN

18111 Nordhoff Street
Northridge, CA 91330
(818) 677-1200
www.csun.edu
[GUIDE PAGE 500 (LA)]
• Take State Highway 118 to the Reseda Boulevard Exit and go south. Left on Nordhoff Street. From there, make a left on Lindley Avenue.
• Visit the Orange Grove in the southeast corner of campus.

Flamingos at the zoo.
Photo by the author .

CHAPTER 4 - THE ZOO

Southern California is home to one of the most famous zoos, the San Diego Zoo, as well as other large (Los Angeles) and small (Orange County, Santa Barbara, and Santa Ana) zoos. For young children, the best zoo is the close zoo that is visited many times. Ask a zookeeper for the names of some of your favorite animals. Get a membership and take a picnic. Go early when it is cool and the animals are awake.

BOOKS FOR YOUR CHILD
- Christelow, Eileen - *Five Little Monkeys Sitting in a Tree*
- Collard III, Sneed B. - *Animal Dads*
- Daly, Kathleen N. - *Wild Animal Babies*
- Hadithi, Mwenye - *Greedy Zebra*
- Jackson, K. - *The Saggy Baggy Elephant*
- Jackson, Kathryn - *Tawny Scrawny Lion*
- Jorgensen, Gail - *Crocodile Beat*
- Martin, Bill, Jr. - *Brown Bear, Brown Bear, What Do You See?*
- Priddy, Roger - *Baby's Book of Animals* (Dorling Kindersley Publishing)

SITE 63 - LOS ANGELES ZOO

ADDRESS
Griffith Park
5333 Zoo Drive
Los Angeles, CA 90027
(323) 644-4200
www.lazoo.org

DIRECTIONS [GUIDE PAGE 564 (LA)]
- Take State Highway 134 west to the Zoo Drive Exit. Follow the road to the zoo.
- Take State Highway 134 east to the Victory Boulevard Exit and turn right at top of offramp. Make a left on Zoo Drive and follow this road to the zoo.

GOOD THINGS TO SEE AND HEAR
The Los Angeles Zoo moved to Griffith Park in 1912 and housed former circus animals. Some are still there, including Ruby (elephant) and Methuselah (alligator). In the last several years, the zoo has undergone extensive improvements and more are underway. New areas include the Winnick Family Children's Zoo, the Red Ape Rain Forest for the orangutans, the Komodo Dragon House, the Neil Papiano Play House, and Mahale Mountain for the chimpanzees. The next new area to open is the Pachyderm Forest that will include an area to view the hippos underwater. Everyone has their favorite animals to see (and smell). Some of the best are the orangutans, hippos, gorillas, camels, giraffes, elephants, flamingos, siamangs (hooting monkeys), snakes in the reptile house-especially the Python, and baby animals in the nursery. Rainy days are some of the best days to go to the zoo, as the animals are quite playful.

Zoos are great places to visit over and over again. This one is no exception. Be ready to lift your little ones up a lot as many exhibits are out of view of a stroller. Note that school day mornings are often crowded with school children. Take advantage of the opportunity to drive by the school buses on your way in or out.

ZOO ANIMALS

ZEBRA

LION

BEAR

ELEPHANT

GIRAFFE

HOURS
Winter:
Daily   10:00 a.m. - 5:00 p.m.
Summer:
Daily   10:00 a.m. - 6:00 p.m.

PARKING
Free

ADMISSION
Adult $10.00
Child (Ages 2-12) $5.00
Under 2   Free

YEARLY MEMBERSHIP
Adult $45.00
Adult (2 People) $55.00
Family $65.00

RELATED PLACES
- Orange County Zoo - Site 65
- Santa Ana Zoo - Site 64
- San Diego Zoo - Site 68
- San Diego Wild Animal Park - Site 69
- Santa Barbara Zoological Gardens - Site 70

CLOSE-BY PLACES
- Glendale Train Station - Site 178
- Griffith Observatory - Site 9
- Griffith Park Pony Rides - Site 95
- Griffith Park Merry-Go-Round - Site 115
- Griffith Park Train Ride - Site 198
- Travel Town Museum - Site 170

YOUR COMMENTS

SITE 65 - SANTA ANA ZOO

ADDRESS
Prentice Park
1801 East Chestnut Avenue
Santa Ana, CA 92701
(714) 835-7484
www.santaanazoo.org

DIRECTIONS [GUIDE PAGE 829 (OC)]
• Take Interstate Highway 5 south to the 4th Street Exit. Go straight on Mabury Street which turns into Elk Lane, and make a left on Chestnut Avenue.
• Take Interstate Highway 5 north to the 1st Street Exit and go west. Make a left on Elk Lane and then a left on Chestnut Avenue.

GOOD THINGS TO SEE AND HEAR
The Santa Ana Zoo is a small zoo that has wonderful primates and macaws (the zoo's main walkway is called "monkey row"), a rain forest exhibit called "Colors of the Amazon" that highlights the wonderful colors of the animals that live in the Amazon; a huge porcupine; and a walk-through aviary. The new Crean Family Farm provides a barnyard adventure with goats, sheep and chickens that can be fed and petted.
Zoofari Express train rides are available on the weekends.

HOURS
Summer:
Monday-Friday   10:00 a.m. - 4:00 p.m.
Saturday-Sunday   10:00 a.m. - 5:00 p.m.
Winter:
Daily   10:00 a.m. - 4:00 p.m.
Train:
Thursday-Sunday   11:00 a.m. - 2:00 p.m.

PARKING
Free

ADMISSION
Adults $6.00
Child (Ages 3-12) $3.00
Under 3   Free
Train Ride $3.00
Elephant Ride $3.00

YEARLY MEMBERSHIP
Adult $29.00
Family $49.00

RELATED PLACES
- Los Angeles Zoo - Site 63
- Orange County Zoo - Site 65
- San Diego Zoo - Site 68
- Santa Barbara Zoological Gardens - Site 70

CLOSE-BY PLACES
- Adventure City - Site 113
- Anaheim Train Station - Site 172
- Anaheim Convention Center - Site 210
- Arrowhead Pond of Anaheim - Site 211
- Discovery Science Center - Site 7
- Disneyland - Site 112

SITE 65 - ORANGE COUNTY ZOO

ADDRESS
Irvine Regional Park
1 Irvine Park Road
Orange, CA 92862
(714) 973-6835 Park
(714) 973-6847 Zoo
www.ocparks.com/oczoo

DIRECTIONS [GUIDE PAGE 800/801 (OC)]
Take Interstate Highway 5 to the Jamboree Road Exit and go north. Jamboree Road ends at Irvine Regional Park.

GOOD THINGS TO SEE AND HEAR
The Orange County Zoo is a small friendly zoo in the middle of Irvine Park. The zoo focuses on animals and plants from the southwestern United States. It includes a pelican, a black bear named Samson who once made the news by hanging out in a family's hot tub, deer, two mountain lions, a porcupine, a beaver, eagles, coyotes, and bobcats.

Since this zoo sits in the middle of Irvine Park, a visit can be combined with a pony ride (see Site 102), a train ride (see Site 200), or a picnic.

HOURS
Park:
Summer:
Daily   7:00 a.m. - 9:00 p.m.
Winter:
Daily   7:00 a.m. - 6:00 p.m.
Zoo:
Daily   10:00 a.m. - 3:30 p.m.

PARKING
Park Entrance:
Weekdays $3.00
Weekends $5.00

ADMISSION

Adult or Child $2.00
Under 2   Free

YEARLY MEMBERSHIP

Family $35.00

RELATED PLACES

- Los Angeles Zoo - Site 63
- San Diego Zoo - Site 68
- San Diego Wild Animal Park - Site 69
- Santa Ana Zoo - Site 64
- Santa Barbara Zoological Gardens - Site 70

CLOSE-BY PLACES

- Green Meadows Farm/Orange County - Site 91
- Irvine Park Railroad - Site 200
- Irvine Regional Park and Nature Center - Site 49
- Irvine Regional Park Pony Rides - Site 102

YOUR COMMENTS

_____
_____
_____
_____
_____

SITE 66 - AMERICA'S TEACHING ZOO AT MOORPARK COLLEGE

ADDRESS

Moorpark College
7075 Campus Road
Moorpark, CA 93021
(805) 378-1441
www.moorparkcollege.edu/zoo

DIRECTIONS [GUIDE PAGE Viii (LA) OR 496 (SB/V)]

Take State Highway 118 west to the Collins Drive Exit. Go right at the light and up a hill. Follow the directions written on blue and white signs.

GOOD THINGS TO SEE AND HEAR

Moorpark College has an exotic animal training and management program for its students. This includes the care and training of animals (including killer whales and dolphins) and the presentation of educational shows utilizing animals. Students in this program offer a short (fifteen minute) demonstration to visitors of some of the practices they have learned with exotic animals. Each show presents a different focus (herbivores, South American animals, etc.) and each student presents four or five different animals. Be sure to sit in the front row as the animals are carried around for close viewing. You can also look at many of the other one hundred fifty animals in their cages or pens, including camels, reptiles, lions, a hyena, and a variety of monkeys. The carnivores are fed at 3:45 p.m.

It can be hot in the summer and there are no snack bars-so come prepared.

HOURS
Saturday-Sunday   11:00 a.m. - 5:00 p.m.

PARKING
Free

ADMISSION
Adult $5.00
Child (Ages 2-12) $4.00
Under 2   Free

RELATED PLACES
• San Diego Wild Animal Park - Site 69
• STAR EcoStation Environmental Science and Wildlife Rescue Center - Site 67

CLOSE-BY PLACES
• Fillmore and Western Railway - Site 203
• Moorpark Train Station - Site 181
• Underwood Family Farms - Site 99

YOUR COMMENTS

_____

_____

_____

_____

SITE 67 - STAR EcoStation Environmental Science and Wildlife Rescue Center

ADDRESS
10101 West Jefferson Boulevard
Culver City, CA 90232
(310) 842-8060
www.ecostation.org

DIRECTIONS [GUIDE PAGE 672 (LA)]
Take Interstate Highway 10 to the La Cienega Boulevard Exit and go south (left at the light after the exit). Make a right on Jefferson Boulevard and go south. The center is on the right side of the street. Parking is in the back.

GOOD THINGS TO SEE AND HEAR

The mission of the EcoStation is to provide state of the art environmental science education and a home for rescued exotic wildlife. The center, built like a Mayan city, is home to a variety of tropical birds (parrots, toucans, and cockatoos), exotic reptiles (iguanas, snakes, and lizards from), and sea animals (fish, eels, sea stars). Visitors are led on a tour that is paced for the age group. Tours leave on the half hour. Children can touch and interact with many of the animals. The sounds from the birds are wonderful.

The EcoStation serves as the main Wildlife Rescue Center for the U.S. Department of the Interior Fish and Wildlife. Special events are good days to avoid as they are crowded. Some tours are given by teenagers which make them especially interesting for young children!

HOURS

Saturday-Sunday   10:00 a.m. - 4:00 p.m.

PARKING

Free

ADMISSION

Adult	$7.00
Child	$5.00
Infants in strollers	Free

YEARLY MEMBERSHIP

Family $55.00

RELATED PLACES

• America's Teaching Zoo at Moorpark College - Site 66
• Natural History Museum of Los Angeles County - Site 1
• Pet Stores-Chapter 2
• San Diego Wild Animal Park - Site 69

CLOSE-BY PLACES

• Santa Monica Pier Carousel - Site 116
• Santa Monica Municipal Airport - Site 161
• Santa Monica Pier Aquarium - Site 75
• Santa Monica Puppet and Magic Center - Site 207
• Santa Monica State Beach - Site 146
• University of California Los Angeles, UCLA - Site 58

YOUR COMMENTS

_____
_____
_____
_____

SITE 68 - SAN DIEGO ZOO

ADDRESS
Balboa Park
2920 Zoo Drive
San Diego, CA 92103
(619) 234-3153
www.sandiegozoo.org

DIRECTIONS [GUIDE PAGE 1269 (SD)]
Take Interstate Highway 5 to the Park Drive Exit and go north. Make a left on Zoo Place.

GOOD THINGS TO SEE AND HEAR
The San Diego Zoo is one of the largest and most famous zoos in America-and has one of the most extensive Children's Zoos. You could spend all day and never leave the Children's Zoo. Highlights beyond the Children's Zoo that make the San Diego Zoo unique are: the Polar Bear Plunge (underwater viewing); Ituri Forest (hippos under water, or duck bottoms); Gorilla Tropics; Tiger River (especially if the tiger is awake); and the camels (very smelly).

Spend most of your time in the Children's Zoo and less, more focused time, visiting a few of your other favorite exhibits.

HOURS
School Year:
Daily   9:00 a.m. - 4:00 p.m.
Summer:
Daily   9:00 a.m. - 8:00 p.m.

PARKING
Free

ADMISSION
Adult $32.00
Child (Ages 3-11) $19.75
Under 3   Free
Including Wild Animal Park and Sea World:
Adult $98.75
Child (Ages 3-11) $74.95
Under 3   Free

YEARLY MEMBERSHIP
Adult $68.00
Adults (2 people) $86.00
Child (Ages 3-11) $21.00
• Includes San Diego Zoo and Wild Animal Park

RELATED PLACES
- Los Angeles Zoo - Site 63
- Orange County Zoo - Site 65
- Santa Ana Zoo - Site 64
- San Diego Wild Animal Park - Site 69
- Santa Barbara Zoological Gardens - Site 70

CLOSE-BY PLACES
- Balboa Park Merry-Go-Round and Butterfly Rides - Site 121
- Bates Nut Farm - Site 101
- Belmont Park Carousel - Site 119
- The Children's Museum of San Diego/Museo de los Niños - Site 12
- San Diego Convention Center - Site 214
- San Diego Model Railroad Museum - Site 202
- San Diego Train Station - Site 185
- Sea World - Site 87
- Seaport Village Carousel - Site 120

YOUR COMMENTS

_____

_____

_____

_____

SITE 69 - SAN DIEGO WILD ANIMAL PARK

ADDRESS
15500 San Pasqual Valley Road
Escondido, CA 92027
(760) 747-8702
www.sandiegozoo.org

DIRECTIONS [GUIDE PAGE 1150/1130/1131 (SD)]
Take Interstate Highway 5 to Highway 78 east, and then go south on Interstate Highway 15. Take the Via Rancho Parkway Exit and go east (turns into Bear Valley Parkway). Make a right on San Pasqual Road and follow the signs. Be on the lookout for an ostrich and a camel farm on the road to the Wild Animal Park.

GOOD THINGS TO SEE AND HEAR
The San Diego Wild Animal Park is a one thousand eight hundred-acre preserve that is home to animals from Africa and Asia. The park takes great pride in its efforts to breed endangered species, especially rhinos and condors. Many of these animals are in huge pens and can be seen on a train ride around the park. The monorail ride is fifty to sixty minutes - maybe too long for toddlers, but a lot of animals can be readily seen. Many activities are centralized near the entrance, including a Petting Kraal, Lorikeet Landing (feed parrot-like birds while they sit on your hand), the Lowland Gorillas, and the Elephant Show. Many of the animals are seen on long walking trails through the park, so bring a stroller, extra water, snacks, and good shoes. On a lucky day, you can feed the giraffes in the Heart of Africa.
If you can avoid a hot day, do it.
There are journals at the beginning of some of the walks with line drawings of the animals you will see as well as words about them. These make great coloring books.

HOURS
Summer:
Daily   9:00 a.m. - 8:00 p.m.
Winter:
Daily   9:00 a.m. - 4:00 p.m.

PARKING
$6.00

ADMISSION
Adult $28.50
Child (Ages 3-11) $17.50
Under 3   Free
Including San Diego Zoo and Sea World:
Adult $98.75
Child (Ages 3-11) $74.95
Under 3   Free

YEARLY MEMBERSHIP

Adult	$68.00
Adults (2 people)	$86.00
Child (Ages 3-11)	$21.00

• Includes San Diego Zoo and Wild Animal Park

RELATED PLACES
• Los Angeles Zoo - Site 63
• San Diego Zoo - Site 68
• Santa Barbara Zoological Gardens - Site 70

CLOSE-BY PLACES
• Children's Discovery Museum of North Country - Site 13
• Legoland - Site 114
• McClellan-Palomar Airport - Site 158

YOUR COMMENTS

_____
_____
_____
_____
_____

SITE 70 - SANTA BARBARA ZOOLOGICAL GARDENS

ADDRESS
500 Niños Drive
Santa Barbara, CA 93103
(805) 962-5339 or (805) 962-6310
www.santabarbarazoo.org

DIRECTIONS [GUIDE PAGE 996 (SB)]
Take U.S. Highway 101 to the Milpas Street Exit. Turn left onto Cabrillo Boulevard, and then left (toward mountains) at Niños Drive.

GOOD THINGS TO SEE AND HEAR
The Santa Barbara Zoo is certainly one of the most beautiful and friendly zoos in the world. It is a smaller zoo with a closer view of many of the animals. Be sure to see the silly lemurs. There is also a small carousel and a train ride.

Have lunch at the hot dog stand just above the elephants.

HOURS
Daily	10:00 a.m. - 5:00 p.m.

PARKING
$2.00

ADMISSION
Adult $9.00
Child (Ages 2-12) $7.00
Under 2 Free

YEARLY MEMBERSHIP
Adult $40.00
Family $65.00

RELATED PLACES
• Los Angeles Zoo - Site 63
• Orange County Zoo - Site 65
• Santa Ana Zoo - Site 64

CLOSE-BY PLACES
• Chase Palm Park Carousel - Site 123
• Kid's World - Site 36
• Santa Barbara Airport - Site 160
• Santa Barbara County Fair and Exposition - Site 110
• Santa Barbara East Beach - Site 143
• Santa Barbara Museum of Natural History - Site 14
• Santa Barbara Train Station - Site 188

YOUR COMMENTS

Children Watch in Amazement as Fish Swim by at the Blue Cavern Exhibit at the Aquarium of the Pacific in Long Beach.
Photo by author, permission to use photo courtesy of Mary Vasiltsova of the Aquarium of the Pacific.

CHAPTER 5 - AQUARIUMS

Being close to the ocean, there are a variety of aquariums and other places that are home to sea creatures in Southern California. The aquariums are all different and while each is worth a visit, the best one is one near your home where you can visit over and over again. Sea World is a big park, but always seems peaceful for young children. The animal rescue centers do not take much time, but are fun for small children. And don't forget about the tide pools!

SEALS AND A SEA LIONS

The difference between a seal and a sea lion is sometimes subtle. Here are the basics:

SEALS (HARBOR SEAL AND NORTHERN ELEPHANT SEAL):
• Lack external ear flaps
• Have small fore flippers with toenails
• Swim with their short rear flippers
• Scoot on land with bellies (can't use back flippers for walking)

SEA LIONS (CALIFORNIA SEA LIONS AND NORTHERN FUR SEAL):
• Have external ear flaps
• Have very large front flippers
• Swim with their front flippers which have no toenails
• Move on land using front and long back flippers

BOOKS FOR YOUR CHILD
• Gunzi, Christiane-*Tide Pool* (Dorling Kindersley Publishing)
• Jaques, Florence Page-*There Once Was a Puffin*
• Lionni, Leo-*Swimmy*
• Raffi-*Baby Beluga*
• Rylant, Cynthia-*The Whale*
• Seuss, Dr.-*McElligot's Pool*
• Seuss, Dr.-*One Fish Two Fish Red Fish Blue Fish*

SITE 71 - LONG BEACH AQUARIUM OF THE PACIFIC

ADDRESS
100 Aquarium Way
Long Beach, CA 90802
(562) 590-3100
www.aquariumofpacific.org

DIRECTIONS [GUIDE PAGE 825 (LA)]
• Take Interstate Highway 710 south into downtown Long Beach. Follow the signs to aquarium.
• Or take the Metro Rail Blue Line - Site 195.

GOOD THINGS TO SEE AND HEAR
The Long Beach Aquarium focuses on three regions of the Pacific Ocean including Southern California/Baja, the Tropical Pacific, and the Northern Pacific. Be sure to see the seals and sea lions, Japanese spider crabs, tropical reef habitat, the puffins, sea turtles, the giant Blue Cavern in the front hall (sit on floor and watch the fish and Moray Eels), and the "Whales: Voices in the Sea" exhibit. The Shark Lagoon allows children to touch real sharks - but be careful not to grab their tail or they will react with a lot of splashing! The Lorikeet Exhibit is a favorite for the colorful birds and the noise they make! They like to land on flowered hair ribbons and dresses so beware (or be prepared!). Afterwards, walk along the water outside the aquarium to see and hear the ships and sea birds.

GOOD THINGS TO SEE AND HEAR (CONTINUED)

Membership or advanced tickets (see website or (800) TICKETS) will help you avoid a long line and wait to get in. Backpacks are better than strollers when the museum is crowded. Be sure to get a "Fish Finder" (brochure with pictures of many of the fish) and involve your toddlers in identifying the fish.

HOURS
Daily   9:00 a.m. - 6:00 p.m.

PARKING
$6.00

ADMISSION
Adult	$18.75
Child (Ages 3-11)	$10.95
Under 3	Free

YEARLY MEMBERSHIP
Adult	$49.00
Adults (2 people)	$79.00
Family	$109.00

RELATED PLACES
• Birch Aquarium at Scripps - Site 88
• Cabrillo Marine Aquarium - Site 72
• Roundhouse Marine Studies Lab and Aquarium - Site 73
• Santa Catalina Island - Site 126
• Santa Monica Pier Aquarium - Site 75
• Tide Pools - Site 77-84

CLOSE-BY PLACES
• Cabrillo Beach Tide Pools - Site 77
• Cabrillo Marine Aquarium - Site 72
• Catalina Terminal/Long Beach-Downtown - Site 127
• Catalina Terminal/Long Beach-Queen Mary - Site 128
• Catalina Terminal/San Pedro-Port of Los Angeles - Site 129
• Long Beach Convention Center - Site 212
• Marine Mammal Care Center at Fort MacArthur - Site 85
• Shoreline Village Carousel - Site 117

YOUR COMMENTS
_____
_____
_____
_____
_____

SITE 72 - CABRILLO MARINE AQUARIUM

ADDRESS
3720 Stephen White Drive
San Pedro, CA 90731
(310) 548-7562
www.cabrilloaq.org

DIRECTIONS [GUIDE PAGE 854 (LA)]
Take Interstate Highway 110 to the Gaffey Exit at the end of the freeway and go south. Make a left (east) on 22nd and then a right (south) on Pacific Avenue. From there turn left (east) on 36th/Stephen White Drive.

GOOD THINGS TO SEE AND HEAR
The Cabrillo Marine Aquarium is divided into Mudflats (crabs, clams, sand dollars, sea stars, and some fish), Rocky Shores, and Open Ocean (sharks, whales, dolphins, sea birds, and jelly fish). Favorites are the lobsters, the hands-on tide pools, the crabs, and the whalebones. Many tanks are low so toddlers don't need to be lifted up to see fish.

Cabrillo Beach is just outside the door and has real tide pools during low tide (see Site 77 in this chapter). The ocean water around Cabrillo Beach is often polluted.

HOURS
Tuesday-Friday   12:00 p.m. - 5:00 p.m.
Saturday-Sunday   10:00 a.m. - 5:00 p.m.

PARKING
$7.00

ADMISSION
Suggested Donation:
Adult: $5.00
Child $1.00

YEARLY MEMBERSHIP
Adult $30.00
Family $40.00

RELATED PLACES
• Birch Aquarium at Scripps - Site 88
• Long Beach Aquarium of the Pacific - Site 71
• Roundhouse Marine Studies Lab and Aquarium - Site 73
• Santa Catalina Island - Site 126
• Santa Monica Pier Aquarium - Site 75
• Tide Pools - Sites 77-84

CLOSE-BY PLACES
- Cabrillo Beach Tide Pools - Site 77
- Catalina Terminal/Long Beach-Downtown - Site 127
- Catalina Terminal/Long Beach-Queen Mary - Site 128
- Catalina Terminal/San Pedro-Port of Los Angeles - Site 129
- Long Beach Aquarium of the Pacific - Site 71
- Long Beach Convention Center - Site 212
- Marine Mammal Care Center at Fort MacArthur - Site 85
- Shoreline Village Carousel - Site 117

YOUR COMMENTS

SITE 73 - ROUNDHOUSE MARINE STUDIES LAB AND AQUARIUM

ADDRESS
Manhattan Beach Pier
Manhattan Beach, CA 92066
(310) 379-8117
www.roundhouseaquarium.org/

DIRECTIONS [GUIDE PAGE 732 (LA)]
Take Interstate Highway 405 to the State Highway 91 west to Pacific Coast Highway 1 north. Make a left on Manhattan Beach Boulevard and go straight for the pier or left or right on Highland Avenue for the beach. Parking at meters and public lots on Highland Avenue.

GOOD THINGS TO SEE AND HEAR
The Roundhouse is a very small round aquarium at the end of the Manhattan Beach Pier. It underwent a renovation in 2002. The exhibits focus on marine life from the Santa Monica Bay and includes a tide pool touch tank, a deep-water tank, a surf surge tank, and a reef tank.

The people fishing at the end of the pier are also fascinating to watch.

HOURS
Monday-Friday	3:00 p.m. - Sunset
Saturday-Sunday	10:00 a.m. - Sunset
Sea Story Time:	
Sunday	11:00 a.m.

PARKING

Varies along the beach
Metered parking at the base of the pier $1.00/hour

ADMISSION

Free
Suggested Donation:
Adult or Child $2.00

YEARLY MEMBERSHIP

Adult or Child $25.00
Family $35.00

RELATED PLACES

- Birch Aquarium at Scripps - Site 88
- Cabrillo Marine Aquarium - Site 72
- Long Beach Aquarium of the Pacific - Site 71
- Santa Catalina Island - Site 126
- Santa Monica Pier Aquarium - Site 75
- Tide Pools - Sites 77-84

CLOSE-BY PLACES

- Hermosa Beach - Site 135
- Manhattan Beach - Site 141
- Redondo Beach - Site 143
- Sea Lab - Site 74
- Seaside Lagoon - Site 147

YOUR COMMENTS

_____
_____
_____
_____
_____

SITE 74 - SEA LAB

ADDRESS

1021 North Harbor Drive
Redondo Beach, CA 90277
(310) 318-7458
www.lacorps.org/about.html?adultcorps.html

DIRECTIONS [GUIDE PAGE 762 (LA)]

Take Interstate Highway 405 to the Crenshaw Boulevard exit. Go south on Crenshaw Boulevard to W. 190th Street. Turn right onto W. 190th Street. W. 190th Street becomes Herondo Street. From Herondo Street turn left onto N. Harbor Drive.

GOOD THINGS TO SEE AND HEAR
The Sea Lab is home to sea creatures rescued from oceanside power plants. Some creatures stay only a short time, and some can no longer survive in the wild and stay longer. Everything is very touchable. Enjoy!

HOURS
Tuesday-Friday	9:00 a.m. - 2:00 p.m.
Saturday	10:00 a.m. - 4:30 p.m.
Sunday	11:00 a.m. - 4:30 p.m.
Touch Tank:	1:00 p.m. - 1:30 p.m.

PARKING
Park on the pier if you can.

ADMISSION
Free
$1.00 for fish food

YEARLY MEMBERSHIP
Adult	$25.00
Family	$40.00

RELATED PLACES
• Birch Aquarium at Scripps - Site 88
• Cabrillo Marine Aquarium - Site 72
• Long Beach Aquarium of the Pacific - Site 71
• Santa Catalina Island - Site 126
• Santa Monica Pier Aquarium - Site 75
• Tide Pools - Sites 77-84

CLOSE-BY PLACES
• Hermosa Beach - Site 135
• Manhattan Beach - Site 141
• Redondo Beach - Site 143
• Roundhouse Marine Studies Lab and Aquarium - Site 73
• Seaside Lagoon - Site 147

SPECIAL EVENTS
• Public Fish Feeding and marine life program   12:00 p.m. Saturday

YOUR COMMENTS

_____
_____
_____
_____
_____
_____

AQUARIUM ANIMALS

SEA LION

OCTOPUS

SHARK

JELLY FISH

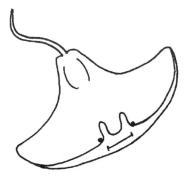

BAT RAY

SITE 75 - SANTA MONICA PIER AQUARIUM

ADDRESS
Under the Santa Monica Pier
1600 Ocean Front Walk
Santa Monica, CA 90401
(310) 393-6149
www.santamonicapier.org

DIRECTIONS [GUIDE PAGE 671 (LA)]
Take Interstate Highway 10 to the 4th Street Exit and go northwest. Make a left on Colorado and park on pier. The center is under the pier.

GOOD THINGS TO SEE AND HEAR
The Santa Monica Pier Aquarium is a very small, very interactive aquarium that displays animals that live in Santa Monica Bay. Tanks with jellyfish, sharks, rays, and an octopus are at eye level. There are usually several touch tanks that are easily accessible to young children, and a new kids' corner full of books and games about marine life.

The Santa Monica Pier Merry-Go-Round is directly above the Santa Monica Pier Aquarium. The Santa Monica Pier Aquarium was started by UCLA and is now run by Heal the Bay.

HOURS
Tuesday-Friday	2:00 p.m. - 5:00 p.m.
Saturday-Sunday	12:00 p.m. - 6:00 p.m.

PARKING
Park on the pier if you can.

ADMISSION
Adult or Child	$5.00
Under 12	Free

YEARLY MEMBERSHIP
Adult	$35.00
Family	$50.00

RELATED PLACES
- Birch Aquarium at Scripps - Site 88
- Cabrillo Marine Aquarium - Site 72
- Long Beach Aquarium of the Pacific - Site 71
- Roundhouse Marine Studies Lab and Aquarium - Site 73
- Santa Catalina Island - Site 126
- Tide Pools - Sites 77-84

CLOSE-BY PLACES
- Santa Monica Pier Carousel - Site 116
- Santa Monica Puppet and Magic Center - Site 207
- Santa Monica State Beach - Site 146
- Santa Monica Municipal Airport - Site 161
- STAR EcoStation Environmental Science and Wildlife Rescue Center - Site 67
- University of California Los Angeles, UCLA - Site 58

YOUR COMMENTS

_____

_____

_____

_____

SITE 76 - LITTLE CORONA DEL MAR TIDE POOLS

ADDRESS
3700 Ocean Boulevard
Corona Del Mar, CA 92625
(949) 644-3151

DIRECTIONS [GUIDE PAGE 919 (OC)]
Take Interstate Highway 405 to the MacArthur Boulevard Exit and go south. Make a left on Pacific Coast Highway 1, a right on Poppy Avenue, and a right on Ocean Boulevard. Park along the streets for free.

GOOD THINGS TO SEE AND HEAR
Southern California has many beaches with tide pools. Our favorite is Little Corona Del Mar. Walk down to the beach (there is a ramp and a bathroom at the half way point). Tide pools are north and south of the end of the ramp.

Frequently the tides are low enough during the day to find sea creatures among the rocks along the shore, including urchins, anemones, sea stars, mussels, keyhole limpets, and barnacles, and maybe even a small octopus if you are lucky (but remember that they squirt a black inky substance when cornered). Look under rocks - nothing can hurt you - and then return the rocks to the same position. Be sure to touch gently and don't remove anything-even empty shells. Wear rubber boots or shoes that can get wet.

The rocks are slippery and sharp, so plan to stay right with your child. Bring dry clothes for adults, two pairs of dry clothes for kids, rubber boots or tennis shoes that can get wet and are good for walking on rocks, a camera, a big snack, jackets, and a towel.

HOURS

To find the best days and times of day, remember that the tides are lowest during a full moon. On the web, look at www.tidelines.com. In the *Los Angeles Times*, look on the "Weather" page. Look at the section called "Sun & Moon and Tides." Here you will find the date of the next full moon and the high and low tides. Look for tides that are at least minus one foot (minus two or minus three feet is better) at an hour of the day when the sun is up. The tides are usually low enough during the two hours preceding and following this time. December and January are usually very good times.

You can also order a neat little tide book and check for days with low tide from Tidelines, Inc., (800) 345-8524 or www.tidelines.com.

PARKING

Free

ADMISSION

Free

RELATED PLACES

- The Beach-Chapter 8
- Birch Aquarium at Scripps - Site 88
- Cabrillo Marine Aquarium - Site 72
- Long Beach Aquarium of the Pacific - Site 71
- Roundhouse Marine Studies Lab and Aquarium - Site 73
- Santa Catalina Island - Site 126
- Santa Monica Pier Aquarium - Site 75

CLOSE-BY PLACES

- Balboa Pavilion Carousel - Site 118
- Catalina Terminal/Newport Beach - Site 131
- Centennial Farm - Site 105
- Corona Del Mar State Beach - Site 134
- John Wayne Airport - Site 156
- Little Corona Del Mar Beach - Site 140
- Newport Beach - Site 142
- Orange County Fair - Site 107
- University of California Irvine, UCI - Site 59

YOUR COMMENTS

_____
_____
_____
_____

Other Tide Pools

Site 77 - Cabrillo Beach Tide Pools

40th Street and Stephen M. White Drive
San Pedro, CA 90731
(310) 548-2914
www.sanpedrochamber.com/champint/cbrobch.htm
[Guide Page 854 (LA)]
• Take Interstate Highway 110 south. From there, go south on Gaffey and make a left (east) on 22nd. Then make a right (south) on Pacific Avenue and a left (east) on 36th/Stephen White Drive. Park at Cabrillo Aquarium.
• Parking is $4.50 weekdays and $5.50 weekends. Tide pools on outer beach. Check for runoff from the Dominguez Channel and the Los Angeles River.

Site 78 - Dana Point Tide Pools

Dana Point Harbor Drive
Dana Point, CA 92629
(949) 923-2255 Harbor
(714) 496-2274 Marine Refuge
www.danapointharbor.com
[Guide Page 971 (OC)]
• Take Interstate Highway 5 to the Camino Las Ramblas Exit and go west. Follow the signs and go along Dana Point Harbor Drive until it ends.
• Tide pools are behind the Ocean Institute downstairs to beach. Check for San Juan Creek Channel runoff.

Site 79 - Doheny State Beach Tide Pools

23500 Dana Point Harbor Drive
Dana Point, CA 92629
(949) 496-2704 Interpretive Center
www.dohenystatebeach.org
[Guide Page 972 (OC)]
• Take Interstate Highway 5 to the Camino Las Ramblas Exit and go west. Follow the signs.
• Tide pools are good on high tide days and easy for little ones. Check for San Juan Creek Channel runoff.

OTHER TIDE POOLS

SITE 80 - DIVER'S COVE TIDE POOLS/ NORTH OF LAGUNA MAIN BEACH

Cliff Drive and Pacific Coast Highway 1
Laguna Beach, CA 92651
(949) 497-9229
www.usc.edu/org/seagrant
[GUIDE PAGE 950 (OC)]
• Take Interstate Highway 405 to the Laguna Canyon Road Exit and go towards the beach. Turn right (north) on Pacific Coast Highway 1 and go to Cliff Drive. From there, turn left to Heisler Park. Diver's Cove is off Heisler Park.

SITE 81 - LA JOLLA SHORES TIDE POOLS

8200 Camino Del Oro
La Jolla, CA 92037
(858) 454-0175
www.sannet.gov/lifeguards/beaches/shores.shtml
[GUIDE PAGE 1227 (SD)]
• Interstate Highway 5 to the La Jolla Village Drive Exit. Make a left at Torrey Pines Road and follow it to La Jolla Shores. Park at Calle Frescota.
• Tide pools are at the base of Bird Rock. See also Birch Aquarium (Site 88 in this chapter).

SITE 82 - LEO CARRILLO STATE BEACH TIDE POOLS

35000 Pacific Coast Highway 1
Malibu, CA 90265
(818) 880-0350
www.parks.ca.gov/default.asp?page_id=616
[GUIDE PAGE 625 (LA) OR 387 (SB/V)]
• Take U.S. Highway 101 to Exit 23. Go south to Pacific Coast Highway 1 and make a right on Pacific Coast Highway 1.
• Tide pools, sea caves and playground. For camping information, call (800) 444-7275.

SITE 83 - LAGUNA BEACH'S HEISLER PARK

West end of Cliff Drive (400 block)
Laguna Beach, CA 92651
(949) 494-6572
www.usc.edu/org/seagrant
[GUIDE PAGE 950 (OC)]
• Take Pacific Coast Highway to Laguna Beach. The park is located at the intersection of Myrtle Street and Pacific Coast Highway, just north of Highway 133.
• One of the best tidepools!.

SITE 84 - POINT DUME BEACH TIDE POOLS

Pacific Coast Highway and Westward Beach Road
Malibu, CA 90265
(310) 457-2525
www.usc.edu/org/seagrant
[GUIDE PAGE 667 (LA)]
• Take Pacific Coast Highway 1 to Malibu. Turn onto Westward Beach Road.
• A cozy family beach with nice tide pools and sometime whale watching.

YOUR COMMENTS

_____
_____
_____
_____

TIDE POOL ANIMALS

ANEMONE

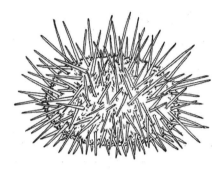

URCHIN

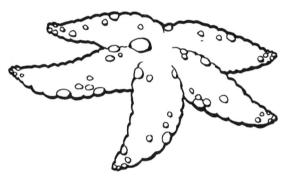

STARFISH

HERMIT CRAB

MUSSEL

SITE 85 - MARINE MAMMAL CARE CENTER AT FORT MACARTHUR

ADDRESS
3601 South Gaffey Street
San Pedro, CA 90731
(310) 547-9888
www.mar3ine.org/

DIRECTIONS [GUIDE PAGE 824/854 (LA)]
Take Interstate Highway 110 south to the end at Gaffey Street. Take Gaffey south to just past 36th Street to the entrance to Fort MacArthur at Angel's Gate on the right. Turn right onto Leavenworth Drive, pass the military museum, and drive until you see the center across the parking lot on the right.

GOOD THINGS TO SEE AND HEAR
The Marine Mammal Care Center is a rescue, rehabilitation, and release facility for injured and sick marine mammals, including harbor seals, fur seals, elephant seals, and sea lions. In other words, this is a hospital for marine mammals. You can usually see seals and sea lions and sometimes other mammals. Most of the animals are rehabilitated and released to the wild. Bring an old clean baby blanket to donate to the seals and sea lions.

There are several marine mammal rescue centers including, starting from the south, Sea World - Site 87, Pacific Marine Mammal Center - Site 86, and the Marine Mammal Care Center at Fort MacArthur, among others in more northern locations.

HOURS
Daily   daylight hours only

PARKING
Free

ADMISSION
Free   (donations accepted

YEARLY MEMBERSHIP
Individual $25.00

RELATED PLACES
• Pacific Marine Mammal Center and Laguna Koi Ponds- Site 86
• Sea World - Site 87

CLOSE-BY PLACES
• Cabrillo Beach Tide Pools - Site 77
• Cabrillo Marine Aquarium - Site 72
• Catalina Terminal/Long Beach-Downtown - Site 127
• Catalina Terminal/Long Beach-Queen Mary - Site 128
• Catalina Terminal/San Pedro-Port of Los Angeles - Site 129
• Long Beach Aquarium of the Pacific - Site 71
• Long Beach Convention Center - Site 212
• Shoreline Village Carousel - Site 117

YOUR COMMENTS

_____

_____

_____

_____

_____

SITE 86 - PACIFIC MARINE MAMMAL CENTER AND LAGUNA KOI PONDS

ADDRESS
20612 Laguna Canyon Road (Sea Lions)
20452 Laguna Canyon Road (Koi)
Laguna Beach, CA 92651
(949) 494-3050 Sea Lions
(949) 494-5107 Koi
www.pacificmmc.org (Sea Lions Information)
www.lagunakoi.com/ (Koi Information)

DIRECTIONS [GUIDE PAGE 920 (OC)]
Take Interstate Highway 405 to the Laguna Canyon Road Exit and go towards the beach. The center is just past El Toro Road and is not right on the beach. Look for Laguna Animal Hospital on the left. The koi ponds are just past that and the Marine Mammal Center is about one-fourth of a mile beyond that; all on the left. Beware there is often a lot of traffic on Laguna Canyon Road on weekends and holidays.

GOOD THINGS TO SEE AND HEAR
Sick and injured seals and sea lions, and elephant seals are rehabilitated and released at the Pacific Marine Mammal Center. The animals are usually found on the beaches by the lifeguards or beach visitors. Bring an old clean baby blanket to donate to the seals and sea lions. Feeding time at the Pacific Marine Mammal Center is 3:00 a.m. - 4:00 p.m. It is fun to watch but very noisy. People working at the center are happy to talk and answer questions. Most of the animals will be released and therefore are not to be talked to, but the babies are usually not released and receive lots of human interaction.

The Laguna Koi Ponds is a small outdoor store that sells koi fish. There are big cement tanks filled with koi fish that may be fed for $.25 for a handful of pellets.

There are several marine mammal rescue centers including, starting from the south, Sea World - Site 87, Pacific Marine Mammal Center, and Marine Mammal Care Center at Fort MacArthur - Site 85, among others in more northern locations.

At the koi ponds, note the prices of the fish!

HOURS
Sea Lions:
Daily   10:00 a.m. - 4:00 p.m.
Koi:
Monday-Saturday   9:00 a.m. - 5:00 p.m.
Sunday   11:00 a.m. - 5:00 p.m.

PARKING
Free

ADMISSION
Free
Donations welcome

YEARLY MEMBERSHIP
Adult $25.00 Pacific Marine Mammal Center

RELATED PLACES
Sea Lions:
• Marine Mammal Care Center at Fort MacArthur - Site 85
• Sea World - Site 87
Koi:
• The Huntington - Site 39

CLOSE-BY PLACES
• Aliso & Wood Canyons Wilderness Park and
      Orange County Natural History Museum - Site 47
• Diver's Cove Tide Pools - Site 80
• Laguna Main Beach - Site 137

YOUR COMMENTS

SITE 87 - SEA WORLD

ADDRESS
1720 South Shores Road
Mission Bay, CA 92109
(800) 257-4258
www.seaworld.com/seaworld/ca/

DIRECTIONS [GUIDE PAGE 1268 (SD)]
Take Interstate Highway 5 to the Sea World Drive Exit and go west. Look for the tall blue needle tower.

GOOD THINGS TO SEE AND HEAR
Sea World is a huge amusement park with some exhibits that are walk-in/ observation and others that are shows. The shows involve sea animals, are fast paced, and keep the attention of most babies and toddlers. Try Shamu Adventure (once during the day and once during the night - they are very different and both great, although the night show is sometimes very loud), Manatee Rescue, Wild

Good Things to See and Hear (Continued)

Arctic, the Dolphin Show, the Sea Lions and Otter Show, Shark Encounter, and Penguin Encounter. Wild Arctic has polar bears, beluga whales and walruses-all up close and underwater through glass. There is a variety of animal encounters where children can feed or pet dolphins, bat rays, and sea stars. In addition, Shamu's Happy Harbor playground is HUGE (two acres) and worth a day in itself-if your child sees this playground, you will be stuck there for a long time. There is a giant sand play area, a toddler bouncing mat, a ball pit, and a tube slide.

Sit up close (but not too close for the whale show or you may get wet) and near an easy exit for the shows just in case. For Shamu's Happy Harbor, bring a bathing suit, a swim diaper, and a towel. There are usually fireworks at night. Be prepared to stay warm in case you stay.

Hours

Summer (Hours Vary Greatly):
Daily   9:00 a.m. - 10:00 p.m.
Winter (Hours Vary Greatly):
Daily   10:00 a.m. - 5:00 p.m.

Parking

$8.00
$14.00 for preferred pass

Admission

Adult $50.95
Child (Ages 3-9) $40.95
Under 3   Free
Including San Diego Zoo and Wild Animal Park:
Adult $98.75
Child (Ages 3-11) $74.95
Under 3   Free
• Check on two day passes or annual passes for the price of one or two day passes.

Yearly Membership

Check website for latest package deals.

Related Places

• Birch Aquarium at Scripps - Site 88
• Cabrillo Marine Aquarium - Site 72
• Pacific Marine Mammal Center and Laguna Koi Ponds- Site 86
• Long Beach Aquarium of the Pacific - Site 71
• Marine Mammal Care Center at Fort MacArthur - Site 85

CLOSE-BY PLACES
- Balboa Park Merry-Go-Round and Butterfly Rides - Site 121
- Bates Nut Farm - Site 101
- Belmont Park Carousel - Site 119
- The Children's Museum of San Diego/Museo de los Niños - Site 12
- San Diego Convention Center - Site 214
- San Diego Train Station - Site 185
- San Diego Model Railroad Museum - Site 202
- San Diego Zoo - Site 68
- Seaport Village Carousel - Site 120

YOUR COMMENTS

SITE 88 - BIRCH AQUARIUM AT SCRIPPS

ADDRESS
2300 Expedition Way
La Jolla, CA 92037
(858) 534-3574
www.aquarium.ucsd.edu

DIRECTIONS [GUIDE PAGE 1227 (SD)]
Take Interstate Highway 5 to the La Jolla Village Drive Exit and go west. Make a left on Expedition Way and go to the end.

GOOD THINGS TO SEE AND HEAR
The Birch Aquarium is part of the Scripps Institute of Oceanography and the University of California San Diego, and is one of the largest oceanographic museums in the country. In spite of this, it feels like a small aquarium providing more time to stare at strange creatures like fish with protrusible jaws, spine fish, and giant clams. The tanks are jammed with ocean life. See the giant octopus, jelly fish, sea horses, and a 55,000-gallon kelp forest with leopard sharks, garibaldi, and giant sea bass. Divers are often in the kelp forest tank; call aquarium for exact times. Visit the Tide Pool Discovery Station and the Shark Tank outside the museum.

Avoid weekday mornings when school children visit the aquarium.

HOURS
Daily   9:00 a.m. - 5:00 p.m.

PARKING
Free

ADMISSION
Adult	$10.00
Child (Ages 3-17)	$6.50
Under 3	Free

YEARLY MEMBERSHIP
Adult	$50.00
Adults (2 People)	$60.00
Family	$66.00

RELATED PLACES
• Cabrillo Marine Aquarium - Site 72
• Long Beach Aquarium of the Pacific - Site 71
• Roundhouse Marine Studies Lab and Aquarium - Site 73
• Santa Catalina Island - Site 126
• Santa Monica Pier Aquarium - Site 75
• Tide Pools - Sites 77-84

CLOSE-BY PLACES
• La Jolla Shores - Site 138
• La Jolla Shores Tide Pools - Site 81

YOUR COMMENTS

SITE 89 - TY WARNER SEA CENTER

ADDRESS
211 Stearns Wharf
Santa Barbara, CA 93101
(805) 962-2526
www.sbnature.org/seacenter/

DIRECTIONS [GUIDE PAGE 996 (SB)]
Take US Highway 101 to Garden Street Exit and exit towards downtown. Turn left onto Garden Street, right onto E Cabrillo Boulevard, and left onto Stearns Wharf.

GOOD THINGS TO SEE AND HEAR

The renovated Sea Center is located on Stearns Wharf and is designed to look and feel like a working marine laboratory. The museum focuses on hands-on exploration of marine life primarily from the Santa Barbara Channel and includes lots of touching of animals along with using laboratory equipment. Look for the Living Beach, a simulated tide pool, the 1,200 gallon Channel Catch Tank, and the Wet Deck where actual samples of the ocean can be captured.

The Sea Center is a facility of the Santa Barbara Museum of Natural History.

HOURS
Daily   10:00 a.m. - 5:00 p.m.

PARKING
On street

ADMISSION
Adult $7.00
Child (Ages 2-12) $4.00
Under 2   Free

YEARLY MEMBERSHIP
Adult $40.00
Family $60.00
Includes membership in the Santa Barbara Museum of Natural History

RELATED PLACES
• Birch Aquarium at Scripps - Site 88
• Cabrillo Marine Aquarium - Site 72
• Long Beach Aquarium of the Pacific - Site 71
• Roundhouse Marine Studies Lab and Aquarium - Site 73
• Santa Catalina Island - Site 126
• Santa Monica Pier Aquarium - Site 75
• Tide Pools - Sites 77-84

CLOSE-BY PLACES
• Chase Palm Park Carousel - Site 123
• Kid's World - Site 36
• Santa Barbara Airport - Site 160
• Santa Barbara County Fair and Exposition - Site 110
• Santa Barbara East Beach - Site 145
• Santa Barbara Museum of Natural History - Site 14
• Santa Barbara Train Station - Site 188
• Santa Barbara Zoological Gardens - Site 70

YOUR COMMENTS

_____

_____

_____

_____

_____

Hugging a Goat at a Petting Farm. Photo by author.

CHAPTER 6 - FARMS AND PONIES

There is not much that is more thrilling to a young child than petting a farm animal. Fortunately, Southern California has a great many petting zoos and county fairs (and now most zoos also have petting sections). Most also have pony rides.

BOOKS FOR YOUR CHILD
- Brown, Margaret Wise-*Big Red Barn*
- Flack, Marjorie-*Ask Mr. Bear*
- Hill, Eric-*Spot Goes to the Farm*
- Hobbie, Holly-*Toot and Puddle*
- Kunhardt, Dorothy-*Pat the Bunny*
- McPhail, David-*The Three Pigs*
- Provensen, Alice and Martin-*Our Animal Friends*

SITE 90 - GREEN MEADOWS FARM/LOS ANGELES COUNTY

ADDRESS
Hansen Dam Equestrian Center
11127 Orcas Avenue
Lakeview Terrace, CA 91342
(800) 493-3276
www.greenmeadowsproductions.com/

DIRECTIONS [GUIDE PAGE 503 (LA)]
From the westbound Interstate Highway 210 exit at Wheatland Street. Go north to Foothill Boulevard and turn left. Turn left on Orcas Avenue.

From the eastbound Interstate Highway 210 exit at Osbourne Street. Go north and veer right onto Foothill Boulevard. Turn right on Orcas Avenue.

SITE 91 - GREEN MEADOWS FARM/ORANGE COUNTY

ADDRESS
Irvine Regional Park
1 Irvine Park Road
Orange, CA 92862
(800) 493-3276
www.greenmeadowsproductions.com

DIRECTIONS [GUIDE PAGE 800/801 (OC)]
Take Interstate Highway 5 to the Jamboree Road Exit and go north. Jamboree Road ends at Irvine Regional Park.

GOOD THINGS TO SEE AND HEAR
Green Meadows sets up a farm in two different parks twice a year - spring and fall (the Orange County farm is usually earlier than the Los Angeles farm). The farm includes about thirty colorful pens full of farm animals from around the world. Children can touch - and often hold - all of the animals including pigs, cows, sheep, goats, camels, ducks, geese, ostriches, llamas, chickens, chicks, ducklings, and water buffalo. Help milk a cow, feed the sheep and goats, and catch a chicken.

A "farmer" guides you around for about two hours at an easy pace that is age appropriate. Two-year-olds (and older) can ride a pony. Avoid weekday morning when all the school children are there on field trips. Bring antibacterial lotion for babies who like to put their hands in their mouths.

HOURS
Spring and Fall (Call ahead for dates in each location):
Monday-Friday   9:30 a.m. - 12:30 p.m.
Some Saturdays   10:00 a.m. - 2:00 p.m.

PARKING
Free

ADMISSION
Adult or Child $10.00
Under 2   Free
• Group rates available

RELATED PLACES
• Centennial Farm - Site 105
• The Farm - Site 96
• Lakewood Pony Rides and Petting Farm - Site 104
• Montebello Barnyard Zoo - Site 103
• Underwood Family Farms - Site 99
• Zoomars Petting Farm - Site 98

CLOSE-BY PLACES
ORANGE COUNTY:
• Irvine Park Railroad - Site 200
• Irvine Regional Park and Nature Center - Site 49
• Irvine Regional Park Pony Rides - Site 102
• Orange County Zoo - Site 65

LOS ANGELES:
• Children's Museum of Los Angeles - Site 11
• San Fernando Valley Fair - Site 108
• Whiteman Airport - Site 164

YOUR COMMENTS

FARM ANIMALS

SHEEP

COW

PONY

PIG

CHICKEN

SITE 92 - SANTA ANITA RACE TRACK MORNING WORKOUT

ADDRESS
Santa Anita Park
285 West Huntington Drive
Arcadia, CA 91007
(626) 574-7223
www.santaanita.com

DIRECTIONS [GUIDE PAGE 567 (LA)]
Take Interstate Highway 210 to the Baldwin Exit and go south. Enter at Gate 8 and follow road to parking area near the west end of main building. Follow the signs to Clocker's Corner.

GOOD THINGS TO SEE AND HEAR
Watch jockeys dressed in colorful gear riding racehorses for their morning workout at "Clocker's Corner." Only a few people are there to watch (compared to the thousands during a racing event) so you can park nearby and watch from so close that you might get splattered with mud! There is plenty of open space in front of the grandstands for moving around. A food stand offers donuts, cereal, and orange juice (and coffee) - you can sit at a table and watch the horses or take your donut up by the fence surrounding the track.

Clocker's Corner morning workouts are year-round except for a short time every two years when the track undergoes maintenance. Racing at Santa Anita is for a short time in the late fall and then again after Christmas.

HOURS
Daily   5:00 a.m. - 10:00 a.m.

PARKING
Free

ADMISSION
Free

RELATED PLACES
• The Fair-Chapter 6
• Griffith Park Pony Rides - Site 95
• Huntington Central Park Equestrian Center - Site 94
• Irvine Regional Park Pony Rides - Site 102
• Lakewood Pony Rides and Petting Farm - Site 104

CLOSE-BY PLACES
• Los Angeles County Arboretum and Botanic Gardens - Site 37
• Pasadena Cruisin Weekly Car Show - Site 35
• Water Play Area - Santa Fe Dam Recreation Area - Site 124
• Wilderness Park and Nature Center - Site 52

SPECIAL EVENTS

Fall Racing   Late September to Early November
Winter Racing   December 26 to Mid-April

YOUR COMMENTS

_____

_____

_____

_____

_____

SITE 93 - OAK GLEN APPLE FARMS

ADDRESS

Oak Glen Road
Oak Glen, CA 92399
(909) 797-6833
www.oakglen.net

DIRECTIONS [GUIDE PAGE 19/31/20C (SB/R)]

Take Interstate Highway 10 east to the Yucaipa Boulevard Exit and go north/northeast. Follow the signs to Oak Glen (left on Bryant Street and right on Oak Glen Road).

GOOD THINGS TO SEE AND HEAR

The Oak Glen Apple Farms are a bit of a drive but you can pick your own apples at any one of a dozen different little farms, so it is worth the trip. If you go early in the season, there are many apples on the low branches so small children can reach them. Or you can use a backpack so your child can reach the higher ones! You pay for what you pick, but the apples are fresh and last a long time, so be generous with your children's wishes to pick one more. You can also pick a pumpkin at many of the farms before Halloween.

The best season is late September through October. Avoid weekends if you can. Oak Tree Village has a collection of shops and restaurants, but is often too busy to be fun for kids. But if it is not, there is a small animal park. Go past the busy farms to the quieter ones, like Riley's, at the end of the string of farms.

HOURS

For Apple Picking September-October:
Monday-Sunday   9:00 a.m. - 5:00 p.m.

PARKING

Free

ADMISSION

Free

Related Places
- Armours Orchard- Site 97
- California Strawberry Festival - Site 55
- Tanaka Farms - Site 100
- Underwood Family Farms - Site 99

Your Comments

_____
_____
_____
_____
_____

Site 94 - Huntington Central Park Equestrian Center

Address
Huntington Central Park
18381 Goldenwest Street
Huntington Beach, CA 92648
(714) 848-6565
www.stockteam.com/horses.html

Directions [Guide Page 857 (OC)]
Take the Interstate Highway 405 to the Brookhurst Street Exit and go south. Make a right on Talbert Avenue and go past the library. Make a left on Goldenwest Street, and the stable is on your right.

Good Things to See and Hear
The Equestrian Center is a riding stable that boards horses and offers a variety of riding rings for its boarders. Although there are no pony rides, this is a very horsy place to walk around. Find a place along the fence and watch the western and English riders. On weekends there are often polo games.

As with all animals, horses can bite. Also be sure to wash hands after being around the barns.

Hours
Daily   No specific times

Parking
Free

Admission
Free

RELATED PLACES
- The Fair-Chapter 6
- The Farm - Site 96
- Griffith Park Pony Rides - Site 95
- Irvine Regional Park Pony Rides - Site 102
- Lakewood Pony Rides and Petting Farm - Site 104
- Santa Anita Race Track Morning Workout - Site 92

CLOSE-BY PLACES
- Bolsa Chica Ecological Reserve - Site 132
- Huntington Beach School Bus Yard - Site 23
- Huntington State Beach and Huntington City Beach - Site 136
- Kite Flying at the Beach - Site 167
- Shipley Nature Center at Huntington Central Park - Site 48

YOUR COMMENTS

SITE 95 - GRIFFITH PARK PONY RIDES

ADDRESS
Griffith Park
Crystal Springs Drive
Los Angeles, CA 90027
(323) 664-3266
www.lacity.org/RAP/dos/parks/griffithPK/attractions.htm

DIRECTIONS [GUIDE PAGE 564 (LA)]
• Take State Highway 134 west to the Zoo Drive Exit. Make a left on Crystal Springs Drive. The ponies are on your left next to the train.
• Take State Highway 134 east to the Victory Boulevard Exit. Turn right at the top of the offramp. Make a left on Zoo Drive. Follow the road onto Crystal Springs Drive. The ponies are on the left next to the train.

GOOD THINGS TO SEE AND HEAR
The Griffith Park Pony Rides offer both slow and fast moving horses. The slow ponies walk in a circle for babies and toddlers. The faster ponies and horses ride around a ring - sometime at a very fast pace - for older toddlers.

Children must be ten months to ride the ponies. Saddles have straps to hold children in place. Parents can walk with the children on the slow pony ride, but not on the fast pony ride.

HOURS
Tuesday-Sunday   10:00 a.m. - 3:00 p.m.

PARKING
Free

ADMISSION
Child (All Ages) $2.00

RELATED PLACES
• The Fair-Chapter 6
• The Farm - Site 96
• Irvine Regional Park Pony Rides - Site 102
• Lakewood Pony Rides and Petting Farm - Site 104
• Underwood Family Farms - Site 99
• Zoomars Petting Farm - Site 98

CLOSE-BY PLACES
• Glendale Train Station - Site 178
• Griffith Observatory - Site 9
• Griffith Park Merry-Go-Round - Site 115
• Griffith Park Train Ride - Site 198
• Los Angeles Zoo - Site 63
• Museum of the American West - Site 3
• Travel Town Museum - Site 170

YOUR COMMENTS

_____
_____
_____
_____
_____

SITE 96 - THE FARM

ADDRESS
8101 Tampa Avenue
Reseda, CA 91335
(818) 341-6805

DIRECTIONS [GUIDE PAGE 530 (LA)]
Take U.S. Highway 101 to the Tampa Avenue Exit and go north. The farm is on your left.

GOOD THINGS TO SEE AND HEAR
The Farm is a very earthy petting farm. Pony rides dominate the center of the farm. On the weekends, young teenagers lead the ponies. Animals are all around - some in their pens, some in the parking lot! There are donkeys, chickens, pigs, ducks, ponies, sheep, goats, a llama, and an emu to pet. Also, there are tractors to climb on. Children can buy food for the animals.

HOURS

Monday-Friday	call for days and hours
Saturday-Sunday	10:00 a.m. - 6:00 p.m.

PARKING

Free

ADMISSION

Adult or Child	$2.00
Pony Rides	$3.00

RELATED PLACES

- Centennial Farm - Site 105
- The Fair-Chapter 6
- Green Meadows Farm - Sites 90-91
- Griffith Park Pony Rides - Site 95
- Irvine Regional Park Pony Rides - Site 102
- Lakewood Pony Rides and Petting Farm - Site 104
- Montebello Barnyard Zoo - Site 103
- Underwood Family Farms - Site 99
- Zoomars Petting Farm - Site 98

CLOSE-BY PLACES

- California State University Northridge, CSUN - Site 62

YOUR COMMENTS

SITE 97 - ARMOURS ORCHARD

ADDRESS

7515 E. Avenue U
Littlerock, CA 91356
(661) 944-3255

DIRECTIONS [GUIDE PAGE 4287 (LA)]

Take Highway 14 to the Pearblossom exit and go east approximately six miles. Turn right onto Highway 138, and continue to 75th Street. Turn left onto 75th Street, and look for a hand made "U Pick Peaches" sign. Go approximately one-fourth of a mile and turn right at Avenue U (this may not be marked, but you can only go right at that point). The farm is a modest house on your immediate left.

GOOD THINGS TO SEE AND HEAR
Pick your own apples, apricots, cherries, peaches and plums depending on the season. The length of the picking season is a function of the weather and the number of people who come to pick. Mid-July is a good time. Big white buckets are provided.

Bring a backpack to help your child reach the fruit.

HOURS
Daily   7:00 a.m. - 12:00 p.m.

PARKING
Free along the street

ADMISSION
One pound   about $1.00 (about four peaches)

RELATED PLACES
• Bates Nut Farm - Site 101
• California Strawberry Festival - Site 55
• Oak Glen Apple Farms - Site 93
• Tanaka Farms - Site 100
• Underwood Family Farm - Site 99

CLOSE-BY PLACES
• Big Rigs at Castaic - Site 34

YOUR COMMENTS

SITE 98 - ZOOMARS PETTING FARM

ADDRESS
Los Rios Historic Section
31791 Los Rios Street
San Juan Capistrano, CA 92675
(949) 831-6550
www.daytrippen.com/zoomerspettingzoo.html

DIRECTIONS [GUIDE PAGE 972 (OC)]
• Take Interstate Highway 5 to the Ortega Highway (State Highway 74) Exit and go west. Make a left at Camino Capistrano and then a right on Verdugo. Park in the garage. The farm is behind the Amtrak Station across the tracks and down a small street to the left.
• Or take Amtrak - Site 193 or Metrolink - Site 194.

GOOD THINGS TO SEE AND HEAR

The Zoomars Petting Farm (formerly the Jones Family Mini-Farm) is a small petting farm in the old part of San Juan Capistrano near the mission. There are goats, sheep, rabbits, pot bellied pigs, horses, and donkeys. Food may be purchased for the animals. There are also pony rides and a very small train ride.

Be sure to wash hands.

HOURS
Daily   10:00 a.m. - 5:00 p.m.

PARKING
Free

ADMISSION
Petting Zoo
Adult	$3.00
Child	$2.00
Under 1	Free

Train
Adult	$3.00
Child	$2.00

RELATED PLACES
- Centennial Farm - Site 105
- The Fair-Chapter 6
- The Farm - Site 96
- Green Meadows Farm - Sites 90-91
- Griffith Park Pony Rides - Site 95
- Irvine Regional Park Pony Rides - Site 102
- Lakewood Pony Rides and Petting Farm - Site 104
- Montebello Barnyard Zoo - Site 103
- Underwood Family Farms - Site 99

CLOSE-BY PLACES
- Catalina Terminal/Dana Point - Site 130
- Dana Point Tide Pools - Site 78
- San Clemente Beach - Site 144
- San Clemente Train Station - Site 184
- San Juan Capistrano Train Station - Site 186

YOUR COMMENTS

SITE 99 - UNDERWOOD FAMILY FARMS

ADDRESS
3370 Sunset Valley Road
Moorpark, CA 93021
(805) 529-3690
www.underwoodfarmmarket.com/

DIRECTIONS [GUIDE PAGE Vi (LA) OR 496 (SB/V)]
Take U.S. Highway 101 to the State Highway 23 Exit and go north. Turn left on Tierra Rejada Road and then a left on Sunset Valley Road (formerly Moorpark Rd).

GOOD THINGS TO SEE AND HEAR
The Underwood Family Farm is a working farm that invites you to come and pick your own fruits and vegetables. Depending on the season, there is a variety of crops available including corn, strawberries, beans, squash, potatoes, tomatoes, and herbs. There are also signs on each row that identify the vegetables or fruit. Smell the different vegetables just after picking and talk about their shape and color. Wagons are available to carry your vegetables and children.

There is also a Farm Animal Center with a petting corral full of goats, donkeys, cows, pigs, and chickens to meet, feed, pet, and smell; a tricycle maze made of bales of straw; and a "Giant Goat Walk" that you have to see to believe. Notice the signs on each pen-there is one for adults and one especially for children. Look for feathers to collect. There are also hay rides and pony rides.

Summer weekdays and winter weekdays after 3:00 p.m. when the school children have left are the most peaceful times to visit. Picnic tables are available in an enclosed area with a sand box and a wooden bus, so bring your lunch and a knife to cut up the vegetables you picked. Shoes are a good idea for walking through the crops, but socks seem to collect stickers. The fields can be hot so bring plenty of water.

HOURS
Daily   9:00 a.m. - 6:00 p.m.
• Closed in December and January

PARKING
Free

ADMISSION
Adult or Child $3.00
Under 2   Free
Pony Rides $4.00
Vegetables and Fruits for Animals:
Carrots $1.00 Per Bag
Pellets $.25 (Bring a lot of quarters)

RELATED PLACES
- Centennial Farm - Site 105
- The Fair-Chapter 6
- The Farm - Site 96
- Green Meadows Farm - Sites 90-91
- Lakewood Pony Rides and Petting Farm - Site 104
- Local Farmer's Markets-Chapter 2
- Montebello Barnyard Zoo - Site 103
- The Original Los Angeles Farmer's Market - Site 32
- Zoomars Petting Farm - Site 98

CLOSE-BY PLACES
- America's Teaching Zoo at Moorpark College - Site 66
- Moorpark Train Station - Site 181
- Fillmore and Western Railway - Site 203

SPECIAL EVENTS
- Fall Harvest Festival in October

YOUR COMMENTS

SITE 100 - TANAKA FARMS

ADDRESS
5380 3/4 University Drive
Irvine, CA 92612
(949) 653-2100
(949) 653-9050
www.tanakafarms.com

DIRECTIONS [GUIDE PAGE 890 (OC)]
Take Interstate Highway 405 to the University Drive Exit and go south to Strawberry Farms Road. The farm is on the corner.

GOOD THINGS TO SEE AND HEAR
Tanaka Farms offers strawberries, pumpkins and other vegetables and fruits to pick. In the spring, come for the strawberries, and in the fall for the pumpkins. There is a corn maze in the fall, a petting zoo, farm exhibits and wagon rides around the farm.
Bring a backpack to help your child reach the fruit.

HOURS
Mid-March through October 31st and Thanksgiving weekend for Christmas trees:
Monday-Friday   9:00 a.m. - 5:30 p.m.
Saturday-Sunday   9:00 a.m. - 5:00 p.m.

Crop Calendar

This is a monthly listing of what crops you can find to pick each month.

January	leeks, salad vegetables
February	leeks, salad vegetables
March	cauliflower, artichokes, celery, strawberries, leeks, salad vegetables
April	cauliflower, artichokes, celery, strawberries, sweet onions, leeks, salad vegetables
May	cauliflower, artichokes, celery, strawberries, sweet onions, blackberries, sweet peas, squash, Valencia oranges, green beans, leeks, salad vegetables
June	cauliflower, artichokes, celery, strawberries, blackberries, sweet peas, squash, Valencia oranges, green beans, apricots, leeks, salad vegetables, raspberries, cucumbers
July	strawberries, squash, Valencia oranges, green beans, leeks, salad vegetables, tomatoes, black-eyed peas, Lima beans, raspberries, cucumbers
August	squash, Valencia oranges, green beans, leeks, salad vegetables, Peppers, tomatoes, black-eyed peas, Lima beans, raspberries, cucumbers
September	squash, Valencia oranges, green beans, leeks, salad vegetables, Peppers, tomatoes, black-eyed peas, Lima beans, raspberries, cucumbers
October	Valencia oranges, green beans, leeks, salad vegetables, pumpkins & gourds, Peppers, tomatoes, black-eyed peas, raspberries, cucumbers
November	green beans, leeks, salad vegetables, pumpkins & gourds, raspberries
December	leeks, salad vegetables

PARKING
Free

ADMISSION
Adult $10.00

RELATED PLACES
• Armours orchard - Site 97
• Bates Nut Farm - Site 101
• California Strawberry Festival - Site 55
• Green Meadows Farm - Site 90-91
• Oak Glen Apple Farms - Site 93
• Underwood Family Farms - Site 99

CLOSE-BY PLACES
- Irvine Park Railroad - Site 200
- Irvine Regional Park and Nature Center - Site 49
- Irvine Regional Park Pony Rides - Site 102
- University of California Irvine - Site 59

YOUR COMMENTS

_____

_____

_____

_____

_____

SITE 101 - BATES NUT FARM

ADDRESS
15954 Woods Valley Road
Valley Center, CA 92082
(760) 749-3333
www.batesnutfarm.biz

DIRECTIONS [GUIDE PAGE 1091 (SD)]
Take Interstate Highway 15 to Highway 78 east. Highway 78 ends at Broadway. Turn right on Broadway and continue to Washington. Turn left on Washington and travel three miles to Calley Parkway. Turn left on Valley Parkway, and continue six miles to Woods Valley Road. Turn right onto Woods Valley Road.

GOOD THINGS TO SEE AND HEAR
Bates Nut Farm is a dry goods store that sells all kinds of nuts surrounded by a 100 acre farm setting that includes a small zoo, a straw maze and a seasonal pumpkin patch.
Bring a backpack to help your child reach the fruit.

HOURS
Daily   9:00 a.m. - 5:00 p.m.

PARKING
Free

ADMISSION
Free
Some seasonal events require reservations and fees. Check the calendar of events on the web page.

RELATED PLACES
- Armours Orchard - Site 97
- California Strawberry Festival - Site 55
- Oak Glen Apple Farms - Site 93
- Tanaka Farms - Site 100
- Underwood Family Farms - Site 99

CLOSE-BY PLACES
- Balboa Park Merry-Go-Round and Butterfly Rides - Site 121
- Belmont Park Carousel - Site 119
- The Children's Museum of San Diego/Museo de los Niños - Site 12
- San Diego Convention Center - Site 214
- San Diego Train Station - Site 185
- San Diego Model Railroad Museum - Site 202
- San Diego Zoo - Site 68
- Sea World - Site 87
- Seaport Village Carousel - Site 120

YOUR COMMENTS

_____

_____

_____

_____

SITE 102 - IRVINE REGIONAL PARK PONY RIDES

ADDRESS
1 Irvine Park Road
Orange, CA 92862
(714) 973-6835 Park
(760) 956-8441 Pony Rides
www.ocparks.com/irvinepark

DIRECTIONS [GUIDE PAGE 800/801/830 (OC)]
Take Interstate Highway 5 to the Jamboree Road Exit and go north. Jamboree Road ends at Irvine Regional Park.

GOOD THINGS TO SEE AND HEAR
Irvine Regional Park is a large park that includes the Orange County Zoo - Site 65, a Nature Center - Site 49, and a Train Ride - Site 200. One of the park's many attractions is a pony ride.

Combine your pony ride with the zoo or a train ride and a picnic. You can also rent a surrey and drive around the park.

HOURS
Park:
Summer:
Daily   7:00 a.m. - 9:00 p.m.
Winter:
Daily   7:00 a.m. - 6:00 p.m.
Pony Rides:
Summer:
Tuesday-Sunday   11:00 a.m. - 4:00 p.m.
Winter:
Saturday-Sunday   11:00 a.m. - 4:00 p.m.

PARKING
Park Entrance:

Weekdays	$3.00
Weekends	$5.00

ADMISSION

All	$3.00

RELATED PLACES
• The Fair-Chapter 6
• The Farm - Site 96
• Griffith Park Pony Rides - Site 95
• Lakewood Pony Rides and Petting Farm - Site 104
• Underwood Family Farms - Site 99
• Zoomars Petting Farm - Site 98

CLOSE-BY PLACES
• Green Meadows Farm/Orange County - Site 91
• Irvine Park Railroad - Site 200
• Irvine Regional Park and Nature Center - Site 49
• Orange County Zoo - Site 65

YOUR COMMENTS

SITE 103 - MONTEBELLO BARNYARD ZOO

ADDRESS
Grant Rea Park
600 Rea Drive
Montebello, CA 90640
(323) 887-4595
www.laavenue.com/barnyard.htm

DIRECTIONS [GUIDE PAGE 676 (LA)]
Take Interstate Highway 605 to the Rose Hills Road/Beverly Boulevard Exit. Follow San Gabriel River Parkway to Beverly Boulevard and make a right on Beverly Boulevard. From there, make a right on Rea Drive. The farm is on the right in Grant Rea Park.

GOOD THINGS TO SEE AND HEAR
The Montebello Barnyard Zoo is easily sighted from Rea Road because of its red barns. The petting zoo includes llamas, emus, cows, sheep, goats, and horses. There is also a duck pond, an aviary with peacocks and doves, and an adorable merry-go-round with little white ponies. The sounds and smells are definitely those of a barnyard. Be sure to wash your hands after petting the animals.

HOURS

Tuesday-Friday	10:00 a.m. - 4:00 p.m.
Saturday-Sunday	10:00 a.m. - 6:00 p.m.

PARKING
Free

ADMISSION

Adult, Child	$2.00
Pony Rides	$2.00
Hay Ride	$2.00
Train	$2.00

RELATED PLACES
- Centennial Farm - Site 105
- The Fair-Chapter 6
- The Farm - Site 96
- Green Meadows Farm - Sites 90-91
- Lakewood Pony Rides and Petting Farm - Site 104
- Underwood Family Farms - Site 99
- Zoomars Petting Farm - Site 98

CLOSE-BY PLACES
- El Monte Airport - Site 153
- Freight Trains - Site 196
- Whittier Narrows Nature Center - Site 46

YOUR COMMENTS

_____

_____

_____

_____

_____

SITE 104 - LAKEWOOD PONY RIDES AND PETTING FARM

ADDRESS
11369 Carson Street
Lakewood, CA 90715
(562) 653-9626

DIRECTIONS [GUIDE PAGE 766 (LA)]
Take Interstate Highway 605 to the Carson Street Exit and go west. Drive for one-fourth of a mile and the entrance is on your right.

GOOD THINGS TO SEE AND HEAR

Three kinds of pony rides are available at Lakewood, including a slow walking ride in a circle, a walking ride that parents lead, and a trotting ride for older toddlers. The petting farm has many enthusiastic goats and sheep along with bunnies, a llama, chickens, and ducks. The setting is farm-like and easy going. Treats for the farm animals can be purchased.

Be sure to feed the goats and sheep from outside the petting farm pen.

HOURS

Wednesday-Sunday 10:00 a.m. - 5:00 p.m.

PARKING

Free

ADMISSION

Petting Farm	$0.50
Pony Rides	$3.00
Cup of Food	$0.50

RELATED PLACES

The Fair - Chapter 6
The Farm - Site 96
Green Meadows Farm - Sites 90-91
Griffith Park Pony Rides - Site 95
Irvine Regional Park Pony Rides - Site 102
Montebello Barnyard Zoo - Site 103
Underwood Family Farms - Site 99
Zoomars Petting Farm - Site 98

CLOSE-BY PLACES

California State University Long Beach, CSULB - Site 61
Cerritos Library - Site 17
El Dorado East Regional Park and Nature Center - Site 50
El Dorado East Regional Park Train Ride - Site 199
Long Beach Airport - Site 157
Norwalk School Bus Yard - Site 26

YOUR COMMENTS

_____
_____
_____
_____
_____

Site 105 - Centennial Farm

Address
Orange County Fairgrounds
88 Fair Drive
Costa Mesa, CA 92626
(714) 708-1618
www.ocfair.com/ocfec/centennialfarm

Directions [Guide Page 859 (OC)]
Take Interstate Highway 405 to State Highway 55 south. Exit Victoria and then proceed to make a right onto Fairview Drive. Make a right on Fair Drive and go though Gate #1 (big main gate). Look for the Millennium Barn.

Good Things to See and Hear
As you approach the Orange County Fairgrounds-home to the Centennial Farm, you will first see the Millennium Barn - a real barn where animals live. Centennial Farm is a working farm with rabbits, pigs, ducks, horses, chickens, and a buffalo. There is a garden that produces food for the animals. In the spring, there are many baby animals. Check the bee observatory in the Bug Barn.

The farm is closed in June and open as part of the fair in July. You may not feed the animals here. Be sure to call ahead as sometimes the farm is closed for other big events at the fairgrounds.

Hours
August-May:
Monday-Friday   1:00 p.m. - 4:00 p.m.
Saturday-Sunday   9:00 a.m. - 4:00 p.m.

Parking
Weekends $3.00
On weekends, park across the street from Gate 1 at Vanguard University for free.

Admission
Free

Related Places
The Fair - Chapter 6
Green Meadows Farm - Sites 90-91
Underwood Family Farms - Site 99

Close-by Places
Balboa Pavilion Carousel - Site 118
Catalina Terminal/Newport Beach - Site 131
Corona Del Mar State Beach - Site 134
John Wayne Airport - Site 156
Little Corona Del Mar Beach - Site 140
Little Corona Del Mar Tide Pools - Site 76
Newport Beach - Site 142
Orange County Fair - Site 107
University of California Irvine, UCI - Site 59

YOUR COMMENTS

_____

_____

_____

_____

SITE 106 - LOS ANGELES COUNTY FAIR

ADDRESS
1101 McKinley Avenue
Pomona, CA 91768
(909) 623-3111
www.Fairplex.com/

DIRECTIONS [GUIDE PAGE 600 (LA)]
• Take Interstate Highway 210 to State Highway 57 south to the Arrow Highway Exit. Go east. Make a right on White Avenue. To get to the closest parking, make a right on McKinley Avenue (Sheraton Suites Hotel).
• Or take the Metrolink train - Site 194.

GOOD THINGS TO SEE AND HEAR
Over three thousand two hundred fairs are held in North America each year; this one is the largest. This is a great place to see and pet all varieties of cows, pigs, sheep, goats, miniature horses, and chickens. Pony rides and petting zoos are near the animal barns. Watch how animals are groomed for shows.

The fair can be hot and crowded, so park close and go early. Focus on the animals and don't stay too long. Ask owners before petting the animals as many can bite. This can be a great day for a baby or toddler. Avoid the rides if you can - there will be plenty of time for that later in life.

HOURS
Mid-September Only:
Wednesday-Sunday 10:00 a.m. or 11:00 a.m. - 10:00 p.m. or 11:00 p.m.
(depending on day of week)

PARKING
$5.00
$7.00-$10.00   Preferred

ADMISSION
Adult $10.00 ($15.00 on Weekends)
Child (Ages 6-12) $6.00 ($8.00 Weekends)
Under 6   Free

RELATED PLACES
- Centennial Farm - Site 105
- The Fair-Chapter 6
- The Farm - Site 96
- Green Meadows Farm - Sites 90-91
- Lakewood Pony Rides and Petting Farm - Site 104
- Montebello Barnyard Zoo - Site 103
- Underwood Family Farms - Site 99
- Zoomars Petting Farm - Site 98

CLOSE-BY PLACES
- Brackett Air Field - Site 149
- Mrs. Nelson's Toy and Book Shop - Site 18
- Puddingstone Reservoir Beach - Site 125
- San Dimas Canyon Park and Nature Center - Site 45

YOUR COMMENTS

_____

_____

_____

_____

OTHER FAIRS IN SOUTHERN CALIFORNIA

SITE 107 - ORANGE COUNTY FAIR

Orange County Fair and Exposition Center
88 Fair Drive
Costa Mesa, CA 92626
(714) 708-3247
www.ocfair.com
[GUIDE PAGE 859/889 (OC)]
• Take Interstate Highway 405 to State Highway 55 south. Exit Victoria and make a right onto Fairview Drive. From there, make a right on Fair Drive and go though Gate #1 (big main gate) and look for the Millennium Barn.
• Usually held in July.

OTHER FAIRS IN SOUTHERN CALIFORNIA

SITE 108 - SAN FERNANDO VALLEY FAIR

Hansen Dam Park
Hansen Dam Sports Center
Lake View Terrace, CA 91342
(818) 557-1600
www.sfvalleyfair.org
[GUIDE PAGE 502 (LA)]
• Take Interstate Highway 210 to the Osborne Exit. Follow the signs to the Hansen Dam Park.
• Usually held in June.

SITE 109 - DEL MAR FAIR

Del Mar Fairgrounds
2260 Jimmy Durante Boulevard
Del Mar, CA 92014
(858) 755-1161
www.sdfair.com/
[GUIDE PAGE 1187 (SD)]
• Take Interstate Highway 5 to the Via de la Valle Exit and go west to Jimmy Durante Boulevard. Make a left on Jimmy Durante Boulevard.
• Usually held June to July.

SITE 110 - SANTA BARBARA COUNTY FAIR AND EXPOSITION

Earl Warren Showgrounds
3400 Calle Real (U.S. Highway 101 at Las Positas Road)
Santa Barbara, CA 93105
(805) 687-0766
www.earlwarren.com
[GUIDE PAGE 995 (SB)]
• Take U.S. Highway 101 to the Las Positas Road Exit and go north.
• Usually held in April.

OTHER FAIRS IN SOUTHERN CALIFORNIA

SITE 111 - VENTURA COUNTY FAIR

Seaside Park and Ventura County Fairgrounds
10 West Harbor Boulevard
Ventura, CA 93001
(805) 648-3376
www.seasidepark.org
[GUIDE PAGE 491 (SB)]
• Take U.S. Highway 101 to the California Street Exit. Go left back over freeway and then make a right on Harbor Boulevard.
• Or take Amtrak (Site 193) or Metrolink - see "Real Train Rides Around Los Angeles in Chapter 10
• Usually held from July to August.

YOUR COMMENTS

The Miniature Ferris Wheel at Adventure City.

Photo by author; permission to use photo courtesy of Allan Ansdell of Adventure City.

CHAPTER 7 - AMUSEMENT

Southern California is the home to some of the most famous amusement parks in the world. Some are best suited for older children, however, many are great for babies and toddlers. Beyond the fancy amusement parks, there are other simpler kinds of amusement like merry-go-rounds and school carnivals.

SITE 112 - DISNEYLAND

ADDRESS
1313 South Harbor Boulevard
Anaheim, CA 90620
(714) 781-4565
www.disneyland.disney.go.com

DIRECTIONS [GUIDE PAGE 768/798 (OC)]
• Take Interstate Highway 5 south to the Ball Road/Disneyland Drive Exit. Go left from the offramp and this road leads directly to the Mickey and Friends Parking structure for the theme park.
• Take Interstate Highway 5 north to the Katella Avenue Exit and turn left (west). Follow the theme park signs to the parking structure.

GOOD THINGS TO SEE AND HEAR
Disneyland was made for kids of all ages, including babies and toddlers. If you love Disneyland, take your baby or toddler. Try Its a Small World, Disneyland Railroad, King Arthur Carrousel, Peter Pan's Flight, Storybook Canal Boats, Enchanted Tiki Room, and the Casey Junior Circus Train. In addition, this is a great place for babies and toddlers to watch people, balloons, and parades.

Avoid Snow White - it is too scary. Focus on a few things and don't try to stay the whole day.

HOURS
Daily   10:00 a.m. - 8:00 p.m.
• Later and earlier hours from Friday to Sunday and daily in summer

PARKING
$9.00

ADMISSION
Adult	$56.00
Child (Ages 3-9)	$46.00
Under 3	Free

YEARLY MEMBERSHIP
Adult or Child $209.00

RELATED PLACES
• Adventure City - Site 113
• Legoland - Site 114
• Merry-Go-Rounds - Sites 115-123

CLOSE-BY PLACES
• Anaheim Convention Center - Site 210
• Anaheim Train Station - Site 172
• Arrowhead Pond of Anaheim - Site 211
• Discovery Science Center - Site 7
• Santa Ana Zoo - Site 64

YOUR COMMENTS

_____
_____
_____
_____
_____

SITE 113 - ADVENTURE CITY

ADDRESS
1238 Beach Boulevard
Stanton, CA 90680
(714) 236-9300
www.adventurecity.com

DIRECTIONS [GUIDE PAGE 767/797 (OC)]
Take Interstate Highway 5 north to the Beach Boulevard Exit and go south (from Interstate Highway 5 south, turn right onto Beach Boulevard). The park is on left, adjacent to Hobby City after you pass Knott's Berry Farm. It is between Ball Road and Cerritos Avenue.

GOOD THINGS TO SEE AND HEAR
Adventure City is a little theme park built just for little kids. Rides include a carousel, airplanes, a train, fire engines that kids crank by hand (best for three-year-olds), fire engines, police cars, and a precious Ferris wheel with moons for each chair. There is also a petting zoo with a tortoise that won't stay home. You can make your own ginger bread cookies, paint your own face (or let mom or dad do it), and play with a great collection of Thomas the Tank Engine trains.

All rides are for toddlers and young children. The roller coasters, the balloon ride, and the bus ride may be too fast for children ages three and under. The Children's Theater is geared for children older than three years, but may still be entertaining for the little ones.

HOURS
Summer:
Monday-Thursday	10:00 a.m. - 5:00 p.m.
Friday	10:00 a.m. - 7:00 p.m.
Saturday	11:00 a.m. - 9:00 p.m.
Sunday	11:00 a.m. - 8:00 p.m.

Winter:
Friday	10:00 a.m. - 5:00 p.m.
Saturday-Sunday	11:00 a.m. - 7:00 p.m.

PARKING
Free

ADMISSION
Adult or Child	$12.95
Under 1	Free

YEARLY MEMBERSHIP
Adult or Child	$39.95

203

RELATED PLACES
- Disneyland - Site 112
- Legoland - Site 114
- Merry-Go-Rounds - Sites 115-123
- School Carnivals-Chapter 7

CLOSE-BY PLACES
- Anaheim Convention Center - Site 210
- Anaheim Train Station - Site 172
- Arrowhead Pond of Anaheim - Site 211
- Discovery Science Center - Site 7
- Disneyland - Site 112
- Santa Ana Zoo - Site 64

YOUR COMMENTS

_____
_____
_____
_____
_____

SITE 114 - LEGOLAND

ADDRESS
1 Legoland Drive
Carlsbad, CA 92008
(760) 918-LEGO
www.lego.com/legoland/california

DIRECTIONS [GUIDE PAGE 1126 (SD)]
Take Interstate Highway 5 to the Cannon Road Exit and go east. Follow the signs to Legoland.

GOOD THINGS TO SEE AND HEAR
Thirty million Legos comprise the park. For toddlers and babies, try Fairy Tale Brook, Water Works. Duplo Playtown, Coast Cruise, Dino Island and Miniland (famous landmarks built entirely with Legos, including Washington D.C., New York, and a farm). In Imagination, there are several locations where you can build with Legos (Build and Test) - try the one with the giant giraffe over the door.

Most of the rides are for children ages three and older, however, the Water Works, Playtown, and Miniland provide plenty to entertain an "under three" for hours. Be aware that most of the rides that are excellent for children ages three and older (thirty-four inches is the key) allow only two people per ride, so make sure you have one adult per young child. The Junior Driving School is for children ages three to five.

HOURS

Summer:
Daily   10:00 a.m. - 8:00 p.m.
Winter:
Thursday-Tuesday   10:00 a.m. - 5:00 p.m.
• Hours vary depending on season and day of the week

PARKING

$4.00

ADMISSION

Adult $46.95
Child (Ages 3-12) $38.95
Under 3   Free

YEARLY MEMBERSHIP

Adult $119.00
Child (Ages 3-12) $99.00
Pass with Saturday to Sunday in July, August, and Holidays Blocked:
Adult: $89.00
Child $69.00

RELATED PLACES

• Adventure City - Site 113
• Disneyland - Site 112
• Merry-Go-Rounds - Sites 115-123

CLOSE-BY PLACES

• Children's Discovery Museum of North Country - Site 13
• McClellan-Palomar Airport - Site 158
• San Diego Wild Animal Park - Site 69

YOUR COMMENTS

SITE 115 - GRIFFITH PARK MERRY-GO-ROUND

ADDRESS
Griffith Park
Mineral Wells Trail
Los Angeles, CA 90027
(323) 665-3051
www.laparks.org/dos/concession/griffith.htm

DIRECTIONS [GUIDE PAGE 564 (LA)]
• Take State Highway 134 west to the Zoo Drive Exit. Make a left on Crystal Springs Drive. The merry-go-round is to the right.
• Take State Highway 134 east to the Victory Boulevard Exit. Turn right at the top of the offramp and then make a left on Zoo Drive. The merry-go-round is to the right.

GOOD THINGS TO SEE AND HEAR
The Griffith Park Merry-Go-Round is an 1800s Spillman Engineering Carousel. As with all merry-go-rounds, the animals are beautifully painted, the ride is fun and the music is delightful. Other merry-go-round makers in southern California include Charles I.D. Looff (Santa Monica Pier Carousel built in 1916), the Looff Company (Seaport Village Carousel built in 1895), and Herschell-Spillman (Balboa Park Merry-Go-Round built in 1910.)

HOURS
Summer:
Daily   11:00 a.m. - 5:00 p.m.
Winter:
Weekends and Holidays 11:00 a.m. - 5:00 p.m.

ADMISSION
$1.00

RELATED PLACES
• Other merry-go-rounds - Site 123
• Adventure City - Site 113
• Disneyland - Site 112

CLOSE-BY PLACES
• Griffith Observatory - Site 9
• Griffith Park Pony Rides - Site 95
• Griffith Park Train Ride - Site 198
• Los Angeles Zoo - Site 63
• Museum of the American West - Site 3
• Travel Town Museum - Site 170

YOUR COMMENTS

_____
_____
_____
_____
_____

SITE 116 - SANTA MONICA PIER CAROUSEL

ADDRESS
200 Santa Monica Pier
Santa Monica, CA 90401
(310) 394-8042
www.santamonicapier.org/

DIRECTIONS [GUIDE PAGE 671 (LA)]
Take Interstate Highway 10 to the 4th Street Exit and go northwest. Make a left on Colorado and park on the pier.

HOURS
Summer:
Sunday-Monday,
Wed.-Thurs.   11:00 a.m. - 7:00 p.m.
Friday, Sat.-Sun.   11:00 a.m. - 9:00 p.m.
Winter:
Saturday-Sunday   10:00 a.m. - 5:00 p.m.

PARKING
$7.00   on the pier

ADMISSION
Adult $1.00
Child $0.50

CLOSE-BY PLACES
• Santa Monica Municipal Airport - Site 161
• Santa Monica Puppetry Center - Site 207
• Santa Monica Pier Aquarium - Site 75

YOUR COMMENTS

_____
_____
_____
_____

SITE 117 - SHORELINE VILLAGE CAROUSEL

ADDRESS
401-435 Shoreline Village Drive
Long Beach, CA 90802
(562) 980-1415
www.shorelinevillage.com

DIRECTIONS [GUIDE PAGE 825 (LA)]
Take Interstate Highway 710 south into downtown Long Beach. Follow Shoreline Drive to Shoreline Village, or park at Aquarium of the Pacific and take the trolley bus.

HOURS
All Year:
Sunday-Thursday   10:00 a.m. - 11:00 p.m.
Friday-Saturday   10:00 a.m. - 12:00 a.m.

ADMISSION
$1.50

CLOSE-BY PLACES
• Long Beach Aquarium of the Pacific - Site 71
• Long Beach Convention Center - Site 212

YOUR COMMENTS
_____
_____
_____
_____

SITE 118 - BALBOA PAVILION CAROUSEL

ADDRESS
Fun Zone
600 East Bay Avenue
Balboa, CA 92661
(949) 673-0408
www.thebalboafunzone.com/

DIRECTIONS [GUIDE PAGE 919 (OC)]
Take Interstate Highway 405 to State Highway 55 south. State Highway 55 turns into Newport Boulevard. Make a left on Balboa Boulevard and go along Balboa Peninsula to the Balboa Pier. Park in the lot. Balboa Fun Zone is in between Palm Street and Washington Street on the Newport Bay side of the peninsula.

HOURS
All Year:
Monday-Thursday   11:00 a.m. - 9:00 p.m.
Friday-Saturday   11:00 a.m. - 10:00 p.m.

ADMISSION
$1.25

CLOSE-BY PLACES
• Catalina Island Terminal / Newport Beach - Site 131
• Newport Beach - Site 142

SITE 119 - BELMONT PARK CAROUSEL

ADDRESS
Belmont Park is on Mission Beach
3190 Mission Boulevard
San Diego, CA 92109
(858) 488-1549
www.belmontpark.com

DIRECTIONS [GUIDE PAGE 1267 (SD)]
Take Interstate Highway 5 to the Sea World Drive Exit and go west to Mission Bay Drive. Make a right on Mission Boulevard.

HOURS
All Year:
Daily   11:00 a.m. - Evening

ADMISSION
$2.00

CLOSE-BY PLACES
• Bates Nut Farm - Site 101
• Sea World - Site 87

SITE 120 - SEAPORT VILLAGE CAROUSEL

ADDRESS
849 West Harbor Drive
San Diego, CA 92101
(619) 235-4014
www.spvillage.com

DIRECTIONS [GUIDE PAGE 1289 (SD)]
• Take Interstate Highway 5 north to the 6th Avenue Exit and go left. Make a right on Ash, and then a left on Pacific Highway, which ends at Seaport Village.
• Take Interstate Highway 5 south to the Front Street Exit. Make a right on Ash Street, and then a left on Pacific Highway, which ends at Seaport Village.

HOURS
Summer:
Daily   10:00 a.m. - 10:00 p.m.
Winter:
Daily   10:00 a.m. - 9:00 p.m.

ADMISSION
$1.00

CLOSE-BY PLACES
• Bates Nut Farm - Site 101
• San Diego Train Station - Site 185

YOUR COMMENTS

_____

_____

_____

_____

_____

_____

SITE 121 - BALBOA PARK MERRY-GO-ROUND AND BUTTERFLY RIDES

ADDRESS
Zoo Place
San Diego, CA 92103
(619) 239-0512
www.balboapark.org

DIRECTIONS [GUIDE PAGE 1289 (SD)]
Take Interstate Highway 5 to the Park Drive Exit and go north. Make a left on Zoo Place. The merry-go-round is next to the zoo.

HOURS
Summer:
Monday-Saturday   11:00 a.m. - 5:30 p.m.
Sunday   11:00 a.m. - 6:00 p.m.
Winter:
Weekends, Holidays 11:00 a.m. - 5:30 p.m.

ADMISSION
$1.50
Under 1   Free

CLOSE-BY PLACES
• Bates Nut Farm - Site 101
• San Diego Model Railroad Museum - Site 202
• San Diego Zoo - Site 68

Your Comments

_____
_____
_____
_____

Site 122 - Westfield Santa Anita Fashion Park

Address
400 S. Baldwin Avenue, Suite 231
Arcadia, CA 91007
(626) 445-6255
http://westfield.com/santaanita/

Directions [Guide Page 567 (LA)]
Take Interstate Highway 210 and exit at Baldwin Avenue. Go south on Baldwin Avenue.

Hours
All Year:
Monday-Saturday   10:00 a.m. - 9:00 p.m.
Sunday   11:00 a.m. - 7:00 p.m.

Admission
$2.00

Close-by Places
• Los Angeles County Arboretum and Botanic Gardens - Site 37
• Pasadena Cruisin' Weekly Car Show - Site 35
• Santa Anita Race Track Morning Workout - Site 92
• Water Play Area - Santa Fe Dam Recreation Area - Site 124
• Wilderness Park and Nature Center - Site 52

Your Comments

_____
_____
_____
_____

SITE 123 - CHASE PALM PARK CAROUSEL

ADDRESS
323 East Cabrillo Boulevard and State Street
Santa Barbara, CA 93101
(805) 963-9463

DIRECTIONS [GUIDE PAGE 996 (SB)]
Take U.S. Highway 101 to the Garden Street Exit and go towards the ocean.
Make a left at end of Garden Street.

HOURS
All Year:
Daily   9:00 a.m. - 9:00 p.m.

ADMISSION
$2.00

CLOSE-BY PLACES
- Kid's World - Site 36
- Santa Barbara Airport - Site 160
- Santa Barbara County Fair and Exposition - Site 110
- Santa Barbara East Beach - Site 145
- Santa Barbara Museum of Natural History - Site 14
- Santa Barbara Train Station - Site 188
- Santa Barbara Zoological Gardens - Site 70

YOUR COMMENTS

_____
_____
_____
_____

SCHOOL CARNIVALS

Nursery Schools, pre-schools and elementary schools often hold school carnivals as fundraisers. The carnivals are geared for young children and are usually not very expensive. There are often petting corrals, booths with games appropriate for young children, crafts, and puppet shows. Contact your local elementary or pre-school for more information.

PHONE BOOK:
Yellow Pages   Look under schools-"Academic-Pre-School" and
                     "Kindergarten."

A Child's Natural Curiosity with Snow
Photo by author.

CHAPTER 8 - WATER

Southern California is beach heaven. There is nothing better and more relaxing than a day at the beach. In addition, there are a few other water-related activities in Southern California of interest to young children, including some lakes, and of course, the mountain snow in the winter. Where else can you go to the snow in the morning and the beach in the afternoon?

BIRD FIELD GUIDES

In many of the water locations you will find birds. Below are a few additional field guides (see also Chapter 3-Gardens and Nature) that focus on birds.

Local Birds of Los Angeles County, Local Birds, Inc., Woodside, CA, 1999,
Birds of Los Angeles, Chris C. Fisher and Herbert Clarke, Lone Pine Publishing, Canada, 1997.
Field Guide to the Birds of North America, National Geographic, Second Edition: Washington, D. C., 1987.
An Introduction to Southern California Birds, Herbert Clarke, Mountain Press Publishing Company, 1989.

BOOKS FOR YOUR CHILD

- Brett, Jan, *The Mitten*
- Gramatky, Hardie, *Little Toot*
- Hill, Eric, *Spot Goes to the Beach*
- Keats, Ezra Jack, *The Snowy Day*
- Kleven, Elisa, *The Puddle Pail*
- McPhail, David, *Snow Lion*
- Raffi, *Down by the Bay*
- Rey, H. A., *Curious George Goes to the Beach*
- Rockwell, Anne, *Boats*

SOMETHING TO DO - ICE

Water can be a gas, a liquid, or a solid (ice). In Southern California, water is usually a liquid, but if you visit the snow, you will find it as a solid. Talk about this with your child so he starts to hear words like liquid and solid. Buy a block of ice or two (or make one in your freezer), a box of salt (or rock salt), and some food coloring. Give them to you child in the backyard after a visit to water and let her explore. Your block of ice may become a beautiful castle. See what happens to it the next day. What happens to the ice after it melts? What happens to the snow on the mountain after it melts? What animals like to live on ice, (the penguins you saw at Sea World or the polar bears you saw at the San Diego Zoo)?

SOMETHING TO MAKE - BINOCULARS

Your toddler can easily make a pair of binoculars (with your help) by stapling together two toilet paper rolls. Add a string for a strap using a hole punch, and let your child decorate the binoculars with stickers or marking pens. The new binoculars will be great fun to take on hikes to hunt for birds. Although they do not magnify, they do focus attention and will therefore help your child see birds. Bring your real binoculars along so you can both look.

SITE 124 - WATER PLAY AREA-SANTA FE DAM RECREATION AREA

ADDRESS
15501 East Arrow Highway
Irwindale, CA 91706
(626) 334-1065
parks.co.la.ca.us/santa_fe_rpark.html

DIRECTIONS [GUIDE PAGE 568/598 (LA)]
Take Interstate Highway 210 to the Irwindale Exit and go south. Make a right on Arrow Highway and then a right into Santa Fe Dam. Make a left after entering the park.

GOOD THINGS TO SEE AND HEAR
The Water Play structure at Santa Fe Dam is a play structure in the middle of a shallow swimming pool that sprays water in all directions. The pool and structure are very clean and friendly, and just right for toddlers and babies.

Parents need to help babies and toddlers as with any play structure. Don't forget your swim diapers.

HOURS
Summer:
Daily   10:30 a.m. - 6:00 p.m.
One and one-half hour sessions start every two hours
May-September:
Saturday-Sunday   10:30 a.m. - 6:00 p.m.

PARKING
$8.00

ADMISSION
Child (Ages 0-12) $1.00

RELATED PLACES
• Puddingstone Reservoir Beach - Site 125
• Sea World - Site 87

CLOSE-BY PLACES
• Los Angeles County Arboretum and Botanic Gardens - Site 37
• Pasadena Cruisin' Weekly Car Show - Site 35
• Santa Anita Race Track Morning Workout - Site 92
• Wilderness Park and Nature Center - Site 52

YOUR COMMENTS
_____
_____
_____
_____

SITE 125 - PUDDINGSTONE RESERVOIR BEACH

ADDRESS
Frank G. Bonelli Regional Park
210 East Via Verde
San Dimas, CA 91773
(909) 599-8411
parks.co.la.ca.us/frank_rpark.html

DIRECTIONS [GUIDE PAGE 600 (LA)]
Take Interstate Highway 210 to State Highway 57 south to the Via Verde Exit. Follow the signs to Bonelli Park, and ask for specific directions to the beach at the gate entrance.

GOOD THINGS TO SEE AND HEAR
The beach on Puddingstone Lake in Bonelli Park is a sand beach that is shallow, clean, friendly, and has many many lifeguards. Airplanes from nearby Brackett Air Field - Site 148 are fun to watch overhead.

No shade is available, so bring an umbrella, a lot of sun block, and swim diapers.

HOURS
Summer Only-June to September:
Daily   10:00 a.m. - 6:00 p.m.

PARKING
Free with Park Fees
• Park in Lot Right Next to Beach

ADMISSION
Vehicle $8.00

YEARLY MEMBERSHIP
Annual Pass $120.00

RELATED PLACES
• The Beach-Chapter 8
• Santa Catalina Island - Site 126
• Water Play Area-Santa Fe Dam Recreation Area - Site 124

CLOSE-BY PLACES
• Brackett Air Field - Site 149
• Los Angeles County Fair - Site 106
• Mrs. Nelson's Toy and Book Shop - Site 18
• Raymond M. Alf Museum - Site 15
• San Dimas Canyon Park and Nature Center - Site 45

YOUR COMMENTS

_____

_____

_____

_____

_____

SITE 126 - SANTA CATALINA ISLAND

ADDRESS
Catalina Island Visitor's Bureau
Avalon, Catalina Island, CA 90704
(310) 510-1520
www.catalina.com

DIRECTIONS
Travel by ferry boat from the following terminals:

SITE 127 - CATALINA TERMINAL/LONG BEACH-DOWNTOWN

To Avalon
Catalina Express
(800) 481-3470
(866) 432-6276 (Catalina Explorers)
www.catalinaexpress.com

[GUIDE PAGE 825 (LA)]
• Take Interstate Highway 710 to the Goldenshore Exit.

SITE 128 - CATALINA TERMINAL/LONG BEACH-QUEEN MARY

To Avalon
Catalina Express
(800) 481-3470
www.catalinaexpress.com

[GUIDE PAGE 825 (LA)]
• Take Interstate Highway 710 until it ends. Follow the signs to the Queen Mary.

SITE 129 - CATALINA TERMINAL/SAN PEDRO-PORT OF LOS ANGELES

To Avalon and Two Harbors
Catalina Express
(800) 481-3470
(800) 641-1004 (Catalina Classic Cruiser)
www.catalinaexpress.com

[GUIDE PAGE 824 (LA)]
• Take Interstate Highway 110 to the Harbor Boulevard Exit and follow signs.

SITE 130 - CATALINA TERMINAL/DANA POINT

To Avalon
Catalina Express
(800) 481-3470
www.catalinaexpress.com

[GUIDE PAGE 971 (OC)]
• Take Interstate Highway 5 to the Pacific Coast Highway 1 Exit. Make a left at Dana Point Harbor Drive and then a left at Golden Lantern.

SITE 131 - CATALINA TERMINAL/NEWPORT BEACH

To Avalon
Catalina Passenger Service/Catalina Flyer
(949) 673-5245
www.catalinainfo.com

[GUIDE PAGE 919 (OC)]
• Take Interstate Highway 405 to State Highway 55. Exit at Newport Boulevard and go south. From there, go east as Main Street turns into Balboa Boulevard. Make a left on Main Street.

GOOD THINGS TO SEE AND HEAR

Catalina Island is located about twenty-two miles off the coast of California. The ferry boats from Long Beach, San Pedro, Dana Point, and Newport Beach go to the towns of Avalon and Two Harbors. The trip out provides great excitement for babies and toddlers. Sit by a window on the upper deck inside if possible. Look for pelicans, seals, and harbor boats - leave from San Pedro to see the most harbor boats.

On Catalina Island, many charming hotels are available, however, a day trip is also a great adventure. Take the Avalon Trolley for $1.00 to the Botanical Gardens and Wrigley Memorial. Go to the beach or take a trip in a glass bottom boat.

There are sand beaches with light waves on either side of the pier in Avalon with little shells, feathers, sea glass, and rocks to collect. Descanso Beach on the other side of the Casino (the big round building) is very rocky and not recommended for small children.

You can get a ride on the glass bottom boat at Catalina Adventure Tours ((562) 432-8828 or www.catalinaadventuretours.com) or Discovery Tours (800) 626-1496 or www.scico.com). There are simple glass bottom boats or Adventure Tours has a fancier yellow "submarine" called the Nautilus. The Nautilus has large round windows and a feeding system that allows your child to push a button to launch food for the fish. The fish come in swarms! You will probably see Garibaldi, Topsmelt, Opaleyes, and Bass. If you look in the seaweed, you may see a bat ray or a small shark. If you look on the sandy bottom, you may see a halibut with both eyes on one side of his head. Be sure to get a Fish Finder when you buy your tickets so you can identify the fish and remember them after your trip.

As with any boat, your child will need constant supervision. If you get seasick, remember the Bonine, but beware of getting sleepy. Never give your child any seasickness medicine. Bring jackets as the boat ride can be chilly. Also bring your usual beach gear (sun block, towels, change of clothes, bathing suits, and of course, swim diapers).

HOURS
Summer (Check Website for Other Times):
First Boat to Avalon   6:30 a.m.
Last Boat from Avalon 9:30 p.m.

PARKING
$10.00 per day

ADMISSION
Catalina Express
Adult	$49.00-$51.00
Child (Ages 2-11)	$37.50-$39.00
Under 2	$3.00

Catalina Explorer
Adult	$41.00

Catalina Classic Cruiser
Adult	$31.50

• Round Trip Boat Ride Prices Vary with Service

RELATED PLACES
• The Beach-Chapter 8
• Birch Aquarium at Scripps - Site 88
• Cabrillo Marine Aquarium - Site 72
• Long Beach Aquarium of the Pacific - Site 71
• Roundhouse Marine Studies Lab and Aquarium - Site 73
• Puddingstone Reservoir Beach - Site 125
• Santa Monica Pier Aquarium - Site 75
• Tide Pools - Sites 77-84

YOUR COMMENTS

_____

_____

_____

_____

SITE 132 - BOLSA CHICA ECOLOGICAL RESERVE

ADDRESS
3842 Warner Avenue-Interpretive Center
Pacific Coast Highway 1 between Warner Avenue and Golden West Street
Huntington Beach, CA 92469
(714) 846-1114
www.bolsachica.org/

DIRECTIONS [GUIDE PAGE 857 (OC)]
• Take Interstate Highway 405 to the Warner Avenue Exit and go west. Make a left on Pacific Coast Highway 1. The Interpretive Center is on the southeast corner of Pacific Coast Highway 1 and Warner Avenue. Then follow Pacific Coast Highway 1 for one mile south to parking lot, which is on the left, to find the Walking Bridge.

GOOD THINGS TO SEE AND HEAR
Bolsa Chica is a protected salt marsh or estuary where the river meets the ocean, and is home to many birds. The wetlands are what are left of a much larger area that has shrunk over time - notice the oil pumps around the reserve. The sticky smelly mud is home to algae, fish, and invertebrates, as well as birds. Nearly half of the birds found in the U.S. have been seen in the Huntington Beach/Bolsa Chica area - you are likely to see pelicans, egrets, plovers, terns, coots, teals, and pintails, as well as sparrows, pigeons, and sea gulls. There is a one and one-half mile nature loop - take it all the way or part of the way, and don't forget your stroller or backpack.

You may not feed these birds. It is often cold and windy - bring a jacket. There are open rails along the Walking Bridge - a stroller or backpack may be best.

HOURS
Daily	Dawn-Dusk
Interpretive Center:	
Tuesday-Friday	10:00 a.m. - 4:00 p.m.
Saturday	9:00 a.m. - 12:00 p.m.
Sunday	12:30 p.m. - 3:30 p.m.

PARKING
$6.00	Interpretive Center
Free	Walking Bridge

ADMISSION
Free	Donations Accepted

YEARLY MEMBERSHIP
Adult	$40.00

RELATED PLACES
- Los Angeles County Arboretum and Botanic Garden - Site 37
- Descanso Gardens - Site 38
- The Huntington - Site 39
- Puddingstone Reservoir Beach - Site 125
- Santa Catalina Island - Site 126
- South Coast Botanical Gardens - Site 40

CLOSE-BY PLACES
- Huntington Beach School Bus Yard - Site 23
- Huntington Central Park Equestrian Center - Site 94
- Huntington State Beach and Huntington City Beach - Site 136
- Kite Flying at the Beach - Site 167
- Shipley Nature Center at Huntington Central Park - Site 48

YOUR COMMENTS

_____

_____

_____

_____

_____

HARBOR BOATS

SAIL BOAT

TUG BOAT

CRUISE SHIP

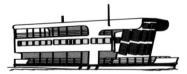

FERRY BOAT

SPEED BOAT

SITE 133 - SNOW IN THE ANGELES NATIONAL FOREST

ADDRESS
Angeles Crest Highway/State Highway 2
Angeles National Forest, CA 91011
(626) 574-5200
www.r5.fs.fed.us/angeles/

DIRECTIONS [GUIDE PAGE 535 (LA)]
Take Interstate Highway 210 to the Angeles Crest Highway/State Highway 2 Exit, go north for about an hour.

GOOD THINGS TO SEE AND HEAR
For Southern Californians, snow is a strange thing. Introduce your child to our local snow by taking him or her up to the Angeles National Forest. The winter months after Christmas are usually good times to find snow. The weekend after a big storm may have a lot of snow, but also may have a lot of visitors (and traffic jams). If you can, go on a weekday. Bring sand toys - they work well in the snow also. Find a place along the road to pull off - you will not need much snow to keep your child's attention long enough to get cold.

Come prepared with extra mittens (for you and your child), hats, boots, snowsuit, and a complete change of clothes or two for after the snow. Bring a small sled with an attached rope, plastic shovels, buckets, a waterproof tarp, and a blanket for a picnic. Don't forget carrots and pieces of coal for your snowman.

Go early as sometimes the roads are closed due to too many cars.

HOURS
Driving time from Interstate Highway 210 to the snow is thirty to sixty minutes, depending on weather and traffic. Be sure to leave enough time to get home during daylight.

PARKING
Along the road

ADMISSION
Free
• Wilderness Pass is REQUIRED. (Purchase at a Forest Service Office or most sports stores)

RELATED PLACES
• Children's Nature Institute - Site 43

CLOSE-BY PLACES
• Descanso Gardens - Site 38
• School Buses/Pasadena Unified School District - Site 19

YOUR COMMENTS

_____

_____

_____

_____

_____

THE BEACH

ADDRESS

Favorite beaches for babies and toddlers are listed in this section. Visit www.usc.edu/org/seagrant for an overall guide to beaches in Los Angeles and Orange Counties. Also try Los Angeles County Department of Beaches and Harbors, (310) 305-9503 or Los Angeles Area Surf and Weather Information (310) 457-9701.

GOOD THINGS TO SEE AND HEAR

Sand, waves, birds, kites, boats, planes, helicopters, lifeguard trucks rolling along the sand, and other children playing in the surf can all be found at the beach. Southern California has endless beaches of all sorts, and most are not as crowded as you might think. The sights, sounds, smells, feel and taste of beaches are fascinating for babies and toddlers.

Shells, feathers, and bottle caps can be collected walking along the beach. Sand crabs can be found down by the water in the very wet sand by digging down where you find little bubbles. Catch them in a bucket and keep them wet. Let them go by putting them back on the wet sand and watch them dig in. Look for the many kinds of sea birds; especially the pelicans. Watch them dive for fish.

Most beaches have a pier - a great place to watch the surfers, the local fishermen and sometimes the sea lions. The pier at Manhattan Beach has a little aquarium at the end of it (Site 73- Roundhouse) and the big Santa Monica pier has a bigger aquarium (Site 75-Santa Monica Pier Aquarium) and a merry-go-round - the one that was in the movie _The Sting_ (Site 116-Santa Monica Pier Carousel).

Your baby may want to eat some sand, it is so salty! A little sand will go right through them, but a big blanket is helpful to keep them off the sand some of the time. If your baby likes a pacifier, use it - it might help minimize the sand they eat.

Pay to park close - it is worth it when you are ready to bring your tired children back to the car through the sand!

Be aware that many of the "mothers'" beaches are among the most polluted in Southern California. Breakwaters usually protect these beaches from currents and surf. With little circulation, the water becomes stagnant and a breeding ground for bacteria. It is best to check Heal the Bay or the Los Angeles County Ocean Water Monitoring Program websites before setting out for one of these beaches. Stay at least one hundred yards from piers, storm drains, and creeks, and avoid the beach for at least seventy-two hours after a rain when the runoff from our city pollutes the water.

BEACH POLLUTION INFORMATION

Heal the Bay
www.healthebay.org/baymap/

Los Angeles County Ocean Water Monitoring Program
phps.dhs.co.la.ca.us/phcommon/public/eh/rechlth/ehrecocdata.cfm

County of San Diego-Department of Environmental Health
www.sdcounty.ca.gov/deh/lwq/beachbay

Orange County Hot Line
www.surfrider.org/beachreport.aspx

Be sure to bring sun block, sand toys (stacking cups, a bucket, and an ice cream scoop), a blanket, a lot of quarters for parking, swim diapers, hats, an umbrella, drinking water (twice as much as you think you will need), snacks (twice as many as you think you will need), and a water bottle to squirt sand out of eyes. Try a snow sled to drag your gear, and a backpack for your child.

HOURS
All

PARKING
Some beaches have parking lots, others have metered parking. Some even have close-by neighborhood streets with free parking although the walk is usually much longer.

ADMISSION
Most beaches are free. The exception of the beaches recommended here is the Seaside Lagoon.

RELATED PLACES
- Bolsa Chica Ecological Reserve - Site 132
- Puddingstone Reservoir Beach - Site 125
- Santa Catalina Island - Site 126
- Tide Pools - Sites 77-84

YOUR COMMENTS

_____

_____

_____

_____

_____

BEST BEACHES FOR CHILDREN

SITE 134 - CORONA DEL MAR STATE BEACH

Ocean Boulevard and Iris Avenue
Newport Beach, CA 92625
(949) 644-3151
www.usc.edu/org/seagrant

[GUIDE PAGE 919 (OC)]
• Take Interstate Highway 405 to the MacArthur Boulevard Exit and go south. Make a left on Pacific Coast Highway 1 and a right on Poppy Avenue. Then make a right on Ocean Boulevard, and follow Ocean Boulevard to its end.
• Beware of runoff from San Diego Creek Channel.

SITE 135 - HERMOSA BEACH

Hermosa and Pier Avenues
Hermosa Beach, CA 90254
Pier-Hermosa Beach Pier
Playgrounds-off 2nd Street and 22nd Street
www.usc.edu/org/seagrant

[GUIDE PAGE 762 (LA)]
• Take Interstate Highway 405 to State Highway 91 and go west to Pacific Coast Highway 1. Go south on Pacific Coast Highway 1 and make a right on Pier Avenue. Go straight for the pier or left or right on Hermosa Avenue for the beach.

SITE 136 - HUNTINGTON STATE BEACH AND HUNTINGTON CITY BEACH

Pacific Coast Highway 1 at Beach Boulevard
Huntington Beach, CA 92647
www.usc.edu/org/seagrant

[GUIDE PAGE 887/888 (OC)]
• Take Interstate Highway 405 to the Ellis Avenue Exit and go west. Veer south on Main Street and follow it to the pier. Areas north and south of pier are good beaches.
• The pier has a kite shop (see Site 167-Kite Flying at the Beach). Beware of ocean pollution and high surf.

SITE 137 - LAGUNA MAIN BEACH

Cliff Drive west of Broadway
Ocean and Laguna Streets
Laguna Beach, CA 92651
www.usc.edu/org/seagrant

[GUIDE PAGE 950 (OC)]
• Take Interstate Highway 405 to the Laguna Canyon Road Exit and go towards the beach. Be aware that there is often a lot of traffic on Laguna Canyon Road on weekends and holidays. For coves, turn right and go anywhere along Pacific Coast Highway 1.
• There are tide pools at Diver's Cove and Crescent Bay (get a tide pool chart at the Visitor's Center). Go north along Pacific Coast Highway 1 for the coves like Shaws, Fishermans, Diver's, and Crescent Bay. Stop at Laguna Koi Ponds and Marine Mammal Center - Site 86 on your way to the beach.

SITE 138 - LA JOLLA SHORES

8200 Camino Del Oro
La Jolla, CA 92037
www.sannet.gov/lifeguards/beaches/shores.shtml

[GUIDE PAGE 1227 (SD)]
• Take Interstate Highway 5 to the La Jolla Village Drive Exit. Make a left at Torrey Pines Road and follow to La Jolla Shores. Park at Calle Frescota.
• The Children's Pool Beach protects seals and provides a close-up viewing of them. You are close to the Birch Aquarium - Site 88.

SITE 139 - LEO CARRILLO STATE BEACH

35000 Pacific Coast Highway 1
Malibu, CA 90265
www.usc.edu/org/seagrant

[GUIDE PAGE 625 (LA) or 387 (SB/V)]
• Take U.S. Highway 101 to State Highway 23. Go south to Pacific Coast Highway 1 and make a right onto Pacific Coast Highway 1.

SITE 140 - LITTLE CORONA DEL MAR BEACH

Poppy and Ocean Avenue
Newport Beach, CA 92625
www.usc.edu/org/seagrant

[GUIDE PAGE 919 (OC)]
• Take Interstate Highway 405 to the MacArthur Boulevard Exit and go south. Make a left on Pacific Coast Highway 1 and a right on Poppy Avenue. From there make a right on Ocean Boulevard.
• Beware of runoff from the San Diego Creek Channel.

SITE 141 - MANHATTAN BEACH

Manhattan Beach Boulevard and North Ocean Drive
Manhattan Beach, CA 92066
www.usc.edu/org/seagrant

[GUIDE PAGE 732 (LA)]
• Take Interstate Highway 405 to State Highway 91 west to Pacific Coast Highway 1 going north. Make a left on Manhattan Beach Boulevard. Go straight towards the pier or left or right on Highland Avenue for the beach.
• At the end of the pier is the Roundhouse Marine Studies Lab and Aquarium - Site 73.

SITE 142 - NEWPORT BEACH

Balboa Boulevard at McFadden Place and Ocean Front Street
Newport Beach, CA 92663
www.usc.edu/org/seagrant
[GUIDE PAGE 918/919 (OC)]
• Take Interstate Highway 405 to State Highway 55 south. State Highway 55 turns into Newport Boulevard. Make a left on Balboa Boulevard and go along the Balboa Peninsula to Balboa Pier.
• There are lots of shells to collect. Beware runoff from the San Diego Creek Channel.

SITE 143 - REDONDO BEACH

Pier at Torrance Boulevard
Redondo Beach, CA 90277
(310) 379-8471
www.usc.edu/org/seagrant

[GUIDE PAGE 762 (LA)]
• Take Interstate Highway 405 to State Highway 91 west to Pacific Coast Highway 1 south. Exit Torrance Boulevard and make a right. Go straight for the pier or left on Catalina Avenue for the beach. Park in lots by pier for $5.00-$7.00, or metered side streets.
• There is often music on the pier in the summer. Seaside Lagoon (Site 147) is to the north, and SEA Lab (Site 74) is close by.

SITE 144 - SAN CLEMENTE BEACH

Pacific Coast Highway 1 below Ole Hanson Beach Club
San Clemente, CA 92676
www.takethebeachtrain.com
www.usc.edu/org/seagrant

[GUIDE PAGE 992 (OC)]
• Take Interstate Highway 5 to the Avenida Pico Exit and go south.
• Or take Metrolink - Site 194 or Amtrak - Site 193. (See "Real Train Rides Around Los Angeles" in Chapter 10).
• The Amtrak/Metrolink Station - Site 184) is located near the Ole Hanson Beach Club. In the summer, take the train.

SITE 145 - SANTA BARBARA EAST BEACH

East Cabrillo Boulevard and Milpas Street
Santa Barbara, CA 93101
www.totalsantabarbara.com/beach.shtml

[GUIDE PAGE 996 (SB)]
• Take U.S. Highway 101 to the Garden Street Exit and go towards the ocean.
• There is a merry-go-round at Chase Palm Park - Site 123. The Ty Warner Sea Center is on Stearns Wharf - this is an excellent hands-on aquarium (site 89). There are grassy areas shaded by palm trees.

SITE 146 - SANTA MONICA STATE BEACH

1600 Ocean Boulevard
Santa Monica, CA 90401
www.pacpark.com

[GUIDE PAGE 671 (LA)]

• Take Interstate Highway 10 to the 4th Street Exit and go northwest. Make a left on Colorado, and park on pier.

• Try the stonewalled sandbox at the foot of the pier. There is a dragon that sprays ocean mist and a concrete ship. The Santa Monica Pier Carousel - Site 116 and the Santa Monica Pier Aquarium - Site 75 are on and under the pier.

SITE 147 - SEASIDE LAGOON

200 Portofino Way
Redondo Beach, CA 90277
(310) 318-0681
www.redondo.org/seasidelagoon

[GUIDE PAGE 762 (LA)]

• Take Interstate Highway 405 to State Highway 91 west to Pacific Coast Highway 1 south. Exit Catalina Avenue and make a right, and then a right on Beryl Street, which turns into Portofino Way.

• Seaside Lagoon is a large, shallow saltwater lagoon heated by the nearby steam-generating plant that is only open in the summer. There is a large sand area, several grassy and shady areas, and a children's playground. The snack bar is provided by Ruby's Restaurant. There is a charge to get in: $4.50 for adults, $3.25 for children, while children under two are free. Redondo Beach is to the south.

SHORE BIRDS

EGRET

PELICAN

SEAGULL

PLOVER

SANDPIPER

Hot Air Balloons at the Temecula Valley Balloon and Wine Festival.

Photo by author; permission to use photo courtesy of Carol Popejoy-Hime of
the Temecula Valley Balloon and Wine Festival.

CHAPTER 9 - FLYING

Now that Los Angeles has cleaned up its air, there are quite a few things to see in the sky. All of the medium to small airports in Southern California are listed - find one that is near your home and make it a regular stop. A visit to the Goodyear Blimp - Site 168 or the Temecula Valley Balloon and Wine Festival - Site 169 takes some planning, but it is worth the effort.

SITE 148- BOB HOPE AIRPORT

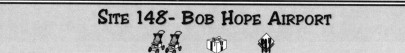

ADDRESS
2627 North Hollywood Way
Sun Valley, CA 91352
(818) 840-8840
www.bobhopeairport.com

DIRECTIONS [GUIDE PAGE 533 (LA)]
Take Interstate Highway 5 north to the Hollywood Way Exit. Turn left under freeway and drive one mile. The entrance is on the right.

GOOD THINGS TO SEE AND HEAR
The Bob Hope Airport was formerly known as the Burbank Airport. Park on the roof of the short term parking structure and watch the airplanes take off and land.

Since you will be on a parking structure, keep children in a stroller or backpack, or in the car.

HOURS
Planes operate from 7:00 a.m. - 10:00 p.m.

PARKING
$2.00   For 1 hour or Fraction Thereof

ADMISSION
None

RELATED PLACES
- Chino Planes of Fame Air Museum - Site 166
- Museum of Flying - Site 165
- Other Airports-Chapter 9

CLOSE-BY PLACES
- Burbank Train Station - Site 173
- Falcon Theater - Site 205
- North Hollywood School Bus Yard - Site 25
- Summer Sounds at the Hollywood Bowl - Site 219

YOUR COMMENTS
_____
_____
_____
_____

FLYING THINGS

AIRPLANE

HELICOPTER

HOT AIR BALLOON

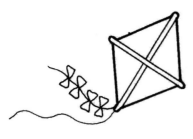

KITE

BLIMP

SITE 149 - BRACKETT AIR FIELD

1615 McKinley Avenue
La Verne, CA 91750
(909) 593-1395
www.pilotage.com/airports/poc/

[GUIDE PAGE 600 (LA)]
• Take Interstate Highway 210 to State Highway 57 south to the Arrow Highway Exit and go east. Make a right on Fairplex Drive, a right on McKinley Avenue and then a right on SkyDoc Park. Watch through the fence.

SITE 150 - CABLE AIRPORT

1739 Benson Avenue
Upland, CA 91786
(909) 982-6021
www.pilotage.com/airports

[GUIDE PAGE 601 (LA)]
• Take Interstate Highway 10 to the Central Avenue Exit and go north. Make a right on Foothill Boulevard, a left on Benson Avenue, a left on 13th street, and then park and walk into the terminal.

SITE 151 - COMPTON AIRPORT

901 West Alondra Boulevard
Compton, CA 90220
(310) 631-8140
www.pilotage.com/airports/cpm/

[GUIDE PAGE 734 (LA)]
• Take Interstate Highway 110 to the Rosecrans Avenue Exit and go east. Make a right on Central Avenue and a left on Alondra Boulevard. The airport is on the left.

SITE 152 - CORONA MUNICIPAL AIRPORT

1901 Aviation Drive
Corona, CA 92880
(909) 736-2289
www.pilotage.com/airports/

[GUIDE PAGE 18-20 (R)]
• Take State Highway 91 to the Maple Exit. Make a right so you are going east on 6th Street. Make a left on Smith and then a left on Butterfield State Drive. The airport is on the right.

SITE 153 - EL MONTE AIRPORT

4233 Santa Anita Avenue
El Monte, CA 91731
(626) 448-6129
www.pilotage.com/airports/emt/

[GUIDE PAGE 597 (LA)]
• Take Interstate Highway 605 to the Ramona Boulevard Exit and go west. Make a right on Santa Anita Avenue, and a left on Lambert Avenue. Park and go into the terminal.

SITE 154 - FULLERTON MUNICIPAL AIRPORT

4011 West Commonwealth
Fullerton, CA 92833
(714) 738-6323
www.pilotage.com/airports/ful/

[GUIDE PAGE 738 (OC)]
• Take Interstate Highway 5 to the Beach Boulevard Exit and go north. Make a right on Commonwealth Avenue. The airport is to your left.

SITE 155 - HAWTHORNE MUNICIPAL AIRPORT/ JACK NORTHROP FIELD

12101 Crenshaw Avenue
Hawthorne, CA 90250
(310) 970-7215
www.PilotAge.com/airports/hhr/

[GUIDE PAGE 733 (LA)]
• Take Interstate Highway 405 to the El Segundo Boulevard Exit and go east. Make a left on Crenshaw Avenue.

SITE 156 - JOHN WAYNE AIRPORT

18601 Airport Way
Santa Ana, CA 92707
(949) 252-5200
www.ocair.com

[GUIDE PAGE 859 (OC)]
• Take Interstate Highway 405 to the MacArthur Boulevard Exit and go south. Follow the signs.
• There are huge windows, including a V-shaped window that provides a close view of take-offs and landings.

SITE 157 - LONG BEACH AIRPORT

4100 Donald Douglas Drive
Long Beach, CA 90808
(562) 570-6555
www.longbeach.gov/airport

[GUIDE PAGE 796 (LA)]
• Take Interstate Highway 405 to the Lakewood Boulevard Exit and go north past Spring Street. Make a left on Donald Douglas Drive. Park and go into the terminal.

SITE 158 - MCCLELLAN-PALOMAR AIRPORT

2198 Palomar Airport Road
Carlsbad, CA 92008
(760) 431-4640
www.pilotage.com/airports/crq

[GUIDE PAGE 1127 (SD)]
• Take Interstate Highway 5 to the Palomar Airport Road Exit and go east.

SITE 159 - ONTARIO INTERNATIONAL AIRPORT

2500 East Airport Drive
Ontario, CA 91761
(909) 937-2700
www.PilotAge.com/airports/ont/

[GUIDE PAGE vii]
• Take Interstate Highway 10 east to the Vineyard Avenue Exit and go south. Follow the signs to parking areas.

SITE 160 - SANTA BARBARA AIRPORT

500 Fowler Road
Goleta, CA 93117
(805) 967-7111
flysba.com

[GUIDE PAGE 994 (SB)]
• Take the U.S. Highway 101 to the Fairview Avenue Exit and go south. Follow the signs.

SITE 161 - SANTA MONICA MUNICIPAL AIRPORT

3200 Donald Douglas Loop South
Santa Monica, CA 90405
(310) 458-8591
www.PilotAge.com/airports/smo/

[GUIDE PAGE 672 (LA)]
• Take Interstate Highway 10 to the Bundy Drive Exit and go south. Make a right on Ocean Park Boulevard and a left on 28th Street.

SITE 162 - TORRANCE MUNICIPAL AIRPORT/ ZAMPERINI FIELD

3115 Airport Drive
Torrance, CA 90505
(310) 784-7914
www.PilotAge.com/airports/toa/

[GUIDE PAGE 793 (LA)]
• Take Interstate Highway 110 to Pacific Coast Highway 1 west. Pass Crenshaw Boulevard, make a right on Zamperini, and go straight to the Zamperini Field parking lot. Go into the terminal.

SITE 163 - VAN NUYS AIRPORT

16700 Roscoe Boulevard or 16461 Sherman Way
Van Nuys, CA 91406
(818) 785-8838
www.PilotAge.com/airports/vny/

[GUIDE PAGE 531 (LA)]
• Take Interstate Highway 405 to the Sherman Way Exit and go west. Follow the signs.

SITE 164 - WHITEMAN AIRPORT

12653 Osborn Street
Pacoima, CA 91331
(818) 896-5271
www.PilotAge.com/airports/whp/

[GUIDE PAGE 502 (LA)]
• Take Interstate Highway 210 to the Osborne Street Exit and go south (changes temporarily into Foothill Boulevard). Follow the signs.

SITE 165 - MUSEUM OF FLYING

ADDRESS
Santa Monica Airport
Santa Monica, CA 90405
www.museumofflying.com/

GOOD THINGS TO SEE AND HEAR
This museum is being renovated and moved into a new hangar at Santa Monica Airport and plans to reopen in 2007. The museum has a variety of small vintage aircraft, especially World War II airplanes. These airplanes can be touched and seen up close. Some take off from the runway right outside the museum. In addition, the Airadventure Children's Interactive Learning Center features many airplanes, cockpits, and simulators for children to climb on. All have buttons to push and levers to pull.

HOURS
Wednesday-Sunday 10:00 a.m. - 5:00 p.m.

PARKING
Free

ADMISSION
Adult	$7.00
Child (Ages 3-17)	$3.00
Under 3	Free

YEARLY MEMBERSHIP
Adult	$35.00
Family	$75.00

RELATED PLACES
• Bob Hope Airport - Site 148
• Chino Planes of Fame Air Museum - Site 166
• Kite Flying at the Beach - Site 167
• Other Airports-Chapter 9

CLOSE-BY PLACES
• STAR EcoStation Environmental Science and Wildlife Rescue Center - Site 67

YOUR COMMENTS

SITE 166 - CHINO PLANES OF FAME AIR MUSEUM

ADDRESS
7000 Merrill Avenue
Chino, CA 91710
(909) 597-3722
www.planesoffame.org

DIRECTIONS [GUIDE PAGE 682 (SB/R)]
Take Highway 91 to Highway 71 and go north. Go north on Euclid and exit at Merrill Avenue. Take a right on Airport Way.

GOOD THINGS TO SEE AND HEAR
The Air Museum has about 100 vintage airplanes along with a hands-on aviation room and a space exhibit with a full-size model of the Apollo 13 capsule.

On Saturday and Sunday a B-17 bomber lands at the museum and your child can sit in it for a small fee.

HOURS
Daily   9:00 a.m. - 5:00 p.m.

PARKING
Free

ADMISSION
Adult $8.95
Child (Ages 5-11) $1.95
Under 5   Free

RELATED PLACES
• Bob Hope Airport - Site 148
• Museum of Flying - Site 165
• Other Airports-Chapter 9

CLOSE-BY PLACES
• Cable Airport - Site 150
• Ontario International Airport - Site 159

YOUR COMMENTS

SITE 167 - KITE FLYING AT THE BEACH

ADDRESS
Huntington State Beach and Huntington City Beach
Pacific Coast Highway 1 at Beach Boulevard
Huntington Beach, CA 92646
(714) 536-3630 Kite Connection
www.usc.edu/org/seagrant (Huntington Beach)
www.kiteconnection.com (Kite Connection)

DIRECTIONS [GUIDE PAGE 857/887/888 (OC)]
Take Interstate Highway 405 to the Ellis Avenue Exit and go west. Veer south on Main Street. Follow it to the pier.

GOOD THINGS TO SEE AND HEAR
Although kites can be flown at most beaches, Huntington Beach is recommended because it has a kite shop on the pier (Kite Connection). Although it is great fun to watch other people's kites, it is the most fun to fly your own (or at least watch mom or dad). Get the simplest kite possible and fly it low.

There are a variety of kite festivals where you can see a lot of kites in the sky at once. Check with Kite Connection for dates.

Keep your kite in your car in case of a windy day.

HOURS
Daylight When it is Windy

PARKING
Prices Vary at Meters on the Street or in Lots

ADMISSION
Free   Kite Prices Vary

RELATED PLACES
 • Goodyear Blimp Airfield - Site 168
 • Temecula Valley Balloon and Wine Festival - Site 169

CLOSE-BY PLACES
 • Bolsa Chica Ecological Reserve - Site 132
 • Huntington Beach School Bus Yard - Site 23
 • Huntington Central Park Equestrian Center - Site 94
 • Huntington State Beach and Huntington City Beach - Site 136
 • Shipley Nature Center at Huntington Central Park - Site 48

YOUR COMMENTS

SITE 168 - GOODYEAR BLIMP AIRFIELD

ADDRESS
19200 South Main Street
Carson, CA 90746
(323) 770-0456
www.goodyearblimp.com/

DIRECTIONS [GUIDE PAGE 764 (LA)]
• Take Interstate Highway 405 north to the Main Street Exit and go north. Drive one block to the airfield, which is on the right.
• Take Interstate Highway 405 south to the Vermont Avenue Exit. Make a left on 190th/Victoria Street (northeast, passing under Interstate Highway 405 and Interstate Highway 110) and then a right (south) Main Street.

GOOD THINGS TO SEE AND HEAR
Get a very close look at the Goodyear Blimp (*The Eagle*, one of three Goodyear blimps in the United States) and watch it land and take off-both exciting feats. On a normal operating day (usually Wednesday to Sunday), the blimp makes about ten flights of about forty-five minutes each starting at about 10:00 a.m. There is a little parking lot with a fence - perhaps you can have a tailgate lunch while you watch. Go in the office and ask what is happening that day. If the blimp is not flying, you may be able to walk out closer to it.

If the blimp is on the ground, you can't miss it. It is one hundred and ninety-two feet long and sixty feet high. Its shape is maintained by gas pressure, not an internal frame. It normally flies between one thousand and one thousand five hundred feet. Sometimes it is away covering big events in the area.

HOURS
Wednesday-Sunday 10:00 a.m. - 8:00 p.m.
• Flights vary greatly in time and day-call ahead for next day's schedule.

PARKING
There is free parking on the west side of the air base, inside chain link fence. This is the best location to watch departures and landings.

ADMISSION
Free

RELATED PLACES
• Kite Flying at the Beach - Site 167
• Temecula Valley Balloon and Wine Festival - Site 169

CLOSE-BY PLACES
• Lomita Railroad Museum - Site 197
• Santa Ana Train Station - Site 187
• South Coast Botanical Gardens - Site 40
• Torrance Municipal Airport/Zamperini Field - Site 162

YOUR COMMENTS

_____
_____
_____
_____
_____

SITE 169 - TEMECULA VALLEY BALLOON AND WINE FESTIVAL

ADDRESS
Lake Skinner
Temecula, CA 9590
(951) 676-6713
www.tvbwf.com

DIRECTIONS [GUIDE PAGE 125/126/116 (SB/R)]
Take Interstate Highway 15 to the Rancho California Road Exit (turns into Warren Road) and make a right at Lake Skinner Park.

GOOD THINGS TO SEE AND HEAR
The Temecula Valley Balloon and Wine Festival focuses on hot air balloons that take off in great numbers on Saturday and Sunday mornings of the festival. There are also Balloon Glows on Friday and Saturday evenings - balloons are tethered to the ground while their pilots ignite the balloon burners causing the balloons to glow with brilliant colors. This is a great time to watch the pilots blow up their balloons so arrive a little early. During the day there is an excellent Kids Fair, including a Discovery Science Tent and live music.

Try camping at the lake to see the evening and early morning shows (but make reservations well in advance). There can be a lot of traffic at the entrance so arrive early.

HOURS
One weekend in May or June (Reservations Required):
Friday   5:00 p.m. - 10:00 p.m.
Saturday   6:00 a.m. - 10:00 p.m.
Sunday   6:00 a.m. - 6:00 p.m.
Morning Balloon Launch: 7:00 a.m.
Balloon Glow:
Friday-Saturday Evening   Sunset

PARKING
$5.00

ADMISSION
Adult $10.00-Friday, $18.00-Saturday, and $15.00-Sunday
Child (Ages 7-12) $5.00 (Free on Friday)
Under 7   Free

RELATED PLACES
• Goodyear Blimp Airfield - Site 168
• Kite Flying at the Beach - Site 167

YOUR COMMENTS

Sitting on the Cow Catcher of a Train at the Travel Town Museum.

Photo by author; permission to use photo courtesy of Tom Breckner of the Travel Town Museum.

CHAPTER 10 - TRAINS, TRAINS, TRAINS

Trains of all sizes - from small toys to thundering Amtraks-are exciting to small children. Southern California has a great variety of trains that you can ride with your child, from smaller children's trains to Metrolink and Amtrak trains. Try one of the trips suggested in this section or make up your own. Because of the Los Angeles and Long Beach ports, there are also a lot of freight trains.

BOOKS FOR YOUR CHILD
- Brown, Margaret Wise - *The Train to Timbuctoo*
- Crews, Donald - *Freight Train*
- Piper, Watty - *The Little Engine that Could*
- Awdry, Wilbert Vere - *Thomas the Tank Engine*
- Ziefert, Harriet - *Train Song*

RAIL SAFETY TIPS

Visit the website www.metro.net/riding_metro/riders_guide/quick_tips-01.htm for train safety tips that are provided courtesy of Warren Morse of the Los Angeles County Metropolitan Transportation Authority.

SAFETY IN THE STATION
While waiting on the platform, always stand away from the edge.
Don't play on the platform or near trains. Pushing and shoving can cause accidents.
Always walk on the platform.
Stay away from the subway's third rail. It carries deadly, high-voltage electricity.

BOARDING THE TRAIN
Watch and listen for the train. Hear the horn or bell? Sing along if you want.
Don't move toward the train until it comes to a complete stop.
Never run after or next to the train. The train always wins.
Let passengers leave the train before you board.
Watch the gap between the platform edge and the train. Don't get caught in that crack!

ON THE TRAIN
Use the handholds and take a seat if available.
Don't lean against the train door and keep your hands clear when it's opening.

LEAVING THE TRAIN
Get ready to exit in advance, so you don't have to rush.
Watch the gap (again) between the train and the platform edge.
Step away from the train after exiting.

WHEN CROSSING TRACKS ON FOOT OR BY CAR
Don't cross tracks when crossing gates are lowered or lights are flashing.
Never use tracks as a shortcut.
Don't be dead wrong. You can't beat the train!
Trains come on any track, at any time, from any direction, so look both ways before crossing.
One train may obstruct your view of another. Don't cross until you can see all tracks clearly.
Trains travel at different speeds - some fast, some slow. Don't take chances when trying to cross.
Metro Rail trains are quiet and fast, so listen for the horn or bell.
Tracks mean Trains! Teach your children to Look, Listen and Live!

Site 170 - Travel Town Museum

Address
Griffith Park
5200 West Zoo Drive
Los Angeles, CA 90027
(323) 662-5874 Museum
(323) 662-9678 Train Ride
www.cityofla.org/RAP/grifmet/tt

Directions [Guide Page 563 (LA)]
• Take State Highway 134 west to the Zoo Drive Exit. Follow the signs.
• Take State Highway 134 east to the Victory Boulevard Exit. Turn right at top of offramp and then make a right on Zoo Drive. Follow the signs.

Good Things to See and Hear
Travel Town is an outdoor museum full of real locomotives, freight cars, cabooses, and passenger cars dating from the late 1800s. Children can walk right up to the huge trains and touch the wheels and cow catchers. All of the trains have been recently renovated, and access has been made safe for children. There is also an HO gage model railroad (open weekends) and a children's train ride.

Watching the children's train go by is almost as much fun as riding it - take a picnic, sit in the grassy area, and watch it go by many times.

Hours
Summer:
Monday-Friday   10:00 a.m. - 5:00 p.m.
Saturday-Sunday   10:00 a.m. - 6:00 p.m.

Parking
Free

Admission
Free
Train Ride:
Adult, Child $2.00
Under 18 months   Free

Related Places
• Fillmore and Western Railway - Site 203
• Freight Trains - Site 196
• Lomita Railroad Museum - Site 197
• Pasadena Model Railroad Club - Site 201
• San Diego Model Railroad Museum - Site 202
• Union Station - Site 171

CLOSE-BY PLACES
- Glendale Train Station - Site 178
- Griffith Observatory - Site 9
- Griffith Park Merry-Go-Round - Site 115
- Griffith Park Pony Rides - Site 95
- Griffith Park Train Ride - Site 198
- Los Angeles Zoo - Site 63

YOUR COMMENTS

SITE 171 - UNION STATION

ADDRESS
Union Station
800 North Alameda Street
Los Angeles, CA 90012
www.westworld.com/~elson/larail/

DIRECTIONS [GUIDE PAGE 634 (LA)]
Take Interstate Highway 110 to the Hill Street Exit and go south. Make a left on Ord Street and then a right on Alameda Street. The station is on the left, just past Cesar Chavez Boulevard.

GOOD THINGS TO SEE AND HEAR
Amtrak trains, Metrolink trains and the Metro Rail Red Line (subway) can all be seen up close at Union Station. Walk into the station, which is the last large passenger railroad terminal built in the United States, and all the way up to the train tracks. Check the schedules for the best arrival and departure times. Hear, smell, and feel the trains as they come into the station. Notice the murals and a mountain-like waterfall that is covered with artifacts from the original Chinatown site under Union Station. Take a ride on the Metro Rail Red Line - Site 195 (subway) and back again. Or ride the train to the beach or a petting farm in San Juan Capistrano (Site 98-Zoomars Petting Farm). See "Real Train Rides Around Los Angeles" in this Chapter for more ideas

Use strollers or backpacks to restrain children for safety around trains. Although it is tempting, do not put a penny on the track; your children will want to do the same!

HOURS
Daily   6:00 a.m. - 11:00 p.m.

PARKING

$10   Parking Over 1 $^1/_2$ Hours

ADMISSION

- Free to Watch Trains
- See Amtrak, Metro Rail, and Metrolink Sections for Ticket Prices

RELATED PLACES

- Amtrak Trains - Site 193
- Fillmore and Western Railway - Site 203
- Freight Trains - Site 196
- Metro Rail Red, Blue, and Green Lines - Site 195
- Metrolink Regional Rail Trains - Site 194
- Other Train Stations-Chapter 10
- Real Train Rides Around Los Angeles-Chapter 10
- Travel Town Museum - Site 170

CLOSE-BY PLACES

- Bob Baker Marionette Theater - Site 204
- Chinatown - Site 30
- Grand Central Market - Site 31
- KLOS Story Theater - Site 206
- Richard J. Riordan Library - Site 16
- Olvera Street - Site 29
- Walt Disney Music Concert Hall - Site 221

YOUR COMMENTS

_____

_____

_____

_____

_____

OTHER TRAIN STATIONS FOR AMTRAK

Below are some other train stations in Southern California. The ones listed are for Amtrak and usually also for Metrolink. There are other Metrolink stations that can be found on the Metrolink webpage.

Visit www.dot.ca.gov/hq/rail/depots/amstas.htm for detailed information about each station.

SITE 172 - ANAHEIM TRAIN STATION

2150 East Katella
Anaheim Stadium
Anaheim, CA 92807
[GUIDE PAGE 799 (OC)]
• Take Interstate Highway 5 to the State Highway 57 north. Exit Katella Avenue, then go west.

SITE 173 - BURBANK TRAIN STATION

3750 Empire Avenue
Burbank, CA 91505
[GUIDE PAGE 533 (LA)]
• Take Interstate Highway 5. Exit Buena Vista Street, then go south. Make a right turn onto Empire Avenue.

SITE 174 - CAMARILLO TRAIN STATION

30 Lewis Road
Camarillo, CA 93010
[GUIDE PAGE 524 (SB/V)]
• Take U.S. Highway 101 north. Exit CA-34/Lewis Road. Turn right onto Daily Drive, then left onto Lewis Road.

SITE 175 - CARPENTERIA TRAIN STATION

Union Pacific Railroad at Linden Avenue
Carpenteria, CA 93013
[GUIDE PAGE 998/1018 (SB/V)]
• Take U.S. Highway 101 north. Exit Casitas Pass Road, then go left. make a right turn onto Carpenteria Avenue. Make a left onto Linden Avenue.

SITE 176 - CHATSWORTH TRAIN STATION

10040 Old Depot Plaza Road
Chatsworth, CA 91311
[GUIDE PAGE 500 (LA)]
• Take State Highway 118. Exit De Soto Avenue, then go south. Make a right turn onto Devonshire Street. Turn left onto Old Depot Plaza Road.

SITE 177 - FULLERTON TRAIN STATION

120 East Santa Fe Avenue
Fullerton, CA 92832
[GUIDE PAGE 738 (OC)]
• Take Interstate Highway 5 south to State Highway 91 west. Exit Harbor Boulevard, go north. Turn right on to Santa Fe Avenue.

SITE 178 - GLENDALE TRAIN STATION

Railroad and Cerritos Avenues
Glendale, CA 91204
[GUIDE PAGE 564 (LA)]
• Take State Highway 134 west. Exit Brand Boulevard and go south. Make a right turn onto Los Feliz Road. Make a left onto Gardena Avenue, then a right on Railroad Street.

SITE 179 - IRVINE TRAIN STATION

15215 Barranca Street
Irvine, CA 92618
[GUIDE PAGE 891 (OC)]
• Take Interstate Highway 5 south to the 133 south toward Laguna Beach. Exit Barranca Parkway, then go left.

SITE 180 - LOS ANGELES/UNION STATION

800 North Alameda Street
Los Angeles, CA 90012
[GUIDE PAGE 634 (LA)]
• Take Interstate Highway 110 to the Hill Street Exit, go south. Turn left onto Ord Street, then a right turn onto Alameda Street.

SITE 181 - MOORPARK TRAIN STATION

High Street at Moorpark Avenue
Moorpark, CA 93021
[GUIDE PAGE 496 (SB/V)]
• Take State Highway 118. Exit Los Angeles Avenue, then turn left. Los Angeles Avenue turns into High Street.

SITE 182 - OCEANSIDE TRAIN STATION

235 South Tremont Avenue
Oceanside, CA 92054
[GUIDE PAGE 1106 (SD)]
• Take Interstate Highway 5. Exit toward Hills Street/Coast Highway. Merge onto the CA-76 west. Make a left turn onto Coast Highway, then a right onto Topeka Street. Also a left turn onto Tremont Avenue.

SITE 183 - OXNARD TRAIN STATION

201 East 4th Street
Oxnard, CA 93030
[GUIDE PAGE 522 (SB/V)]
• Take U.S. Highway 101 north. Exit Vineyard Avenue. Go toward left, then make a left turn onto Oxnard Boulevard.

SITE 184 - SAN CLEMENTE TRAIN STATION

Municipal Pier (Summer Only)
San Clemente, CA 92676
[GUIDE PAGE 992 (OC)]
• Take State Highway 55. Exit Avenida Pico, then go south. Train Station is near Ole Hanson Beach Club.

SITE 185 - SAN DIEGO TRAIN STATION

1050 Kettner Boulevard
San Diego, CA 92101
[GUIDE PAGE 1289 (SD)]
• Take State Highway 55. Exit Front Street and go right. Then make a right turn onto Broadway, and a right turn onto Kettner Boulevard.

SITE 186 - SAN JUAN CAPISTRANO TRAIN STATION

26701 Verdugo Street
San Juan Capistrano, CA 92675
[GUIDE PAGE 972 (OC)]
• Take Interstate Highway 5 south to the Ortega Highway Exit and go right. Make a left turn onto Camino Capistrano, then a right turn onto Verdugo Street.

SITE 187 - SANTA ANA TRAIN STATION

1000 East Santa Ana Boulevard
Santa Ana, CA 92701
[GUIDE PAGE 829 (OC)]
• Take Interstate Highway 5 to the Santa Ana Boulevard Exit and go west.

SITE 188 - SANTA BARBARA TRAIN STATION

209 State Street
Santa Barbara, CA 93101
[GUIDE PAGE 996 (SB)]
• Take U.S. Highway 101 north to the Garden Street Exit, then go right. Make a left turn onto Gutierrez Street, then a left turn onto State Street.

Site 189 - Simi Valley Train Station

5000 Los Angeles Avenue
Simi Valley, CA 93063
[GUIDE PAGE 498 (SB/V)]
• Take State Highway 118 to the Stearns Street Exit, then go left. Make a right turn onto Los Angeles Avenue.

Site 190 - Solana Beach Train Station

105 South Cedros Avenue
Solana Beach, CA 92075
[GUIDE PAGE 1167 (SD)]
• Take Interstate Highway 5 south to the Lomas Santa Fe Drive Exit, then go right. Make a left turn onto Cedros Avenue.

Site 191 - Van Nuys Train Station

7720 Van Nuys Boulevard
Van Nuys, CA 91405
[GUIDE PAGE 532]
• Take State Highway 170. Exit Sherman Way (west). Make a right turn onto Van Nuys Boulevard.

Site 192 - Ventura Train Station

Harbor Boulevard and Figueroa Street
Ventura, CA 93001
[GUIDE PAGE 491 (SB/V)]
• Take U.S. Highway 101. Exit California Street, then go right. Make a left turn onto Thompson Boulevard, then a left turn onto Figueroa Street.

Your Comments

_____
_____
_____
_____
_____

FREIGHT TRAINS

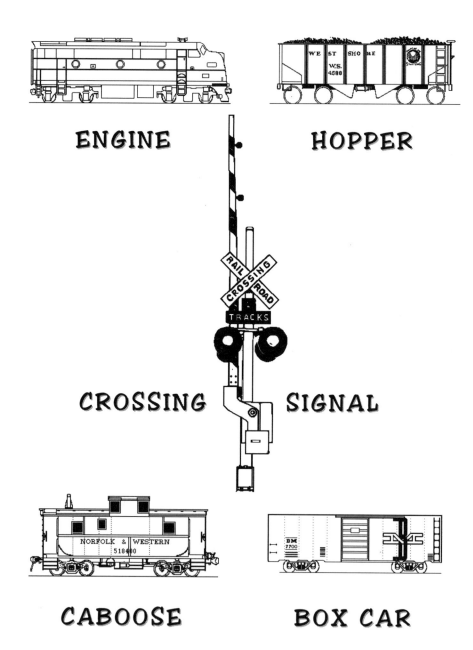

ENGINE   HOPPER

CROSSING   SIGNAL

CABOOSE   BOX CAR

SITE 193 - AMTRAK TRAINS

ADDRESS
Union Station
800 North Alameda Street
Los Angeles, CA 90012
(800) 872-7245
www.amtrakcalifornia.com

• Or see Sites 172 to 192 for the location of other Southern California train stations.

DIRECTIONS [GUIDE PAGE 634 (LA)]
Take Interstate Highway 110 to the Hill Street Exit and go south. Make a left on Ord Street and then a right on Alameda Street.

GOOD THINGS TO SEE AND HEAR
Amtrak provides train transportation across the United States. Amtrak's main home in Los Angeles is Union Station. The trains can also be seen at many other stations around Southern California - Sites 171 to 192. To ride an Amtrak train, see the section "Real Train Rides Around Los Angeles" in this chapter for suggested destinations. You may also download the current Amtrak Pacific Surfliner Timetable from the Amtrak website. Once you decide where you are going, call Amtrak to make a reservation.

Use strollers or backpacks to restrain children for safety around trains. Although it is tempting, do not put a penny on the tack; your children will want to do the same!

HOURS
See Train Schedules

PARKING
Varies with Station

ADMISSION
Free to Watch Trains
• Check Website for Amtrak Ticket Prices and Reservations

YEARLY MEMBERSHIP
• 45-Day 10-Ride Ticket Available
• Unlimited Monthly Ticket Available

RELATED PLACES
• Fillmore and Western Railway - Site 203
• Metro Rail Red, Blue, and Green Lines - Site 195
• Metrolink Regional Rail Trains - Site 194
• Other Train Stations-Chapter 10
• Real Train Rides Around Los Angeles-Chapter 10
• Union Station - Site 171 & 180

CLOSE-BY PLACES
- Chinatown - Site 30
- Grand Central Market - Site 31
- Local Fire Department-Chapter 2
- Richard J. Riordan Central Library - Site 16
- Metrolink Regional Rail Trains - Site 194
- Metro Rail Red, Blue, Green, and Gold Lines - Site 195
- Olvera Street - Site 29

YOUR COMMENTS

SITE 194 - METROLINK REGIONAL RAIL TRAINS

ADDRESS
Union Station
800 North Alameda Street
Los Angeles, CA 90012
(800) 371-5465
www.metrolinktrains.com

• Or see Sites 172 to 192 and page 258 for the location of other Southern California Metrolink train stations.

DIRECTIONS [GUIDE PAGE 634 (LA)]
Take Interstate Highway 110 to the Hill Street Exit and make a left on Ord Street. From there, make a right on Alameda Street to Union Station.

GOOD THINGS TO SEE AND HEAR
Metrolink is a long distance commuter service that operates five lines between Union Station and Oxnard, Lancaster, Oceanside, Riverside, and San Bernardino. A sixth route connects San Bernardino and Riverside with Orange County. Most of these lines only operate on weekdays. The San Bernardino Line operates Saturday and Sunday, and the Antelope Valley Line operates Saturday. These regional trains are real train size, very clean, have very large picture windows, and come and go frequently.

Go to your local Metrolink train station and purchase a round-trip ticket between two places that are not too far away (see the section "Real Train Rides Around Los Angeles" in this chapter). Tickets are purchased in a Ticket Vending Machine at the station and the honor system is used (e.g. the tickets are not collected but may be asked for by a conductor). Enjoy the ride.

The Coaster Regional Rail Train operates between Oceanside and San Diego; call (619) 685-4900 or visit www.gonctd.com/coaster/coasters.html for more information.

Use strollers or backpacks for safety around trains. For round trips, make sure return trains are available when you need them. Tickets are purchased in vending machines at the station; bring coins and $1.00 and $5.00 bills. All real trains are safest with two adults when traveling with small children. Avoid rush hour.

HOURS
Daily   6:00 a.m. - 11:00 p.m.
Non-commuter Times 8:30 a.m. - 3:30 p.m. and 7:00 p.m. - 8:00 p.m.

PARKING
$10   Rate for over 1¹/₂ hours at Union Station

ADMISSION TO RIDE
Roundtrip During Non-Commuter Times:
Adult $5.20
Child (Ages 6-18) $3.70
Under 6   Free*
* One Free Child Per Adult

YEARLY MEMBERSHIP
Ten trip tickets and monthly passes are available

RELATED PLACES
• Amtrak Trains - Site 193
• Fillmore and Western Railway - Site 203
• Metro Rail Red, Blue, Green, and Gold Lines - Site 195
• Other Train Stations-Chapter 10
• Real Train Rides Around Los Angeles- Chapter 10
• Union Station - Site 171 & 180

CLOSE-BY PLACES
• Chinatown - Site 30
• Grand Central Market - Site 31
• Local Fire Department-Chapter 2
• Richard J. Riordan Central Library - Site 16
• Olvera Street - Site 29

YOUR COMMENTS

_____
_____
_____
_____
_____

METROLINK LINES MAP

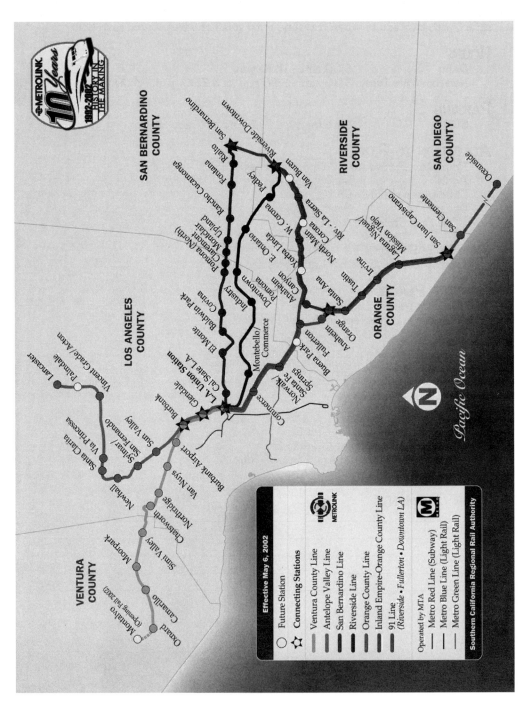

METROLINK STATIONS

SOUTHERN CALIFORNIA'S COMMUTER TRAIN SYSTEM

In 1991, Los Angeles, Orange, Riverside, San Bernardino and Ventura Counties formed the Southern California Regional Rail Authority to develop Metrolink, a regional commuter train system.

Today, Metrolink trains serve 51 stations in Southern California, carrying thousands of long-distance commuters to centers of employment such as Burbank, Glendale, Irvine and Downtown Los Angeles. Trains are also popular with group travelers, taking students on field trips and families to fun recreational destinations throughout the region.

For more information call (800) 371-LINK or visit www.metrolinktrains.com. Discover the Metrolink advantage!

LINES AND STATION LOCATIONS

SAN BERNARDINO LINE
Trains run from San Bernardino to Los Angeles, paralleling the San Bernardino Freeway (I-10). The 57-mile commute from San Bernardino to Los Angeles takes 1 hour and 25 minutes.

- **SAN BERNARDINO**
  1204 W. 3rd Street
- **RIALTO**
  261 S. Palm Avenue
- **FONTANA**
  16777 Orange Way
- **RANCHO CUCAMONGA**
  11208 Azusa Court
- **UPLAND**
  300 East A Street
- **MONTCLAIR**
  5091 Richton Street
- **CLAREMONT**
  200 W. 1st Street
- **POMONA (NORTH)**
  205 Santa Fe Street
- **COVINA**
  600 N. Citrus Avenue
- **BALDWIN PARK**
  3825 Downing Avenue
- **EL MONTE**
  10925 Railroad Street
- **CAL STATE L.A.**
  5150 State University Drive
- **L.A. UNION STATION**
  800 N. Alameda Street

ANTELOPE VALLEY LINE
Trains run from Lancaster to Los Angeles, paralleling the Antelope Valley Freeway (State Route 14) and Golden State Freeway (I-5). The 76-mile trip takes 1 hour and 40 minutes.

- **LANCASTER**
  44812 N. Sierra Highway
- **VINCENT GRADE/ACTON**
  730 W. Sierra Highway
- **VIA PRINCESSA**
  19201 Via Princessa
- **SANTA CLARITA**
  22122 Soledad Canyon Road
- **NEWHALL**
  24300 Railroad Ave
- **SYLMAR / SAN FERNANDO**
  12219 Frank Modugno Drive
- **SUN VALLEY**
  8360 San Fernando Road
- **BURBANK**
  201 N. Front Street
- **GLENDALE**
  400 W. Cerritos Avenue
- **L.A. UNION STATION**
  800 N. Alameda Street

RIVERSIDE LINE
Trains run from Riverside to Los Angeles, paralleling the Pomona Freeway (60). The 59-mile trip takes 1 hour and 15 minutes.

- **RIVERSIDE - DOWNTOWN**
  4066 Vine Street
- **PEDLEY**
  6001 Pedley Road
- **EAST ONTARIO**
  3330 E. Francis Street
- **DOWNTOWN POMONA**
  101 W. 1st Street
- **INDUSTRY**
  600 S. Brea Canyon Road
- **MONTEBELLO / COMMERCE**
  2000 Flotilla Street
- **L.A. UNION STATION**
  800 N. Alameda Street

VENTURA COUNTY LINE
Trains run from Oxnard to Los Angeles, paralleling the Ventura Freeway (101) and the Simi Valley Freeway (118). The 66-mile trip takes 1 hour and 30 minutes.

- **OXNARD**
  201 East 4th Street
- **CAMARILLO**
  30 Lewis Road
- **MOORPARK**
  300 High Street
- **SIMI VALLEY**
  5050 Los Angeles Avenue
- **CHATSWORTH**
  10046 Old Depot Plaza Road
- **NORTHRIDGE**
  8775 Wilbur Avenue
- **VAN NUYS**
  7720 Van Nuys Boulevard
- **BURBANK AIRPORT**
  3750 Empire Avenue
- **BURBANK**
  201 N. Front Street
- **GLENDALE**
  400 W. Cerritos Avenue
- **L.A. UNION STATION**
  800 N. Alameda Street

ORANGE COUNTY LINE
Trains run from Oceanside to Los Angeles, paralleling the Santa Ana Freeway (I-5). The 87-mile trip takes 1 hour and 45 minutes.

- **OCEANSIDE**
  235 S. Tremont Street
- **SAN CLEMENTE**
  1850 Avenida Estacion
- **SAN JUAN CAPISTRANO**
  26701 Verdugo Street
- **LAGUNA NIGUEL/MISSION VIEJO**
  28200 Forbes Road
- **IRVINE**
  15215 Barranca Parkway
- **TUSTIN**
  2975 Edinger Avenue
- **SANTA ANA**
  1000 E. Santa Ana Boulevard
- **ORANGE**
  194 N. Atchison Street
- **ANAHEIM**
  2150 E. Katella Avenue
- **FULLERTON**
  120 E. Santa Fe Avenue
- **NORWALK / SANTA FE SPRINGS**
  12700 Imperial Highway
- **COMMERCE**
  6433 26th Street
- **L.A. UNION STATION**
  800 N. Alameda Street

INLAND EMPIRE - ORANGE COUNTY LINE
Trains run from San Bernardino to San Juan Capistrano, paralleling the Riverside Freeway (91), the Costa Mesa Freeway (55) and the Santa Ana Freeway (I-5). The 59-mile trip takes 1 hour and 35 minutes.

- **SAN BERNARDINO**
  1204 W. 3rd Street
- **RIVERSIDE - DOWNTOWN**
  4066 Vine Street
- **RIVERSIDE - LA SIERRA**
  10901 Indiana Avenue
- **WEST CORONA**
  155 S. Auto Center Drive
- **ANAHEIM CANYON**
  1039 Pacificenter Drive
- **ORANGE**
  194 N. Atchison Street
- **SANTA ANA**
  1000 E. Santa Ana Boulevard
- **TUSTIN**
  2975 Edinger Avenue
- **IRVINE**
  15215 Barranca Parkway
- **LAGUNA NIGUEL/MISSION VIEJO**
  28200 Forbes Road
- **SAN JUAN CAPISTRANO**
  26701 Verdugo Street

91 LINE (RIVERSIDE • FULLERTON • DOWNTOWN LA)
The 60-mile line connects the commuters from Riverside to Los Angeles via Fullerton, paralleling the Riverside Freeway (91) and the Santa Ana Freeway (I-5). Travel time to L.A. is 1 hour and 30 minutes.

- **RIVERSIDE - DOWNTOWN**
  4066 Vine Street
- **RIVERSIDE - LA SIERRA**
  10901 Indiana Avenue
- **WEST CORONA**
  155 S. Auto Center Drive
- **FULLERTON**
  120 E. Santa Fe Avenue
- **NORWALK / SANTA FE SPRINGS**
  12700 Imperial Highway
- **COMMERCE**
  6433 26th Street
- **L.A. UNION STATION**
  800 N. Alameda Street

METROLINK

For more information on Metrolink call (800) 371-LINK, or (800) 698-4TDD for speech & hearing impaired customers, or visit www.metrolinktrains.com.

SITE 195 - METRO RAIL RED, BLUE, GREEN, AND GOLD LINES

ADDRESS
Los Angeles Metropolitan Transportation Authority
One Gateway Plaza
Los Angeles, CA 90012
(800) 266-6883
www.mta.net

• or see Metro Rail map on page 264 for locations of other Metro Rail Stations.

DIRECTIONS [GUIDE PAGE 634 (LA)]
Take Interstate Highway 110 to the Hill Street Exit and make a left on Ord Street. From there, make a right on Alameda Street to Union Station.

GOOD THINGS TO SEE AND HEAR
Metro Rail is a city rail system that includes both street level and subway trains, and operates in the Los Angeles area. The Blue, Green, and Gold Lines are light rails. The Blue Line runs north and south. The Green Line runs east and west. The Gold Line runs northeast from Union Station to Pasadena. The Red Line is Los Angeles' subway and is the only one that leaves from Union Station. The trains are connected at Transit Stations. Look for public art at each station. Trains run every six to fifteen minutes.

Blue Line (Street Level):
  • Downtown Los Angeles to Long Beach
  • Connects with Red Line at the 7th Street Transit Station and Green Line at the Imperial/Wilmington Station
Red Line (Subway):
  • Union Station to Wilshire/Western Station
  • Connects with Blue Line at the 7th Street Transit Station and Gold Line at Union Station
Green Line (Elevated):
  • Norwalk to Los Angeles Airport area and Redondo Beach
  • Connects with Blue Line at the Imperial/Wilmington Station
Gold Line (Street Level):
  • Union Station to Pasadena
  • Connects with Red Line at Union Station

Use strollers or backpacks for safety around trains. For round trips, make sure return trains are available when you need them. Tickets are purchased in vending machines at the station; bring coins and $1.00 and $5.00 bills. All real trains are safest with two adults when traveling with small children. Avoid rush hour.

The Gold Line is being extended eastward from Pasadena. Look for opportunities to watch the construction.

HOURS
Daily   5:00 a.m. - 11:00 p.m.
• Six to fifteen minute wait between trains depending on time of day.

PARKING

$8   Rate for over 1½ hours at Union Station
      Less or free at other stations

ADMISSION

Adult or Child $1.35 Oneway
Under 5   Free (Two Per Adult)
Transfer $0.25
Cash Accepted   Coins, $1.00 and $5.00 Bills Only

YEARLY MEMBERSHIP

Weekly Pass $11.00
Monthly Pass $42.00

RELATED PLACES

• Amtrak Trains - Site 193
• Fillmore and Western Railway - Site 203
• Metrolink Regional Rail Trains - Site 194
• Other Train Stations-Chapter 10
• Real Train Rides Around Los Angeles-Chapter 10
• Union Station - Site 171 & 180

CLOSE-BY PLACES

• Chinatown - Site 30
• Grand Central Market - Site 31
• Local Fire Department-Chapter 2
• Richard J. Riordan Central Library - Site 16
• Olvera Street - Site 29

YOUR COMMENTS

_____
_____
_____
_____
_____

REAL TRAIN RIDES AROUND LOS ANGELES

Take a ride on a real train. There are interesting places to go on Amtrak - Site 193, Metrolink - Site 194, or Metro Rail - Site 195 Trains. On Amtrak, be sure to find the Sight Seer Lounge and encourage your children to watch for the rail yards, train stations, and shipping yards (talk them through the journey of a freight box from manufacturer to train to ship to train to store). Remember that most Metrolink trains only operate on weekdays (see Site 194). Here are some suggestions:

The California Strawberry Festival (Site 55)
• Amtrak from your local station to Oxnard Station, free shuttle bus

Chinatown (Site 30)
• Metrolink from your local station to Union Station
• Metro Rail Gold Line to Chinatown Station
• Or Metro Rail Gold Line from Pasadena to Chinatown Station

Kidspace Museum (Site 4)
• Metro Rail Gold Line to Del Mar Station

Long Beach Aquarium of the Pacific (Site 71)
• Metro Rail Blue Line to 1st Street and Pine Station (one stop beyond 1st Street)
• Note: It is a very long ride - one hour - through Los Angeles from Union Station to the aquarium with twenty stops along the Blue Line route. Start closer to the end of the line.
• Long Beach Passport Shuttle to the aquarium

Los Angeles County Fair (Site 106)
• Metrolink (San Bernardino Line) to Pomona Station

Olvera Street (Site 29)
• Metrolink from your local station to Union Station

Richard J. Riordan Central Library (Site 16)
• Metrolink from your local station to Union Station
• Metro Rail Red Line to Pershing Square Station
• Exit onto 5th Street

San Clemente Beach (Summer Only) (Site 144)
• Amtrak from your local Amtrak station to San Clemente Beach
• Or Metrolink Beach Train from your local station to San Clemente Beach (909) 787-7938
www.takethebeachtrain.com
• Adult $15.00, Child (Ages 2-15) $10.00, and Children (Ages Under 2) Free

San Diego
• Amtrak (Pacific Surfliner) to San Diego Station
• The duration is about two hours and forty-five minutes

Santa Barbara
• Amtrak (Pacific Surfliner) to Santa Barbara Station
• The duration is about three hours and thirty minutes

Staples Center (Site 217) and Los Angeles Convention Center (Site 215)
• Metrolink from your local station to Union Station
• Metro Rail Red Line to 7th Street Transfer Station
• Metro Rail Blue Line to Pico Station

Through Freight Train Yards (Site 196)
• Metrolink (Riverside Line) from Union Station to Montebello/Commerce Station and back
• Or Metrolink (Orange County Line or 91 Line) from Union Station to Commerce Station and back
• Or Metrolink from Commerce Station to Union Station and back

Tournament of Roses Parade® (Site 216)
• Metro Rail Gold Line to Lake, Allen, or Sierra Madre Villa Stations

Ventura County Fair (Site 111)
• Amtrak from your local station to Ventura Station
• Or Metrolink (Ventura County Line) from your local station to Seaside Park (special service available during fair time)

Zoomars Petting Farm (Site 98 and San Juan Capistrano Station (Site 186)
• Metrolink from your local station to Union Station
• Amtrak to San Juan Capistrano Station
• Or Metrolink from your local station to San Juan Capistrano Station

YOUR COMMENTS

_____

_____

_____

_____

_____

METRO RAIL LINES MAP

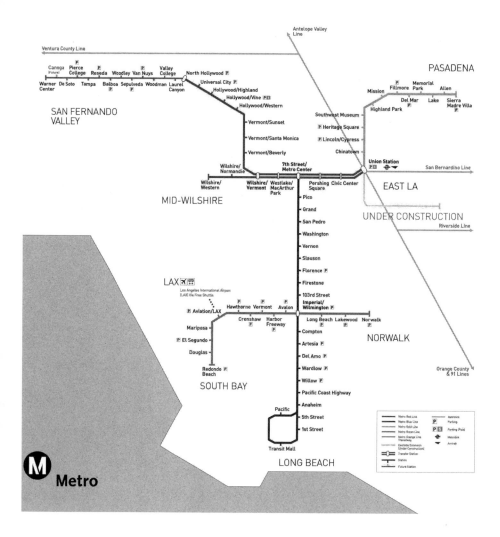

LOCAL TRANSIT CONNECTIONS

To take a bus between the train station and your destination, here are a few numbers:

- *DASH (Downtown Los Angeles)*
  (213) 808-2273
  www.ladottransit.com/dash/routes/downtown/downtown.html

- *Foothill Transit (San Gabriel/Pomona Valleys)*
  (800) 743-3463
  www.foothilltransit.org/

- *Glendale Beeline (Glendale)*
  (818) 548-3960
  www.glendale-online.com/transportation/beeline/

- *Laguna Beach Transit (Laguna Beach)*
  (949) 497-0746
  www.lagunabeachcity.net/government/departments/publicworks/
  services/transit.htm

- *Long Beach Transit (Long Beach)*
  (562) 591-2301
  www.lbtransit.com/

- *Los Angeles County Metropolitan Transportation Authority*
  (800) COMMUTE
  www.mta.net/

- *Moorpark City Bus*
  (805) 517-6257
  www.ci.moorpark.ca.us/rideguide.htm

- *Orange County Transportation Authority*
  (714) 636-7433
  www.octa.net/

- *San Diego Transit*
  (619) 233-3004
  www.sdcommute.com/

- *Santa Barbara Metro Transit*
  (805) 683-3702
  www.sbmtd.gov/

YOUR COMMENTS

_____

_____

_____

_____

_____

SITE 196 - FREIGHT TRAINS

ADDRESS
26th Street and Garfield Avenue
City of Commerce, CA 90040
(323) 722-4805
www.uprr.com (Union Pacific Railway)
www.bnsf.com (Burlington Northern-Santa Fe Railway)
www.acta.org (Alameda Corridor Transportation Authority)

DIRECTIONS [GUIDE PAGE 676 (LA)]
• Take Interstate Highway 5 north or south to the Garfield Avenue Exit and go south to 26th Street (right next to freeway). From there, turn right. Follow along the fence to watch trains from your car, or go to the end of the street to Metrolink Station and park.
• Or take the train (see "Real Train Rides Around Los Angeles in this Chapter)

GOOD THINGS TO SEE AND HEAR
Union Pacific (UP RR) and Burlington Northern-Santa Fe (BNSF) railways transport goods to and from the ports of Long Beach and Los Angeles. Freight trains are concentrated in the Union Pacific (UP RR) and Burlington Northern-Santa Fe (BNSF RR) Railroad Yards in the City of Commerce - you can see them from the Interstate Highway 710. There is a Metrolink Station (Commerce) at 26th and Garfield Avenue-one of many good locations to watch and listen to the freight trains in Los Angeles, (recommended by the City of Commerce). You can see about eight parallel tracks, many of which have trains that are waiting to go - tank cars, box cars, hoppers, and engines. Freight trains, Metrolink, and Amtrak trains all pass this location. It is also a good place to watch airplanes from LAX in the sky. Watch from your car (roll down the windows to hear the trains), sit behind the fence at the Metrolink stop, or take Metrolink to Union Station and back (see "Real Train Rides Around Los Angeles in this Chapter).

Freight trains also run north/south from east Los Angeles to the ports of Long Beach and Los Angeles along the Alameda Corridor. This corridor runs along Alameda Street through Vernon and Huntington Park [**Guide Page 674**]; Walnut Park, Southgate, and Lynwood [**Guide Page 704**]; Compton [**Guide Page 734/735**]; Rancho Dominguez and Carson [**Guide Page 765/764**] and Wilmington [**Guide Page 794**] where the tracks split to the two shipping ports [**Guide Page 824/825**]. From State Highway 91 in Compton south for ten miles, the Alameda Corridor ducks into the Mid-Corridor Trench where the tracks run in a thirty-three-foot deep trench. Another good place to look for freight trains is in the Simi Valley, Moorpark, Camarillo, or Oxnard Stations (Sites 189, 181, 174, 183) as all north/south bound freight trains must travel along these tracks.

Trains go VERY fast and the tracks are right there. Be sure your child is restrained and watch the trains from a very safe distance behind the yellow line, or better yet, behind the fence. Avoid the temptation to put pennies on the track.

HOURS
All

PARKING
Free

ADMISSION
Free

RELATED PLACES
• Other Train Stations-Chapter 10
• Travel Town Museum - Site 170

CLOSE-BY PLACES
• El Monte Airport - Site 153
• Montebello Barnyard Zoo - Site 103
• Whittier Narrows Nature Center - Site 46

YOUR COMMENTS

_____

_____

_____

_____

_____

SITE 197 - LOMITA RAILROAD MUSEUM

ADDRESS
2137 West 250th Street
Lomita, CA 90717
(310) 326-6255
www.lomita-rr.org

DIRECTIONS [GUIDE PAGE 793 (LA)]
• Take Interstate Highway 110 to Pacific Coast Highway 1 west. From there, go north on Narbonne Avenue and make a right on 250th Street. The museum is on the left.

GOOD THINGS TO SEE AND HEAR
Dedicated to the era of the steam engine, the Lomita Railroad Museum is in a station that is a copy of Boston and Maine's Greenwood Station, which was built before the turn-of-the-century. On display are a Southern Pacific Railroad steam locomotive, a "whaleback" tender, a 1910 Union Pacific Railroad caboose (or "bobber"), and a modern all-steel Santa Fe caboose - all of which may be climbed on. Across the street is a small park that is part of the museum. On display are a 1923 Union Oil tank car and a 1931 Union Pacific wood box car.

The museum is small and has many "do not touch" signs. It is a very nice little museum if you are already in the area.

HOURS
Wednesday-Sunday 10:00 a.m. - 5:00 p.m.

PARKING
Free

ADMISSION
Adult $4.00

Child (under 12) $2.00

RELATED PLACES
• Fillmore and Western Railway - Site 203

• Freight Trains - Site 196

• Travel Town Museum - Site 170

CLOSE-BY PLACES
• Goodyear Blimp Airfield - Site 168

• Santa Ana Train Station - Site 187

• South Coast Botanical Gardens - Site 40

• Torrance Municipal Airport/Zamperini Field - Site 162

YOUR COMMENTS

_____

_____

_____

_____

_____

SITE 198 - GRIFFITH PARK TRAIN RIDE

ADDRESS
Griffith Park

Crystal Springs Drive

Los Angeles, CA 90027

(323) 664-6788

www.lacity.org/RAP/dos/parks/griffithPK/sorailroad.htm

DIRECTIONS [GUIDE PAGE 564 (LA)]
• Take State Highway 134 west to the Zoo Drive Exit. Make a left on Crystal Springs Drive. The train is on your left next to ponies.

• Take State Highway 134 east to the Victory Boulevard Exit. Turn right at top of the offramp. Make a left on Zoo Drive and follow the road onto Crystal Springs Drive. The train is on your left next to ponies.

GOOD THINGS TO SEE AND HEAR
The Griffith Park Train is a children's train that you can ride. It is one of the best train routes in Los Angeles because you can see Snow White and the Seven Dwarfs, cross a rickety red bridge, and pass through an old Western town.

Plan to ride several times. The Griffith Park Pony Rides (Site 95) are essentially at the same location.

HOURS
Monday-Friday	10:00 a.m. - 4:30 p.m.
Saturday-Sunday	10:00 a.m. - 5:00 p.m.

PARKING
Free

ADMISSION
Adult	$2.00
Child	$1.50
Under 18 months	Free

RELATED PLACES
- Travel Town Museum - Site 170
- El Dorado East Regional Park Train Ride - Site 199
- Irvine Park Railroad - Site 200
- Fillmore and Western Railway - Site 203
- Disneyland - Site 112
- Adventure City - Site 113
- Santa Ana Zoo - Site 64
- Santa Barbara Zoological Gardens - Site 70
- Descanso Gardens - Site 38

CLOSE-BY PLACES
- Glendale Train Station - Site 178
- Griffith Observatory - Site 9
- Griffith Park Merry-Go-Round - Site 115
- Griffith Park Pony Rides - Site 95
- Los Angeles Zoo - Site 63
- Travel Town Museum - Site 170

YOUR COMMENTS

SITE 199 - EL DORADO EAST REGIONAL PARK TRAIN RIDE

ADDRESS
7550 East Spring Street
Long Beach, CA 90815
(562) 570-1771 Park
(562) 496-4228 Train
www.longbeach.gov/park/facilities/parks/el_dorado_regional_park.asp

DIRECTIONS [GUIDE PAGE 766/796 (LA)]
Take Interstate Highway 605 to the Spring Street/Cerritos Exit and go west to the park entrance.

GOOD THINGS TO SEE AND HEAR
The El Dorado East Regional Park Train Ride is a children's train ride. Notice the statue of Ferdinand the Bull.

El Dorado Park has several sections - ask for a map when you enter the park. El Dorado East Regional Park is north of Spring Street and east of the San Gabriel River and has lakes and the train. To the south of Spring Street is the one hundred-acre El Dorado Nature Center (Site 51).

HOURS
Park:
Daily   7:00 a.m. - Dusk
Train: Hours Vary-Call Ahead

PARKING
Weekdays $3.00 Per Vehicle
Weekends $5.00 Per Vehicle

ADMISSION
Train $2.00

YEARLY MEMBERSHIP
Annual Vehicle Pass $35.00

RELATED PLACES
• Adventure City - Site 113
• Descanso Gardens - Site 38
• Disneyland - Site 112
• Fillmore and Western Railway - Site 203
• Griffith Park Train Ride - Site 198
• Irvine Park Railroad - Site 200
• Santa Ana Zoo - Site 64
• Santa Barbara Zoological Gardens - Site 70
• Travel Town Museum - Site 170

CLOSE-BY PLACES
• California State University Long Beach, CSULB - Site 61
• Cerritos Library - Site 17
• El Dorado East Regional Park and Nature Center - Site 50
• Lakewood Pony Rides and Petting Farm - Site 104
• Long Beach Airport - Site 157
• Norwalk School Bus Yard - Site 26

BOOKS
• Lawson, Robert and Munro Leaf-Ferdinand the Bull

YOUR COMMENTS

SITE 200 - IRVINE PARK RAILROAD

ADDRESS
Irvine Regional Park
1 Irvine Park Road
Orange, CA 92862
(714) 973-6835 Park
(714) 997-3968 Train
www.irvineparkrr.com

DIRECTIONS [GUIDE PAGE 800/801 (OC)]
Take Interstate Highway 5 to the Jamboree Road Exit and go north. Jamboree Road ends at Irvine Regional Park.

GOOD THINGS TO SEE AND HEAR
The Irvine Park children's train goes around the Irvine Regional Park (Site 49). The train depot is old-fashioned.

The Irvine Park Railroad is in a large regional park that includes the Orange County Zoo - Site 65, Pony Rides - Site 102 and a Nature Center - Site 49. You may want to combine your train ride with a pony ride, a trip to the nature center, or a picnic.

HOURS
Park:
Summer:
Daily   7:00 a.m. - 9:00 p.m.
Winter:
Daily   7:00 a.m. - 6:00 p.m.
Train:
Daily   10:00 a.m. - 4:00 p.m.

PARKING
Park Entrance:
Weekdays $3.00
Weekends $5.00

ADMISSION
All $3.00

RELATED PLACES
- Adventure City - Site 113
- Descanso Gardens - Site 38
- Disneyland - Site 112
- El Dorado East Regional Park Train Ride - Site 199
- Fillmore and Western Railway - Site 203
- Griffith Park Train Ride - Site 198
- Santa Ana Zoo - Site 64
- Santa Barbara Zoological Gardens - Site 70
- Travel Town Museum - Site 170

CLOSE-BY PLACES
- Green Meadows Farm/Orange County - Site 91
- Irvine Regional Park and Nature Center - Site 49
- Irvine Regional Park Pony Rides - Site 102
- Orange County Zoo - Site 65

YOUR COMMENTS

SITE 201 - PASADENA MODEL RAILROAD CLUB

ADDRESS
5458 Alhambra Avenue
Los Angeles, CA 90032
(323) 222-1718
www.pmRRc.org/

DIRECTIONS [GUIDE PAGE 595 (LA)]
Take Interstate Highway 210 to the Fair Oaks Avenue Exit and go south. Make a right on Huntington Drive and then a left on Fremont Avenue. From there make a right on Mission Road. Mission Road becomes Alhambra Avenue. The Club is on the left just past Warwick. Park behind the club if no parking is available on Alhambra Avenue.

GOOD THINGS TO SEE AND HEAR
The Pasadena Model Railroad Club operates the Sierra Pacific Lines, one of the largest HO scale operating model railroads in the world covering almost five thousand square feet. The railroad has over thirty thousand feet of hand-laid steel rail and can operate up to ten trains with up to sixty cars each. Trains include steam diesels, modern and old freight trains, classic passenger trains, and Amtrak. The layout includes breathtaking scenery and operating signals. Thirty operators are required to run the full layout.

The train layout is in the center of the room and visitors can walk around the entire extent and view through windows. Be prepared to carry your child for a long time. I do not recommend visiting the club at night alone with your children.

HOURS
Second Tuesday	7:30 p.m. - 10:00 p.m.
Second Saturday	1:00 p.m. - 5:00 p.m.
	7:00 p.m. - 10:00 p.m.

PARKING
Free

ADMISSION
Adult	$3.00
Child	$1.00
Under 10	Free

YEARLY MEMBERSHIP
Adult	$20.00

RELATED PLACES
• Children's Museum at La Habra - Site 2
• San Diego Model Railroad Museum - Site 202
• Travel Town Museum - Site 170

CLOSE-BY PLACES
• Green Meadows Farm/Los Angeles County - Site 90

SPECIAL EVENTS
Spring Open House	April or May
Fall Open House	October or November

YOUR COMMENTS
_____
_____
_____
_____
_____

OTHER MODEL RAILROAD CLUBS
There are a lot of model railroad clubs in Southern California - most can be visited during certain hours each month. Try this website for the latest:
• www.cwrr.com/nmra/Cluba-AE.html#CA

SITE 202 - SAN DIEGO MODEL RAILROAD MUSEUM

ADDRESS
Balboa Park
1649 El Prado
San Diego, CA 92101
(619) 696-0199
www.sdmodelrailroadm.com

DIRECTIONS [GUIDE PAGE 1289 (SD)]
Take Interstate Highway 5 to the Park Boulevard Exit and go north. Turn left at Space Theater Way. The museum is in the basement of Casa de Balboa.

GOOD THINGS TO SEE AND HEAR
The San Diego Model Railroad Museum is the world's largest operating model railroad museum with five enormous scale model layouts depicting railroads of the southwest in O, HO, and N scales. The museum also features a Toy Train Gallery with interactive O gauge and O-27 gauge "Lionel" style toy trains, and, of course, a Brio set.

This is a great side trip if you are visiting the San Diego Zoo (Site 68) or Sea World (Site 87).

HOURS
Tuesday-Friday	11:00 a.m. - 4:00 p.m.
Saturday-Sunday	11:00 a.m. - 5:00 p.m.

PARKING
Free

ADMISSION
Adult	$5.00
Under 15	Free

YEARLY MEMBERSHIP
Adult or Child	$20.00
Family	$30.00

RELATED PLACES
• Travel Town Museum - Site 170
• Children's Museum at La Habra - Site 2

CLOSE-BY PLACES
• Balboa Park Merry-Go-Round and Butterfly Rides - Site 121
• Belmont Park Carousel - Site 119
• The Children's Museum of San Diego/Museo de los Niños - Site 12
• San Diego Zoo - Site 68
• Sea World - Site 87
• Seaport Village Carousel - Site 120
• San Diego Train Station - Site 185
• San Diego Convention Center - Site 214

YOUR COMMENTS

_____

_____

_____

_____

_____

SITE 203 - FILLMORE AND WESTERN RAILWAY

ADDRESS
250 Central Avenue
Fillmore, CA 93016
(805) 524-2546
www.fwry.com

DIRECTIONS [GUIDE PAGE 456 (SB/V)]
Take Interstate Highway 5 north to State Highway 126 west. Take the Central Avenue Exit and go north.

GOOD THINGS TO SEE AND HEAR
The Fillmore and Western Railway runs a full-size vintage train that regularly travels from Fillmore to Santa Paula and back (two and one-half hours round trip total). In October, a special train, the Pumpkinliner, is available that travels from Fillmore to a nearby pumpkin patch where you can pick your own pumpkin. The trip is only about fifteen minutes one-way, and an hour at the pumpkin patch is more than adequate. In December, the Christmas Tree Train stops at a tree farm where you can cut your own tree and bring it back on the train. The North Pole Express travels in the evening, includes a story time and carolers, and takes Santa to the North Pole. Try the shorter holiday trips. Enjoy the sounds of the train wheels on the tracks, the train whistle, and the bells at the street intersections. Feel the rumbling of the train's wheels. Walk through the train as it is moving to see the different cars. Sometimes special trains visit the Fillmore and Western Railway station including Thomas the Tank Engine and the Little Engine That Could.

The drive along State Highway 126 offers lots of orchards and crops, and, of course, farm stands.

If you take the long train ride to Santa Paula, bring an activity with you, as if you were going on a long car trip. The windows are open; so be careful with children because they can easily fall through. Also bring sun block.

HOURS
Saturday   12:00 p.m.
Sunday   12:00 p.m.
• Times for Holiday Trains Vary

PARKING
Free

ADMISSION
Adult $20.00
Child (Ages 4-12) $10.00
Under 4 $6.00
• Prices for Holiday Trains Vary

RELATED PLACES
• Travel Town Museum - Site 170
• Union Station - Site 171
• Other Train Stations-Chapter 10
• Amtrak Trains - Site 193
• Metrolink Regional Rail Trains - Site 194
• Real Train Rides Around Los Angeles-Chapter 10

CLOSE-BY PLACES
• America's Teaching Zoo at Moorpark College - Site 66
• Moorpark Train Station - Site 181
• Underwood Family Farms - Site 99

SPECIAL EVENTS
The Pumpkinliner   October Weekends
Christmas Tree Trains   December Weekends

YOUR COMMENTS

_____
_____
_____
_____

Puppetolio's Puppets and puppeteer Steve Meltzer.
Photo courtesy of Steve Meltzer.

CHAPTER 11 - ENTERTAINMENT

Music helps to develop math skills when children listen to the rhythms and the beats, and language skills when children hear the rhymes and the words of songs. There are many ways to introduce your child to different kinds of music, from summer concerts in the park to big shows at the Hollywood Bowl. In addition to the places listed, you may know of a coffee house that often has music, or may run across someone playing a guitar at the farmer's market. All of these experiences help your child to enjoy and learn from music.

For seating locations at various venues, check the website or the front of your Yellow Pages phone book (usually blue pages titled "Theater and Stadium Seating") for seating charts.

BOOKS FOR YOUR CHILD
- Emerson, Sally, Moira MacLean, Colin MacLean-*The Kingfisher Nursery Rhyme Songbook: With Easy Music to Play for Piano and Guitar*
- Kapp, Richard-*Metropolitan Museum of Art's Lullabies: An Illustrated Songbook*
- Orozco, Jose-Luis-*De Colores and Other Latin American Folk Songs for Children*

SITE 204 – BOB BAKER MARIONETTE THEATER

ADDRESS
1345 West First Street
Los Angeles, CA 90026
(213) 250-9995
www.bobbakermarionettes.com

DIRECTIONS [GUIDE PAGE 634 (LA)]
Take Interstate Highway 110 to the 6th Street Exit and go east. Make a left on Figueroa Street, and then a left on 1st Street.

GOOD THINGS TO SEE AND HEAR
The Bob Baker Marionette Theater is a large, open, carpeted theater so children can run around before the show, and sit on the floor during the show. Many beautifully crafted marionettes participate in the show and interact with the children in the first row. The show is unique, creative, and enchanting for all ages.

Bring a snack or drink for entertainment in the middle of the show in case your child gets fidgety. Ice cream is provided after the show in a wildly decorated room.

HOURS
Tuesday-Friday   10:30 a.m.
Saturday   10:30 a.m. & 2:30 p.m.
Sunday   2:30 p.m.
• Reservations Required

PARKING
Free

ADMISSION
Adult or Child $10.00
Under 2   Free
• Includes Refreshments
• Reservations Required

RELATED PLACES
• Other Children's Theaters–Chapter 11

CLOSE-BY PLACES
• Chinatown - Site 30
• Grand Central Market - Site 31
• KLOS Story Theater - Site 206
• Olvera Street - Site 29
• Richard J. Riordan Central Library - Site 16
• Union Station - Site 171
• Walt Disney Music Concert Hall - Site 221

SPECIAL EVENTS
• Christmas Show   Call for Dates

OTHER CHILDREN'S THEATERS

Most theaters suggest shows that are for children ages three and up so judge for yourself if your toddler is ready. Current shows are listed in the *Los Angeles Times* Calendar Weekend and parenting magazines (see section "More Information on Upcoming Events" in Chapter 13). The theaters listed below are good places to start. Call for information on specific shows.

SITE 205 - FALCON THEATER

4252 Riverside Drive
Burbank, CA 91505
(818) 955-8101
www.falcontheater.com

[GUIDE PAGE 563 (LA)]

• Take State Highway 134 to the Hollywood Way Exit. Make a left at Alameda which becomes Riverside Drive. The theater is on the left. Park in the back.
• The Falcon Theater has plays for small children that are presented periodically. The shows change frequently so call to find shows that are appropriate for toddlers.

SITE 206 - KLOS STORY THEATER

Los Angeles Central Library
630 west 5th Street
Los Angeles, CA 90071
(213) 228-7250
www.lapl.org/kidspath/events/calendar/

[GUIDE PAGE 634 (LA)]

• Take Interstate Highway 110 to the 6th Street Exit. Go east on 6th. From there, make a left on Grand Avenue, and then a left on 5th Street.
• There is a storytime and a puppet show at various times during the week.

SITE 207 - SANTA MONICA PUPPETRY CENTER

1255 2nd. Street
Santa Monica, CA 90401
(310) 656-0483
www.puppetmagic.com

[GUIDE PAGE 67 (LA)]

• Take Interstate Highway 10 to the 4th Street Exit and go northwest (right). Make a left on Colorado Avenue, and then a right on 2nd Street. Park in the lot.
• Puppetolio and other puppet shows are presented in a small theater. There is a museum with hundreds of beautiful puppets and a store. The puppet show is recommended for children age three years and up.

YOUR COMMENTS

_____

_____

_____

_____

SITE 208 - IMAX THEATER AT THE CALIFORNIA SCIENCE CENTER

ADDRESS
Exposition Park
700 State Drive
Los Angeles, CA 90037
(213) 744-2014
www.casciencectr.org

DIRECTIONS [GUIDE PAGE 674 (LA)]
• Take Interstate Highway 110 south to the Exposition Boulevard Exit. Make a left on Flower Street (first light), and park on right.
• Take Interstate Highway 110 north to the Martin Luther King Jr. Boulevard Exit and go left. Make a right on Flower Street, and park on left.

GOOD THINGS TO SEE AND HEAR
The IMAX theater screen is seven stories high and ninety feet wide. The audience is immersed in the movie. Animals appear life-size. The 2-D movies with animal themes that are favorites for babies and toddlers - look for movies about whales and sharks, African animals, and Alaskan animals. Although some of the movies have loud sounds (like the Space Shuttle blast-offs), none of the movies are scary or inappropriate for small children.

Avoid 3-D movies for children under three. Movies are only thirty to forty minutes, but sit near an easy escape and bring a snack.

HOURS
Daily   10:00 a.m. - 8:00 p.m.
• Call or Check Website for Show Times

PARKING
$6.00

ADMISSION
Adult $8.00
Child (Ages 4-12) $4.75
Under 4   Free

RELATED PLACES
• Bob Baker Marionette Theater - Site 204
• Ringling Bros. and Barnum & Bailey Circus - Site 217
• Summer Sounds at the Hollywood Bowl - Site 219

CLOSE-BY PLACES
• Natural History Museum of Los Angeles County - Site 1
• Exposition Park Rose Garden - Site 41
• Los Angeles Memorial Sports Arena - Site 213
• University of Southern California, USC - Site 57

YOUR COMMENTS

_____

_____

_____

_____

_____

_____

SITE 209 - LOS ANGELES CONVENTION CENTER

ADDRESS
1201 South Figueroa Street
Los Angeles, CA 9082
(213) 741-1151 Convention Center
(310) 444-1850 Auto Show
lacclink.com/

DIRECTIONS [GUIDE PAGE 634 (LA)]
• Take Interstate Highway 110 north to the 9th Street Exit and go east. Make a right on Figueroa Street, and then a right on 11th Street.
• Or take Interstate Highway 110 south to the Olympic Boulevard Exit. Make a left at bottom of offramp onto Blaine Street. Make a left on 11th Street.
• Or take the Metro Rail Blue Line - Site 195.

GOOD THINGS TO SEE AND HEAR
The Los Angeles Convention Center hosts big shows that are fun for babies and toddlers-especially the Auto Show (www.laautoshow.com/) and the Boat Show (www.scma.com/show_info.htm). The shiny new cars and colorful boats are fascinating. Also try Yeah Baby! Family Expo-a show about babies (www.yeahbabyexpo.com), or a dog show. Depending on your personal interest, try others. There is an Events Schedule on each convention center's website.

Depending on when you go, shows can be crowded so try a backpack rather than a stroller. Gather the brochures from the Auto Show - they make great books.

HOURS
Call or Check Website for Show Times

PARKING
$7.00

ADMISSION
Varies with show. Usually children are free with a paying adult.

RELATED PLACES
• Petersen Automotive Museum - Site 5
• Convention Centers and Sports Arenas-Chapter 11

CLOSE-BY PLACES
- Natural History Museum of Los Angeles County - Site 1
- IMAX Theater at the California Science Center - Site 208
- Exposition Park Rose Garden - Site 41

OTHER CONVENTION CENTERS AND SPORTS ARENAS

SITE 210 - ANAHEIM CONVENTION CENTER

800 West Katella Avenue
Anaheim, CA 92802
(714) 765-8950
www.anaheimconventioncenter.com
[GUIDE PAGE 799 (OC)]
- Take Interstate Highway 5 to the Katella Avenue Avenue and go west.

SITE 211 - ARROWHEAD POND OF ANAHEIM

2695 East Katella Avenue
Anaheim, CA 92806
(714) 704-2400
www.arrowheadpond.com
[GUIDE PAGE 799 (OC)]
- Take Interstate Highway 5 to the Katella Avenue Exit and go east.

SITE 212 - LONG BEACH CONVENTION CENTER

300 East Ocean Boulevard
Long Beach, CA 90802
(562) 436-3636
www.longbeachcc.com/
[GUIDE PAGE 825 (LA)]
- Take Interstate Highway 710 and follow south to its end. The freeway turns into Shoreline Drive. From there, make a left on Pine Avenue.

SITE 213 - LOS ANGELES MEMORIAL SPORTS ARENA

3939 South Figueroa Street
Los Angeles, CA 90007
(213) 748-6136
www.lacoliseum.com/
[GUIDE PAGE 674 (LA)]
• Take Interstate Highway 110 south to the Exposition Boulevard Exit. Make a left on Flower Street (first light) and then park on right.
• Or Take Interstate Highway 110 north to the Martin Luther King Jr. Boulevard Exit and go left. Make a right on Flower Street. Park on the left.

SITE 214 - SAN DIEGO CONVENTION CENTER

111 West Harbor Drive
San Diego, CA 92101
(619) 525-5000
www.sdccc.org

[GUIDE PAGE 1289 (SD)]
• Take Interstate Highway 5 to the Front Street Exit and go south. Make a left on Harbor Drive.

SITE 215 - STAPLES CENTER

1111 South Figueroa Street
Los Angeles, CA 90015
(213) 742-7340
www.staplescenter.com

[GUIDE PAGE 634 (LA)]
• Take Interstate Highway 110 north to the 9th Street Exit and go east. Make a right on Figueroa Street and then a right on 11th Street.
• Take Interstate Highway 110 south to the Olympic Boulevard Exit. Make a left at bottom of the offramp onto Blaine Street. From there, make a left on 11th Street.

YOUR COMMENTS

SITE 216 - TOURNAMENT OF ROSES® PARADE

ADDRESS
Colorado Blvd and Sierra Madre Boulevard
Pasadena, CA 91184
www.tournamentofroses.com
(626) 449-4100

DIRECTIONS [GUIDE PAGE 566 (LA)]
Take Interstate Highway 210 to any of these exits: Allen Avenue, Hill Street, Lake Street, or Altadena Drive. Park and walk south to Colorado Boulevard.

PRE- AND POST-PARADE ACTIVITIES:
There are at least two locations where children are welcome to watch the float decorating without having to stand in a long line or pay. These are in South Pasadena and Sierra Madre. You can also see the floats after the parade, however, be aware of long lines.

PRE-PARADE FLOAT DECORATING IN SOUTH PASADENA:
• Take Interstate Highway 210 to the Fair Oaks Avenue Exit and go south into South Pasadena. Go to the parking lot behind Rite Aid.

PRE-PARADE FLOAT DECORATING IN SIERRA MADRE:
• Take Interstate Highway 210 to the Santa Anita Avenue Exit and go north. Make a left on Sierra Madre Boulevard and go to the parking lot and big building behind Sierra Vista Park.

POST-PARADE FLOAT VIEWING:
• Interstate Highway 210 to the Sierra Madre Boulevard Exit and go north. Make a left onto Altadena Drive. Park near Victory Park.

GOOD THINGS TO SEE AND HEAR
The Rose Parade is world famous and is very different in person from what you see on TV. All of the floats must be covered with flowers, leaves, seeds, or fruit. Sit close (e.g. on the street) so you can see the flowers and the people's faces. There are also marching bands from schools around the country, and horses of all sorts with dazzling decorations on their manes and hoofs. Before the parade, visit one of the floats as it is being decorated. After the parade, for the day of and the day following the parade, the floats are parked in Victory Park. This is a good chance to get a close look at the flowers, seeds, and leaves that make up the floats.

The parade route is very crowded. People start lining up the day before and many people sleep out all night. The best for young children is to get a group of families and assign adults to guard your marked off spot in shifts for the night. Bring the young children in the morning, along with coffee and goodies for those who spent the night. Sit on the south side of Colorado Boulevard to avoid the sun in your eyes.

HOURS

The parade arrives at different locations at different times. Check your newspaper for exact times.

PARKING

Free (but difficult)
• Close parking is sometimes available for about $10.00.

ADMISSION

Free unless you sit in the bleachers.

RELATED PLACES

• Descanso Gardens - Site 38
• Exposition Park Rose Garden - Site 41
• The Huntington - Site 39
• Musical Circus Pasadena Symphony - Site 220

CLOSE-BY PLACES

• California Institute of Technology, Caltech - Site 56
• Doggie Day Camp at PETsMART - Site 28
• Eaton Canyon County Park and Nature Center - Site 44
• The Huntington - Site 39
• Kidspace Museum - Site 4
• Pasadena Civic Auditorium - Site 220

YOUR COMMENTS

_____
_____
_____
_____
_____

SITE 217 – RINGLING BROS. AND BARNUM & BAILEY CIRCUS

ADDRESS
The Greatest Show on Earth
www.ringling.com

DIRECTIONS
Usually in the following locations:

Arrowhead Pond of Anaheim
2695 East Katella Avenue
Anaheim, CA 92806
www.arrowheadpond.com
(714) 704-2400
[GUIDE PAGE 799 (OC)]
• Take Interstate Highway 5 to the Katella Avenue Exit and go east.

Los Angeles Memorial Sports Arena
3939 South Figueroa Street
Los Angeles, CA 90007
(213) 748-6136
www.lacoliseum.com/
[GUIDE PAGE 674 (LA)]
• Take Interstate Highway 110 south to the Exposition Boulevard Exit. Make a left on Flower Street (first light), and park on the right.
• Take Interstate Highway 110 north to the Martin Luther King Jr. Boulevard Exit and go left. Make a right on Flower Street, and park on the left.

GOOD THINGS TO SEE AND HEAR
Everybody loves the circus-including babies and toddlers! The elephants, tigers, and dogs are always a favorite. The clowns, some of the high wire acts, the parade of elephants, menagerie of animals, and circus performers at the beginning and end of the show are also exciting.

Ringing Brothers offers a "Baby's First Circus" free ticket for children under one year. Invest in good seats and go to the pre-show activities. You can meet the clowns and some of the other circus stars, and often see an elephant up close. Don't worry if you don't make it though the whole circus show. Walk around to where the animals enter the arena and watch the elephants arrive. In the last few years, the circus has invited the public to visit the animals after the show. The elephants are in open outdoor roped-off areas and can be watched eating and sometimes getting a bath.

Over the years I have found the circus to fluctuate between a good old circus and a show that is very flashy and high tech.

There are usually bilingual show options. Be sure to check if you want or do not want this option.

HOURS
Usually in June, July or August. Call for information.

PARKING
$5.00-$10.00 Depending on Location

ADMISSION
Call for Information

RELATED PLACES
• America's Teaching Zoo at Moorpark College - Site 66
• Los Angeles Zoo - Site 63
• Orange County Zoo - Site 65
• Santa Ana Zoo - Site 64
• Santa Barbara Zoological Gardens - Site 70
• San Diego Zoo - Site 68
• San Diego Wild Animal Park - Site 69

BOOKS FOR YOUR CHILD
Hill, Eric-*Spot Goes to the Circus*

SITE 218 - FAERY HUNT

ADDRESS
Franklin Canyon Park
Sooky Goldman Nature Center Parking Lot
2600 Franklin Canyon Drive
Beverly Hill, CA 90210
(818) 324-6802
http://www.afaeryhunt.com/

DIRECTIONS [GUIDE PAGE 592 (LA)]
Take U.S. Highway 101 to the Coldwater Canyon Boulevard Exit and go south. At the intersection of Coldwater Canyon and Mulholland Drive make a 90 degree turn right onto Franklin Canyon Drive. Road signs read "Road Closed 800 Feet" "Sunset to Sunrise"; this is the park entrance. Stay on the paved surface to reach the Sooky Goldman Nature Center parking lot.

GOOD THINGS TO SEE AND HEAR
The Faery Hunt is an interactive adventure in which children hunt for faeries, including Pilliwiggin, Darrig the Troll, Belfiana and Bailey Binkerelli, a dog, in Magical Franklin Canyon. Come dressed in your favorite faery outfit (including Peter Pan) and join the fun.

Don't forget to bring your camera, hats and sunblock!

A Faery Hunt will be opening in Orange County-check the website for updates.

HOURS
Saturdays   various times in the morning (call ahead for schedule and
reservations)

PARKING
Free (Look for the "Faery" sign for parking

ADMISSION
• Adult or Child $10.00 suggested contribution
• Advance Early Reservations are Recommended

RELATED PLACES
• Bob Baker Marionette Theater - Site 204
• Other Children's Theaters–Chapter 11

CLOSE-BY PLACES
• Children's Book World - Site 18
• Zimmer Children's Museum - Site 10

YOUR COMMENTS

SITE 219 - SUMMER SOUNDS AT THE HOLLYWOOD BOWL

ADDRESS
2301 North Highland Avenue
Hollywood, CA 90078
(323) 850-2000 Summer Sounds Information
(323) 850-2058 Hollywood Bowl Museum
hollywoodbowl.com/event/summersounds.cfm

DIRECTIONS [GUIDE PAGE 593 (LA)]
Take U.S. Highway 101 north to the Highland Avenue Exit. Circle to the right
under the freeway, and go straight across the main street into the parking lot.

GOOD THINGS TO SEE AND HEAR
The Hollywood Bowl hosts a series of concerts and workshops for children
each summer. The shows are thirty to forty-five minutes long on the Summer
Sounds Stage (covered and shady) in front of the Hollywood Bowl. Each week a different artist performs two shows daily for five days of the week. There are usually
six weeks of shows. The shows are geared for young children. Recent shows
included West African drums, Caribbean and New Orleans blues, Irish music, Latin

jazz rhythms, sounds of Vietnam, and family folk tales and fables. The show is hosted by Dave (David Prather), an enthusiastic actor, storyteller, and master of ceremonies who participates to a greater or lesser degree, depending on the performers. He provides a nice constant figure from week to week, which children seem to appreciate. Young musicians and dancers are often included in the show. After the show, children can participate in an art project in a nearby parking lot (also covered). Visit the Hollywood Bowl Museum which has hands-on musical instruments upstairs, or see the Hollywood Bowl Orchestra rehearse (usually on Tuesdays and Thursdays 9:30 a.m. to 12:15 p.m. only).

The gift store has a wonderful collection of musical instruments for children.

HOURS

Summer Only (July and August):
Monday-Friday   10:00 a.m. and 11:15 a.m.

PARKING

Free

ADMISSION

Adult or Child $5.00
Entire Series $30.00
Baby in arms   Free
Art Workshops: $3.00 (must be at least 3 years of age)
• Advance Early Reservations are Recommended

RELATED PLACES

• Bob Baker Marionette Theater - Site 204
• Music in the Park-Chapter 11
• Musical Circus Pasadena Symphony - Site 220
• Other Children's Theaters-Chapter 11

CLOSE-BY PLACES

• Bob Hope Airport - Site 148
• Burbank Train Station - Site 173
• Falcon Theater - Site 205
• Museum of the American West - Site 3
• North Hollywood School Bus Yard - Site 25

YOUR COMMENTS

_____
_____
_____
_____

SITE 220 - MUSICAL CIRCUS PASADENA SYMPHONY

ADDRESS
Pasadena Civic Auditorium
300 East Green Street
Pasadena, CA 91101
(626) 793-7172 extension 10
www.pasadenasymphony.org/circus.htm

DIRECTIONS [GUIDE PAGE 565 (LA)]
Take Interstate Highway 210 to the Fair Oaks Avenue Exit and go south. Make a left on Green Street.

GOOD THINGS TO SEE AND HEAR
On some Saturdays, the Pasadena Symphony hosts an open house at the Pasadena Civic Auditorium. Children are invited to talk to the musicians, see their instruments, and play similar instruments. Then a special show is presented by an invited guest (not the symphony). Finally, children are invited to watch the Pasadena Symphony practice.

Call ahead for dates.

HOURS
Saturday of Concert:
Instrument Play   8:30 a.m. - 9:00 a.m.
Special Performance   9:00 a.m. - 10:00 a.m.
Symphony Rehearsal 9:30 a.m. - 12:00 p.m.

PARKING
$7.00   Lot Parking
Free   Street Parking

ADMISSION
Free

RELATED PLACES
• Bob Baker Marionette Theater - Site 204
• Music in the Park-Chapter 11
• Summer Sounds at the Hollywood Bowl - Site 219
• Other Children's Theaters-Chapter 11

CLOSE-BY PLACES
• California Institute of Technology, Caltech - Site 56
• Doggie Day Camp at PETsMART - Site 28
• Eaton Canyon County Park and Nature Center - Site 44
• The Huntington - Site 39
• Kidspace Museum - Site 4
• Music-Chapter 11
• Tournament of Roses® Parade and Float Viewing - Site 216

YOUR COMMENTS

_____

_____

_____

_____

_____

_____

SITE 221 - WALT DISNEY CONCERT HALL-
TOYOTA SYMPHONIES FOR YOUTH

Walt Disney Concert Hall
111 South Grand Avenue
Los Angeles, CA 90012
(323) 850-2000
wdch.laphil.com/tix/series_youth_2006.cfm
www.musiccenter.org/education

DIRECTIONS [GUIDE PAGE 634 (LA)]
• Take Interstate Highway 110 to the 6th Street Exit and go east. Make a left on Figueroa Street, right on 1st Street, right on Grand Avenue and right on Second Street.

GOOD THINGS TO SEE AND HEAR
Each year the Toyota Symphonies for Youth includes six one-hour Saturday morning concerts performed by the Los Angeles Philharmonic. Before the concert, children can participate in musical, drama and art activities.

The age limit is three and older.

Also try the Pillow Theater which offers performances for children age three to six while they sit on big colorful pillows. Call ahead for tickets. The show is followed by a hands-on art workshop in the Blue Ribbon Garden.

HOURS
Summer Saturdays:
Musical Playground 10:00 a.m.
Concert   11:00 a.m.

PARKING
$8.00   Below concert hall off Second Street

ADMISSION
Adult/Child $60.00 for 8 concerts

RELATED PLACES

- Bob Baker Marionette Theater - Site 204
- Music in the Park-Chapter 11
- Other Children's Theaters-Chapter 11
- Summer Sounds at the Hollywood Bowl - Site 219

CLOSE-BY PLACES

- Chinatown - Site 30
- Grand Central Market - Site 31
- KLOS Story Theater - Site 206
- Olvera Street - Site 29
- Richard J. Riordan Central Library - Site 16
- Union Station - Site 171

YOUR COMMENTS

MUSIC IN THE PARK

More and more parks are hosting free Summer concerts in the evenings. These concerts offer a pleasant opportunity to have a picnic and listen to some music.

Call for schedules and locations. The Los Angeles County Arts Commission offers a variety of free concerts in public sites, including parks and libraries. Visit www.lacountyarts.org/free.html for more information on performance dates and times. Other summer concerts are listed below. For your local areas, contact:

Phone Book
White Pages   City Government Offices (front of phone book, look under "Chamber of Commerce," "City Hall," and "Parks and Recreation")

ALTADENA
Farnsworth Park Amphitheater
(626) 798-6335
• Summer Concert Series

ARCADIA
Los Angeles County Arboretum and
   Botanical Gardens - Site 37
(626) 821-3222
• Festival on the Green
• Cal Phil Family Night

ARCADIA
City Hall West Lawn
240 West Huntington Drive
• Free Summer Concerts

GLENDORA
160 N. Wabash Avenue
(626) 914-8200
• Summer Series of Concerts in the
   Park

HUNTINGTON BEACH
Huntington Beach Pier
   and Amphitheater
(714) 969-3492
surfcity.usa.com
• Family Entertainment

LA CANADA/FLINTRIDGE
Memorial Park
(818) 790-8880 City Hall
• Free Summer Concerts

LA CANADA FLINTRIDGE
Descanso Gardens - Site 38
(626) 792-7677
www.pasadenaPOPS.org

LA CANADA FLINTRIDGE
Memorial Park
1301 Foothill Boulevard
• Free Concerts

LAKEWOOD
Del Valle Park
(562) 429-0545
• Lakewood Summer Concerts in the Park

LOS ANGELES
Griffith Park
4800 Carousel Drive
(213) 955-6976 or (800) 440-4536
symphonyintheglen.org/
• Symphony in the Glen

LOS ANGELES
Olvera Street - Site 29
(213) 625-5045
• Concert Series

LOS ANGELES
Original Los Angeles Farmer's
   Market (Site 33)
(323) 933-9211
www.farmersmarketla.com/
• Twilight Summer Music Festival

LOS ANGELES
California Plaza
350 S. Grand Avenue
www.grandperformances.org
• *Grand Performances Summer Concert
   Series*

MANHATTAN BEACH
Polliwog Park
Manhattan Beach Boulevard and
   Redondo Avenue(323) 933-9211
www.ci.manhattan-beach.ca.us/
parksrec/cultural_arts/concerts.html

MARINA DEL REY
Fisherman's Village
13755 Fiji Way
(310) 822-6866
• Free Sunday Concerts

MARINA DEL REY
Chase Park
13650 Mindanao Way
(310) 305-9545
• Hot Summer Nights

MONROVIA
Monrovia Library Park
321 South Myrtle
(818) 359-3231
• Free Summer Concerts

PASADENA
Levitt Pavilion
88 E. Holly Street
(626) 683-3230
www.levittpavilionpasadena.org/
• Levitt Pavilion Concert Series

PASADENA
Kidspace Children's Museum - Site 4
(626) 449-9144
• Concerts on the Green

PASADENA
One Colorado Courtyard
Colorado Boulevard between Fair Oaks
   and Delacey
(626) 564-1066
• Street Show

REDONDO BEACH
Redondo Beach Pier - Site 143
• Concerts on the Pier

ROWLAND HEIGHTS
Schabarum Park
17250 Colima Road
(626) 336-4937
• Concerts in the Park

SAN DIEGO
Spreckels Organ Pavilion
Balboa Park
(619) 235-1100
www.balboapark.org/
• Year-Round Sunday Afternoon Concerts
• Twilight in the Park Concert Series

SAN DIMAS
Frank G. Bonelli Park
(909) 599-8411
• Family Music Festival

SAN MARINO
Lacy Park
(626) 299-7014
• Concerts in the Park

SIERRA MADRE
Memorial Park Bandshell
222 West Sierra Madre Boulevard
(626) 355-7135
www.sierramadrechamber.com/events/
• Concert in the Park

SOUTH PASADENA
Garfield Park,
Mission Street west of Fair Oaks
(626) 403-7360
• Concerts in the Park

TEMPLE CITY
Temple City Park Arts Pavilion
970 Las Tunas Drive
(626) 286-3101 Chamber of Commerce
• Free Summer Concerts

VENTURA
Ventura Harbor Village
Spinnaker and Harbor
(805) 644-0169
• Free Music Concerts

WARNER PARK
Valley Cultural Center
(818) 704-1358
• Concerts in the Park

CHAPTER 12 - CALENDAR OF EVENTS

Southern California's year-round climate is mild, yet each month has something new to offer. This calendar of events may give you some ideas for new adventures or new things to discover on your usual outings. Included are "Things to Look For", such as migratory birds and trees that are in bloom, "Holidays", "Special Events at Places in This Book", along with a reference to the site numbers, and "Other Events"; including the address, phone number, and web site if available.

In addition to the events listed for each month, mark your calendars with regular events such as monthly free days at museums, library story hours, and farmer's market days in your town. For special events, call for the exact times and locations (and reservations if necessary) as these vary greatly from year to year.

JANUARY

THINGS TO LOOK FOR
- Camellias
- Gray Whale Migration
- Lettuce
- Low Tide
- Migratory Birds

HOLIDAYS
- Chinese New Year
- Epiphany, The Three King's Day
- Martin Luther King, Jr. Day
- New Year's Day

SPECIAL EVENTS AT PLACES IN THIS BOOK
- Auto Show at the LA Convention Center - Site 209
- Chinese New Years Parade in Chinatown - Site 30
- Los Tres Reyes Celebration on Olvera Street - Site 29
- Tournament of Roses® Parade in Pasadena - Site 216
- Yeah, Baby Show at the LA Convention Center - Site 209

FEBRUARY

THINGS TO LOOK FOR
- Camellias
- Gray Whale Migration
- Lettuce
- Migratory Birds
- Tulips

HOLIDAYS
- Abraham Lincoln's Birthday
- Chinese New Year
- Eid al-Adha
- George Washington's Birthday
- Groundhog Day
- Lunar New Year
- Muhurran (sometimes in March)
- Valentine's Day

SPECIAL EVENTS AT PLACES IN THIS BOOK
- Fat Tuesday celebration on Olvera Street in Los Angeles - Site 29
- Mardi Gras at the Original Los Angeles Farmers Market - Site 32
- Boat Show at the Los Angeles Convention Center - Site 209

OTHER EVENTS
- **Camellia Festival and Parade**
Children's parade with floats decorated with camellias
9701 Las Tunas Drive
Temple City, CA 91780-1834
(626) 285-2171
www.templecitychamber.org/cam_fest_history.html

MARCH

THINGS TO LOOK FOR
- Artichokes
- Cauliflower
- Celery
- Daffodils
- Flowering Deciduous Trees
- Migratory Birds
- Peacock Mating Season
- Strawberries
- Tulips
- Wisteria

HOLIDAYS
- Ash Wednesday
- Easter (sometimes in April)
- First Day of Spring or Spring Equinox
- Good Friday (sometimes in April)
- Mardi Gras
- Muharran (sometimes in February)
- Palm Sunday (sometimes in April)
- Passover (sometimes in April)
- Purim
- St. Patrick's Day

SPECIAL EVENTS AT PLACES IN THIS BOOK
- Arcadia Insect Fair in the Arboretum - Site 37
- Blessing of the Animals on Olvera Street in Los Angeles - Site 29
- Easter Celebration in the Original Los Angeles Farmer's Market - Site 32
- Kite Festivals - Site 167
- St. Patrick's Day Celebration at the Original LA Farmer's Market - Site 32
- Tulip Mania and Easter Egg Hunt in the Descanso Gardens - Site 38

APRIL

THINGS TO LOOK FOR
- Artichokes
- Azaleas
- Caterpillars
- Cauliflower
- Celery
- Colorful Breeding Plumage on Ducks
- Iris
- Ladybugs
- Lilacs
- Magnolias
- Peacock Mating Season
- Roses
- Strawberries
- Sweet Onions
- Tadpoles
- Tulips
- Wildflowers
- Wisteria

HOLIDAYS
- April Fools' Day
- Daylight Savings Time Begins
- Earth Day
- Easter (sometimes in March)
- Good Friday (sometimes in March)
- Holocaust Remembrance Day
- Palm Sunday (sometimes in March)
- Passover (sometimes in March)

SPECIAL EVENTS AT PLACES IN THIS BOOK
- Green Meadows Farm-Orange County - Site 91
- Pasadena Model Railroad Club's Spring Open House - Site 201
- Santa Barbara County Fair and Expo - Site 110
- Tulip Mania and Easter Egg Hunt in Descanso Gardens - Site 38

OTHER EVENTS

• Poppies in Bloom-Poppy Reserve
15101 Lancaster Road
Lancaster, CA 93536
(661) 724-1180
www.parks.ca.gov/default.asp?page_id=627

• California Poppy Festival
Lancaster City Park
43011 North 10th Street West
Lancaster, CA 93534
www.poppyfestival.com

• Wildflowers in Bloom
totalescape.com/active/leisure/wildflwr.html
www.desertusa.com/wildflo/ca.html
www.theodorepayne.org/

• Los Angeles Times Festival of Books
University of California Los Angeles Campus
Los Angeles, CA 90095
(800) 528-4637
www.latimes.com/extras/festivalofbooks/

MAY

THINGS TO LOOK FOR
- Artichokes
- Beans
- Blackberries
- Cauliflower
- Celery
- Dogwood
- Jacaranda Trees
- Ladybugs
- Onions
- Peacock Mating Season
- Peas
- Roses
- Squash
- Strawberries

HOLIDAYS
- Armed Forces Day
- Cinco de Mayo
- May Day
- Mawlid al-Nabi
- Memorial Day
- Mother's Day

SPECIAL EVENTS AT PLACES IN THIS BOOK
- California Strawberry Festival - Site 55
- Children's Nature Institute's Kid's Festival - Site 43
- Cinco de Mayo Celebrations on Olvera Street in Los Angeles - Site 29
- Cinco de Mayo Celebrations at the Original LA Farmer's Market - Site 32
- Gilmore Heritage Auto Show, Original Los Angeles Farmer's Market - Site 32
- Green Meadows Farm in Los Angeles - Site 90
- Insect Fair at the Natural History Museum of Los Angeles County - Site 1
- Temecula Valley Balloon and Wine Festival - Site 169
- University of California Los Angeles Pow Wow - Site 58

OTHER EVENTS
NASA/JPL Open House
4800 Oak Grove Drive
Pasadena, CA 91109
(818) 354-0112
www.jpl.nasa.gov/pso/oh.html

Children's Day Celebration
Plaza of Japanese American Cultural and Community Center
Los Angeles, CA 900
(213) 628-2725

Garden Grove Strawberry Festival
The Village Green
Garden Grove, CA 92

Santa Barbara Children's Festival
Alameda Park
Santa Barbara, CA 93840
(805) 897-2574

JUNE

THINGS TO LOOK FOR
- Apricots
- Artichokes
- Beans
- Blackberries
- Cauliflower
- Celery
- Cucumbers
- Jacaranda Trees
- Ladybugs
- Peacock Mating Season
- Peas
- Raspberries
- Roses
- Squash
- Strawberries
- Summer Annuals

HOLIDAYS
- Father's Day
- First Day of Summer or Summer Solstice
- Flag Day
- Shavuot

SPECIAL EVENTS AT PLACES IN THIS BOOK
- Del Mar Fair - Site 109
- Pasadena Pops Children's Concert at Descanso Gardens - Site 38
- San Fernando Valley Fair - Site 108
- Summer Concerts - Chapter 11
- Summer Sounds at the Hollywood Bowl - Site 219
- Temecula Valley Balloon and Wine Festival - Site 169

JULY

THINGS TO LOOK FOR
- Apricots
- Beans
- Black-Eyed Peas
- Crepe Myrtle
- Cucumbers
- Ladybugs
- Roses
- Peacock Mating Season
- Raspberries
- Squash
- Strawberries
- Summer Annuals and Perennials
- Tomatoes

HOLIDAYS
- Independence Day or 4th of July

SPECIAL EVENTS AT PLACES IN THIS BOOK
- Festival on the Green at the Arboretum - Site 37
- Fourth of July Celebrations on Olvera Street in Los Angeles - Site 29
- Kite Festivals - Site 167
- Summer Sounds at the Hollywood Bowl - Site 219
- Orange County Fair - Site 107
- Ringling Bros. and Barnum & Bailey Circus - Site 217
- Summer Concerts - Chapter 11

OTHER EVENTS
- *U.S. Open Sandcastle Competition*
  City of Imperial Beach
  (619) 424-6663

FOURTH OF JULY FIREWORKS LIST

Check your newspaper or call (800) 900-3473 (Los Angeles County Fire Department) or check one of the local TV network news websites.

Internet:

Los Angeles Fire Department   www.lafd.org/july4.htm

Orange County Fire Department   www.ocfa.org/allriskcomsafety/
fireworks.pdf

San Diego Fire Department   www.firesafe.com/sdfd.html

Santa Barbara Fire Department   ci.santa-barbara.ca.us/departments/fire/

Phone Book:

White Pages: County Government Offices
(front of phone book, look under "Fire Department")

Alhambra	Almansor Park, 800 South Almansor Street	(626) 570-5044
Aliso Viejo	Grand Park at Aliso Viejo Town Center	(949) 362-5890
Aliso Viejo	Pacific Park Drive	(949) 362-5890
Anaheim	Disneyland, 1313 South Harbor Boulevard	(714) 781-4565
Anaheim	Peralta Canyon Park, 115 North Piney	(714) 974-0859
Anaheim	Angel Stadium, 2000 Gene Autry Way	(714) 634-2000
Artesia	Artesia Community Park 12000 South Street	
Avalon	Via Casino Way to Crescent Avenue	(310) 510-1520
Baldwin Park	Sierra Vista High School	(626) 960-7741
	3600 Frazier Street	
Baldwin Park	Baldwin Park High School.	(626) 960-1955
	3900 Puente Avenue	
Bell Gardens	John Anson Ford Park, Scout Avenue and	(562) 806-7600
	Florence Avenue	
Bellflower	Thompson Park, 14001 Bellflower Boulevard	(562) 952-6601
Buena Park	Bellis Park, 7171 Eighth Street	
Buena Park	Knott's Berry Farm, 8039 Beach Boulevard	(714) 220-5200
Burbank	Starlight Bowl, 1249 Lockheed View Drive	(818) 525-3721
Calabasas	Calabasas High School	(818) 222-7177
	22855 Mulholland Highway	
Carlsbad	Legoland, 1 Legoland Drive	(760) 918-5346
Catalina Island	Avalon Bay	(310) 510-1520
Cerritos	Whitney High School, 16800 Shoemaker Avenue	
City of Orange	Fed Kelly Stadium Emadino High School	
	3920 Spring	
Claremont	Claremont McKenna College, Burns Stadium	
	890 Columbia Avenue	
Claremont	Pomona College 6th Street and Mills Avenue	(909) 621-8000
Commerce	Rosewood Park, 2433 Commerce Way	(323) 887-4434
Culver City	Culver City High School, 4300 Elenda Avenue	(310) 390-7717
Dana Point	Lantern Bay Park, 25 Dana Point Harbor Drive	(949) 248-3530
Dana Point	The Ocean Institute	(949) 496-2274
	24200 Dana Point Harbor Drive	
Del Mar	Del Mar Fairgrounds	(858) 755-1161
El Segundo	El Segundo Recreational Park, 401 Sheldon Street	
Fillmore	Fillmore High School, 555 Central Avenue	(805) 524-1500

Fountain Valley	Mile Square Park, Warner and Euclid Streets	(714) 688-0542
Fullerton	Fullerton High School Stadium, 700 North Lemon	(714) 738-6545
Gardena	Rowley Park, 13220 South Van Ness Avenue	(310) 515-9456
Glendora	Citrus College, 1000 West Foothill Boulevard	(626) 914-8549
Hollywood Bowl	2301 North Highland Avenue	(323) 850-2000
Huntington Beach	Huntington Beach Pier Plaza	(714) 374-1535
	Pacific Coast Highway and Main Street	(714) 536-5486
Huntington Park	Huntington Park High School	(323) 584-6218
	6020 Miles Avenue	
Inglewood	Edward Vincent Jr. Park, 700 Warren Lane	(310) 412-5210
Irvine	Laguna Beach Monument Point, Heisler Park on Cliff Drive	
Irvine	Verizon Wireless Amphitheater	(714) 755-5799
	8808 Irvine Center Drive	
Irvine	Irvine High School, 4321 Walnut Avenue	(949) 724-0488
Irwindale	Irwindale Rock Quarry, 5050 North Irwindale Avenue	
La Crescenta	Crescenta Valley High School	(818) 248-4957
	4400 Ramsdell Avenue	
La Habra	La Habra High School	(562) 905-9708
	801 West Highlander Avenue	
La Mirada	La Mirada High School, 13520 Adelfa Drive	(562) 943-0231
La Puente	La Puente High School, North Glendora Avenue	
	and Nelson Avenue	
La Puente	Victory Outreach Church, 454 Coberta Avenue	
La Verne	Bonita High School, 3102 D Street	
Laguna Beach	Heisler Park, Main Beach	(800) 877-1115
Laguna Hills	Laguna Hills Community Sports Complex,	(949) 707-2680
	Alicia Pkwy	
Laguna Niguel	Regional Park, 28241 La Paz Road	(949) 425-5100
Lakeview Terrace	Hansen Dam Sports Center,	(818) 987-9001
	Foothill Boulevard and Osborne Street	
Lawndale	Leuzinger High School, 4118 West Rosecrans Avenue	
Long Beach	Long Beach Aquarium, 100 Aquarium Way	
Long Beach	Queen Mary, 1126 Queens Highway	(562) 435-3511
Long Beach	Veterans Stadium, 5000 Lew Davis Drive	
Los Alamitos	Joint Forces Training Base,	(714) 229-6780
	11200 Lexington Drive at Katella Avenue	
Los Angeles	Dodger Stadium, 1000 Elysian Park Avenue	(323) 224-1459
Los Angeles	Los Angeles Memorial Coliseum	(213) 473-7008
	3911 S. Figueroa Street	
Lynwood	Lynwood City Park, Bullis Road and Century Boulevard	
Malibu	Barge-Off Shore, Pacific Coast Highway 1	(310) 456-2489
Marina Del Rey	12483 Fiji Way	(310) 305-9545
Maywood	Maywood City Park, Heliotrope and 58th Streets	(323) 562-5005
Mission Viejo	Mission Viejo Youth Athletic Park,	(949) 830-7066
	Olympiad Road near Marguerite Parkway	
Montebello	Grant Rea Park, 600 North Rea Drive	
Monterey Park	Barnes Park, 320 South McPherrin Avenue	(626) 307-1388
Moorpark	Arroyo Vista Community Park,	(805) 517-6300
	4550 Tierra Rejada Road	
Newport Beach	Newport Dunes Resort, 1131 Back Bay Drive	(949) 729-3863
Northridge	Cal State Northridge, North Campus Stadium	(818) 677-1200
Norwalk	Cerritos College, 11110 East Alondra Boulevard	

Norwalk	Norwalk Civic Center, Imperial Highway and Avenue Manuel Salinas	
Orange	Fred Kelly Stadium at El Modena High School	(714) 744-7278
	3920 Spring Street	
Pacific Palisades	Palisades High School, 15777 Bowdoin Street	
Palmdale	Palmdale High School, 2137 East Avenue R	(661) 267-5611
Palos Verdes Estates	Rolling Hills Prep School, 300A Paseo Del Mar	
Pasadena	Rose Bowl, 1001 Rose Bowl Drive	(626) 792-7677
Pico Rivera	El Rancho High School, 6501 South Passons Boulevard	
Placentia	Bradford Stadium, 500 North Bradford	
Pomona	Fairplex, 1101 West McKinley Avenue	(909) 865-4047
Pomona	Lanterman Developmental Center	(909) 620-2156
	3530 West Pomona Boulevard	
Rancho Santa Margarita	Lago Santa Margarita, Avenida de Las Fundereras	
Redondo Beach	Redondo Beach Pier, Pacific Coast Highway 1	
Rosemead	Rosemead Park, Encinitas Avenue and Mission Avenue	
San Clemente	End of San Clemente Pier	
San Fernando	Recreation Park, 208 Park Avenue	
San Juan Capistrano	San Juan Capistrano Sports Park,	(949) 493-5911
	25925 Camino Del Avion	
San Marino	Lacy Park, 1485 Virginia Road	(626) 564-6000
San Pedro	Cabrillo Beach, Pacific Avenue and Stephen White Drive	
Santa Ana	Centennial Regional Park, Edinger and Fairview	(714) 571-4200
Santa Clarita	Citrus Street and Magic Mountain Park Way	
Santa Clarita	Stevenson Ranch, 26233 Faulkner Drive	
Santa Clarita	Valencia Boulevard at McBean Parkway	(661) 259-2489
Santa Fe Springs	Los Nietos Park, 11143 Charlesworth Road	
Sierra Madre	Memorial Park, 232 West Sierra Madre Boulevard	
Simi Valley	Simi Valley High School, 5400 Cochran Street	(805) 584-4400
South El Monte	South El Monte High School,	(626) 442-0218
	1001 Durfee Avenue	
South Gate	South Gate City Park, 4900 Southern Avenue	(323) 635-7938
South Pasadena	Garfield Park, Mission Street and Marengo Avenue	
Studio City	CBS Studio Center, 4024 Radford Avenue	(818) 655-7744
Sunland-Tujunga	Verdugo Hills High School	(818) 352-4433
	10625 Plainview Avenue	
Torrance	Torrance Beach Paseo de la Plaza	(310) 372-2166
Tustin	Tustin High Northrop Field, 1171 El Camino Real	(714) 573-3325
Valencia	Valencia Town Center	(661) 286-4018
	24201 W. Valencia Boulevard	
Valencia	Six Flags Magic Mountain Park Park	(661) 255-4100
Venice Beach	Venice Beach Rec. Center	(310) 399-2775
	1800 Ocean Front Walk	
Walnut	Rowland High School	(818) 965-3448
	2000 South Otterbein Avenue	
Walnut	Walnut High School,	(909) 598-5605
	400 North Pierre Road and La Puente Road	
West Covina	Cameron Park, 1305 East Cameron Avenue	(626) 814-8430
West Hollywood	Plummer Park, 7377 Santa Monica Boulevard	
Westminster	Westminster High School Stadium,	(714) 895-2860
	14325 Golden West Street	

Whittier	Friendly Hills Country Club	(562) 945-8250
	8500 Villa Verde Drive	
Whittier	York Park, 9110 Santa Fe Springs Road	(562) 945-8250
Woodland Hills	Pierce College, 6201 Winnetka Avenue	(818) 703-7859
Woodland Hills	Warner Park, 5800 Topanga Canyon Boulevard	(818) 704-1358
Yorba Linda	Valley View Sports Park, 4756 Valley View	(714) 961-7160
Yucaipa	Yucaipa High School Football Stadium	
	33000 Yucaipa Boulevard	

AUGUST

THINGS TO LOOK FOR
- Beans
- Black-eyed Peas
- Crepe Myrtle
- Cucumbers
- Ladybugs
- Peppers
- Raspberries
- Roses
- Squash
- Summer Annuals and Perennials
- Tomatoes

SPECIAL EVENTS AT PLACES IN THIS BOOK
- Summer Concerts - Chapter 11
- Summer Sounds at the Hollywood Bowl - Site 219
- Ventura County Fair - Site 111

OTHER EVENTS
- **Courtyard Kid's Festival**
  Japanese American National Museum
  Little Tokyo
  369 East First Street
  Los Angeles, CA 90012
  (213) 625-0414
  www.janm.org

- **African Marketplace and Cultural Faire**
  Exposition Park
  2520 West View Street
  Los Angeles, CA 90016
  (323) 734-1164
  www.africanmarketplace.org

- **Pow Wow**
  Southern California Indian Center
  (714) 962-6673

SEPTEMBER

THINGS TO LOOK FOR
- Acorns
- Apples
- Beans
- Black-eyed Peas
- Cucumbers
- Peppers
- Raspberries
- Roses
- Squash
- Tomatoes

HOLIDAYS
- First Day of Autumn or Fall Equinox
- Grandparent's Day
- Labor Day
- Mexican Independence Day
- Moon Festival
- Ramadan Begins (sometimes in October)
- Rosh Hashanah
- Yom Kippur (sometimes in October)

SPECIAL EVENTS AT PLACES IN THIS BOOK
- Kite Festivals - Site 167
- Los Angeles County Fair - Site 106
- Los Angeles City Birthday Celebration on Olvera Street in LA - Site 29
- Mexican Independence Celebration on Olvera Street in Los Angeles - Site 29

OTHER EVENTS
- **The Hart of the West Intertribal Pow Wow**
  William South Hart Park
  24151 San Fernando Road
  Newhall, CA 91321
  (661) 254-4584
  www.hart-friends.org

- **Newport Beach Sandcastle Contest**
  Ocean Avenue and Iris Avenue
  Newport Beach, CA 92625
  (949) 729-4400

- **Watts Tower Day of the Drum Festival**
  Watts Tower State Historic Park
  1765 East 107th Street
  Los Angeles, CA 90002
  (213) 847-4646

OCTOBER

THINGS TO LOOK FOR
- Acorns
- Apples
- Beans
- Black-eyed Peas
- Camellias
- Cucumbers
- Gourds
- Migratory Birds
- Raspberries
- Tomatoes
- Peppers
- Pumpkins

HOLIDAYS
- Columbus Day
- Daylight Savings Time Ends
- Diwali-Southeast Asian Festival of Lights (sometimes in November)
- Eid al-Fitr (Ramadan ends) (sometimes in November)
- Halloween
- Ramadan Begins (sometimes in September)
- Sukkot
- Yom Kippur (sometimes in September)

SPECIAL EVENTS AT PLACES IN THIS BOOK
- Fall Festival, Bates Nut Farm - Site 101
- Fall Festival, Original Los Angeles Farmer's Market - Site 32
- Fall Festival, Tanaka Farms - Site 100
- Pumpkinliner, Fillmore and Western Railway - Site 203
- Underwood Family Farm Fall Harvest Festival - Site 99

OTHER EVENTS
- **Pumpkin City's Pumpkin Farm**
  24203 Avenida de Carlota
  Laguna Hills, CA 92653
  (949) 768-1103

- **Pumpkin Patch**
  Cal Polytechnic University
  3801 West Temple Avenue
  Pomona, CA 91768
  (909) 869-2215

- **Calabasas Pumpkin Festival**
  De Anza Park
  37010 Lost Hills Road
  Calabasas, CA 91302
  (818) 880-6461

• **Lombardi Ranch Pumpkin Patch**
29527 Bouquet Canyon Road
Saugus, CA 91390
(661) 296-8697
www.lombardiranch.com
or go to www.pumpkinpatchesandmore.org to find a pumpkin patch near you

• **Industry Hills Pro Rodeo**
16000 Temple Avenue
City of Industry, CA 91744
(626) 961-6892

NOVEMBER

THINGS TO LOOK FOR
• Acorns
• Beans
• Camellias
• Gourds
• Migratory Birds
• Pumpkins
• Raspberries
• Toyon Berries

HOLIDAYS
• Chanukah or Festival of Lights (sometimes in December)
• Dia de los Muertos (Day of the Dead)
• Diwali-Southeast Asian Festival of Lights (sometimes in October)
• Eid al-Fitr (Ramadan ends) (sometimes in October)
• Election Day
• Thanksgiving Day
• Veteran's Day

SPECIAL EVENTS AT PLACES IN THIS BOOK
• Dia de Los Muertos on Olvera Street in Los Angeles - Site 29
• Rosebud Parade in Pasadena - Site 4

OTHER EVENTS
• **Mother Goose Parade**
Mother Goose Parade Association
480 North Magnolia Avenue, Suite 106
El Cajon, CA 92020
(619) 444-8712
www.mothergooseparade.com

• **Cal Stewards Toy Train Meet**
300 East Green Street
Pasadena, CA 91101
(626) 449-7360
www.ttos.org

• *Intertribal Marketplace*
Southwest Museum
234 Museum Drive
Los Angeles, CA 90065
(323) 221-2164

DECEMBER

THINGS TO LOOK FOR
- Berries
- Camellias
- Ginkgo
- Lettuce
- Low Tide
- Migratory Birds

HOLIDAYS
- Christmas Day
- First Day of Winter or Winter Solstice
- Chanukah or Festival of Lights (sometimes in November)
- Kwanzaa
- New Years Eve

SPECIAL EVENTS AT PLACES IN THIS BOOK
- Annual Christmas Festival at the Descanso Gardens - Site 38
- Bob Baker Marionette Theater Christmas Show - Site 204
- Christmas Tree Train, Fillmore and Western Railway - Site 203
- Holiday Lights - Chapter 12
- Holiday Festival at the Original Los Angeles Farmer's Market - Site 32
- Las Posadas (Mexican Christmas Festival) on Olvera Street in LA - Site 29
- Rose Bowl Float Decorating in Pasadena - Site 216

OTHER EVENTS
• *Annual Los Angeles County Holiday Celebration*
Dorothy Chandler Pavilion
135 North Grand Avenue
Los Angeles, CA 90012
(213) 974-1396
www.laphil.org

HOLIDAY LIGHTS

Here are a few great locations to see holiday lights. Watch the *Los Angeles Times* Calendar section for updated information or check their website in December (www.calendarlive.com).

Altadena	Christmas Tree Lane, Santa Rosa Avenue between Woodbury Road and Altadena Drive
Beverly Hills	Mansion of Lights, 9463 Sunset Boulevard
Burbank	Dick Norton's House, 513 North Florence South
Cerritos	Patterson and Kamppila Homes, Castle Place and Kings Row Avenue
Covina	Animated Christmas Display, 923 East Edgecomb Street
Eagle Rock	The Meltons, 4364 York Boulevard
Glendora	Who-ville, 1400 block of south Glendora Avenue
Hancock Park	Rimpau Boulevard, 301 Rimpau Boulevard and 3rd. Street
Hancock Park	Windsor Boulevard, 276 Windsor Avenue
Hawthorne	Williams House, 4117 West 138th Street
Hollywood	Hollywood Boulevard
Inglewood	South 5th Avenue between Century Boulevard and Arbor Vitae Street
La Cañada Flintridge	Illian House, 4951 Indianola Way
La Cañada Flintridge	Descanso Gardens, 1418 Descanso Drive
La Mirada	Wilkinson's Yard, 14371 Ramo Drive
Long Beach	Christmas Tree Lane, Daisy Avenue between 20th Street and Pacific Coast Highway 1
Los Angeles	Griffith Park Festival of Lights, Crystal Springs Drive • To drive, start at Crystal Springs Drive North of Los Feliz Boulevard • To walk, park at the Los Angeles Zoo
Los Angeles	Armstrong Avenue, 2700 block of Armstrong Avenue between West Silver Lake Drive and Lakewood Avenue
Naples	Waterfront homes, Bay Shore Walk
Pasadena	Upper Hastings Ranch, large area North of Sierra Madre Boulevard and west of Michillinda Avenue
San Marino	St. Albans Road
Torrance	Sleepy Hollow Area, Doris Way, Robert Road, Reese Road, Carol Drive and Linda Drive
Venice	Sculptor's House, 911 Marco Place
Whittier	Canopy of Lights, Greenleaf Avenue and Philadelphia Street
Woodland Hills	Candy Cane Lane and Candle Light Lane, U.S. Highway 101, Oxnard Street, Penfield Avenue and Jumilla Avenue

CHAPTER 13 - HANDY REFERENCES

MORE INFORMATION ON UPCOMING EVENTS

Websites for Upcoming Events
- www.downtownla.com/
- www.pasadenacal.com/
- www.culturela.org/
- www.gocitykids.com

Free Family Newspapers
Los Angeles Family Magazine
  (818) 881-FAMILY
  www.lafamily.com

L.A. Parent Magazine and e book
  (818) 846-0400
  www.LAParent.com

Los Angeles Times Thursday Calendar Weekend
  www.calendarlive.com/

The Orange Cat
  (949) 757-1404
  www.theorangecat.org

Parenting-Orange County
  (714) 771-7454
  www.parentingoc.com

Santa Barbara Family Life
  (805) 965-4545
  www.sbfamilylife.com

San Diego Family Magazine
  (619) 685-6970
  www.sandiegofamily.com

San Gabriel Valley Family
(818) 881-FAMILY
www.lafamily.com

South Bay Family Magazine
(818) 881-FAMILY
www.lafamily.com

Ventura County Parent
(805) 498-6889
www.vcparent.com

Ventura Family Magazine
(818) 881-FAMILY
www.lafamily.com

LIST OF SITES AND THEIR THOMAS BROS. MAP PAGE

SITE #	SITE NAME	THOMAS BROS. MAP PAGE #
1	Natural History Museum of Los Angeles County	674 (LA)
2	Children's Museum at La Habra	708 (LA)
3	Museum of the American West	564 (LA)
4	Kidspace Museum	565 (LA)
5	Petersen Automotive Museum	633 (LA)
6	La Brea Tar Pits and Page Museum	633 (LA)
7	Discovery Science Center	799 (OC)
8	Boone Children's Gallery, LACMA	633 (LA)
9	Griffith Observatory	593 (LA)
10	Zimmer Children's Museum	633 (LA)
11	Children's Museum of Los Angeles	502 (LA)
12	The Children's Museum of San Diego, Museo de los Niños	1289 (SD)
13	Children's Discovery Museum of North Country	1106 (SD)
14	Santa Barbara Museum of Natural History	995 (SB)
15	Raymond M. Alf Museum	571 (LA)
16	Richard J. Riordan Central Library	634 (LA)
17	Cerritos Library	767 (LA)
18a	Adventures for Kids	491 (SB/V)
18b	Blue Chair Children's Books	569 (LA)
18c	Bookstar-Culver City	672 (LA)
18d	Bookstar-Los Angeles	632 (LA)
18e	Bookstar-Studio City	562 (LA)
18f	Bright Child	671 (LA)
18g	Catch Our Rainbow Books	793 (LA)
18h	Chevalier's Books	593 (LA)
18i	Children's Book World	632 (LA)
18j	Dutton's Beverly Hills Books	632 (LA)
18k	Dutton's Brentwood Bookstore	631 (LA)
18l	Every Picture Tells a Story	631 (LA)
18m	Mrs. Nelson's Toy and Book Shop	600 (LA)
18n	Once Upon a Time	534 (LA)
18o	San Marino Toy and Book Shoppe	566 (LA)
18p	Storyopolis	562 (LA)
18q	Village Books	631 (LA)
18r	Vroman's	566 (LA)
18s	Whale of a Tale	889 (OC)
19	School Buses - Pasadena Unified School District	535 (LA)
20	Bonita Unified School District Bus Yard	570/600 (LA)
21	Los Angeles Unified School District Lot in Gardena	734-764 (LA)
22	Carson and Rosewood School Bus Yards	734 (LA)
23	Huntington Beach School Bus Yard	857 (OC)
24	Mission Viejo School Bus Yard	891 (OC)
25	North Hollywood School Bus Yard	532 (LA)
26	Norwalk School Bus Yard	736 (LA)
27	Anaheim Union High School District Bus Yard	768 (OC)
28	Doggie Day Camp at PETsMART	566 (LA)
29	Olvera Street	634 (LA)
30	Chinatown	634 (LA)
31	Grand Central Market	634 (LA)
32	The Original Los Angeles Farmer's Market	633 (LA)
33	Sunshine Valley Landfill	481 (LA)
34	Big Rigs at Castaic	4369 (LA)
35	Pasadena Cruisin' Weekly Car Show	566 (LA)
36	Kid's World	996 (SB)
37	Los Angeles County Arboretum and Botanic Gardens	567 (LA)

SITE #	SITE NAME	THOMAS BROS. MAP PAGE #
38	Descanso Gardens	535 (LA)
39	The Huntington	566 (LA)
40	South Coast Botanical Gardens	793 (LA)
41	Exposition Park Rose Garden	674 (LA)
42	Hopkins Wilderness Park	763 (LA)
43	Children's Nature Institute	N/A
44	Eaton Canyon County Park and Nature Center	566 (LA)
45	San Dimas Canyon Park and Nature Center	570 (LA)
46	Whittier Narrows Nature Center	637 (LA)
47	Aliso & Wood Canyons Wilderness Park and Orange County Natural History Museum	921/951 (OC)
48	Shipley Nature Center at Huntington Central Park	857 (OC)
49	Irvine Regional Park and Nature Center	800/801 (OC)
50	El Dorado East Regional Park and Nature Center	766/796 (LA)
51	Audubon Nature Center at Debs Park	595 (LA)
52	Wilderness Park and Nature Center	537 (LA)
53	Sooky Goldman Nature Center	592 (LA)
54	ENC Native Butterfly House	889 (OC)
55	California Strawberry Festival	522 (SB/V)
56	California Institute of Technology, Caltech	566 (LA)
57	University of Southern California, USC	634 (LA)
58	University of California Los Angeles, UCLA	632 (LA)
59	University of California Irvine, UCI	889/890 (OC)
60	California State University Fullerton, CSUF	739 (OC)
61	California State University Long Beach, CSULB	796 (LA)
62	California State University Northridge, CSUN	500 (LA)
63	Los Angeles Zoo	564 (LA)
64	Santa Ana Zoo	829 (OC)
65	Orange County Zoo	800/801 (OC)
66	America's Teaching Zoo at Moorpark College	VIII (LA)
67	STAR EcoStation Environmental Science and Wildlife Rescue Center	672 (LA)
68	San Diego Zoo	1269 (SD)
69	San Diego Wild Animal Park	1150/1130/1131 (SD)
70	Santa Barbara Zoological Gardens	996 (SB)
71	Long Beach Aquarium of the Pacific	825 (LA)
72	Cabrillo Marine Aquarium	854 (LA)
73	Roundhouse Marine Studies Lab and Aquarium	732 (LA)
74	Sea Lab	762 (LA)
75	Santa Monica Pier Aquarium	671 (LA)
76	Little Corona Del Mar Tide Pools	919 (OC)
77	Cabrillo Beach Tide Pools	854 (LA)
78	Dana Point Tide Pools	971 (OC)
79	Doheny State Beach Tide Pools	972 (OC)
80	Diver's Cove Tide Pools/ North of Laguna Main Beach	950 (OC)
81	La Jolla Shores Tide Pools	1227 (SD)
82	Leo Carrillo State Beach Tide Pools	625 (LA)
83	Laguna Beach's Heisler Park	950 (OC)
84	Point Dume Beach Tide Pools	667 (LA)
85	Marine Mammal Care Center at Fort MacArthur	854 (LA)
86	Pacific Marine Mammal Center and Laguna Koi Ponds	920 (OC)
87	Sea World	1268 (SD)
88	Birch Aquarium at Scripps	1227 (SD)
89	Ty Warner Sea Center	996 (SB/V)
90	Green Meadows Farm/Los Angeles County	503 (LA)
91	Green Meadows Farm/Orange County	800/801 (OC)
92	Santa Anita Race Track Morning Workout	567 (LA)
93	Oak Glen Apple Farms	19/31/20C (SB/R)
94	Huntington Central Park Equestrian Center	857 (OC)

SITE #	SITE NAME	THOMAS BROS. MAP PAGE #
95	Griffith Park Pony Rides	564 (LA)
96	The Farm	530 (LA)
97	Armours Orchard	4287 (LA)
98	Zoomars Petting Farm	972 (OC)
99	Underwood Family Farms	VI (LA) or 496 (SB/V)
100	Tanaka Farms	890 (OC)
101	Bates Nut Farm	1091 (SD)
102	Irvine Regional Park Pony Rides	800/801 (OC)
103	Montebello Barnyard Zoo	676 (LA)
104	Lakewood Pony Rides and Petting Farm	766 (LA)
105	Centennial Farm	859 (OC)
106	Los Angeles County Fair	600 (LA)
107	Orange County Fair	859 (OC)
108	San Fernando Valley Fair	502 (LA)
109	Del Mar Fair	1187 (SD)
110	Santa Barbara County Fair and Exposition	995 (SB)
111	Ventura County Fair	491 (SB)
112	Disneyland	768/798 (OC)
113	Adventure City	767/797 (OC)
114	Legoland	1126 (SD)
115	Griffith Park Merry-Go-Round	564 (LA)
116	Santa Monica Pier Carousel	671 (LA)
117	Shoreline Village Carousel	825 (LA)
118	Balboa Pavilion Carouosel	919 (OC)
119	Belmont Park Carousel	1267 (SD)
120	Seaport Village Carousel	1289 (SD)
121	Balboa Park Merry-Go-Round and Butterfly Rides	1289 (SD)
122	Westfield Santa Anita Fashion Park	567 (LA)
123	Chase Palm Park Carousel	996 (SB)
124	Water Play Area/Santa Fe Dam Recreation Area	568/598 (LA)
125	Puddingstone Reservoir Beach	600 (LA)
126	Santa Catalina Island	N/A
127	Catalina Terminal/Long Beach-Downtown	825 (LA)
128	Catalina Terminal/Long Beach-Queen Mary	825 (LA)
129	Catalina Terminal/San Pedro-Port of Los Angeles	824 (LA)
130	Catalina Terminal/Dana Point	971 (OC)
131	Catalina Terminal/Newport Beach	919 (OC)
132	Bolsa Chica Ecological Reserve	857 (OC)
133	The Snow in the Angeles National Forest	535 (LA)
134	Corona Del Mar State Beach	919 (OC)
135	Hermosa Beach	762 (LA)
136	Huntington State Beach and Huntington City Beach	887/888 (OC)
137	Laguna Main Beach	950 (OC)
138	La Jolla Shores	1227 (SD)
139	Leo Carrillo State Beach	625 (LA) 387 (SB/V)
140	Little Corona Del Mar Beach	919 (OC)
141	Manhattan Beach	732 (LA)
142	Newport Beach	918/919 (OC)
143	Redondo Beach	762 (LA)
144	San Clemente Beach	992 (OC)
145	Santa Barbara East Beach	996 (SB)
146	Santa Monica State Beach	671 (LA)
147	Seaside Lagoon	762 (LA)
148	Bob Hope Airport	533 (LA)
149	Brackett Air Field	600 (LA)
150	Cable Airport	601 (LA)
151	Compton Airport	734 (LA)
152	Corona Municipal Airport	18-20 (R)

SITE #	SITE NAME	THOMAS BROS. MAP PAGE #
153	El Monte Airport	597 (LA)
154	Fullerton Municipal Airport	738 (OC)
155	Hawthorne Municipal/Jack Northrop Field	733 (LA)
156	John Wayne Airport	859 (OC)
157	Long Beach Airport	795 (LA)
158	McClellan-Palomar Airport	1127 (SD)
159	Ontario International Airport	VII (LA)
160	Santa Barbara Airport	994 (SB)
161	Santa Monica Municipal Airport	672 (LA)
162	Torrance Municipal Airport/Zamperini Field	793 (LA)
163	Van Nuys Airport	531 (LA)
164	Whiteman Airport	502 (LA)
165	Museum of Flying	672 (LA)
166	Chino Planes of Fame Air Museum	682 (SB/R)
167	Kite Flying at the Beach	887/857/888 (OC)
168	Goodyear Blimp Airfield	764 (LA)
169	Temecula Valley Balloon and Wine Festival	125/126/116 (SB/R)
170	Travel Town Museum	563 (LA)
171	Union Station	634 (LA)
172	Anaheim Train Station	799 (OC)
173	Burbank Train Station	533 (LA)
174	Camarillo Train Station	524 (SB/V)
175	Carpenteria Train Station	998/1018 (SB/V)
176	Chatsworth Train Station	500 (LA)
177	Fullerton Train Station	738 (OC)
178	Glendale Train Station	564 (LA)
179	Irvine Train Station	891 (OC)
180	Los Angeles/Union Station	634 (LA)
181	Moorpark Train Station	496 (SB/V)
182	Oceanside Train Station	1106 (SD)
183	Oxnard Train Station	522 (SB/V)
184	San Clemente Train Station	992 (OC)
185	San Diego Train Station	1289 (SD)
186	San Juan Capistrano Train Station	972 (OC)
187	Santa Ana Train Station	829 (OC)
188	Santa Barbara Train Station	996 (SB)
189	Simi Valley Train Station	498 (SB/V)
190	Solana Beach Train Station	1167 (SD)
191	Van Nuys Train Station	532 (LA)
192	Ventura Train Station	491 (SB/V)
193	Amtrak Trains	634 (LA)
194	Metrolink Regional Rail Trains	N/A
195	Metro Rail Red, Blue, Green and Gold Lines	N/A
196	Freight Trains	676 (LA)
197	Lomita Railroad Museum	793 (LA)
198	Griffith Park Train Ride	564 (LA)
199	El Dorado East Regional Park Train Ride	766/796 (LA)
200	Irvine Park Railroad	800/801 (OC)
201	Pasadena Model Railroad Museum	595 (LA)
202	San Diego Model Railroad Museum	1289 (SD)
203	Fillmore and Western Railway	456 (SB/V)
204	Bob Baker Marionette Theater	634 (LA)
205	Falcon Theater	563 (LA)
206	KLOS Story Theater	634 (LA)
207	Santa Monica Puppetry Center	671 (LA)
208	IMAX Theater at the California Science Center	674 (LA)
209	Los Angeles Convention Center	634 (LA)
210	Anaheim Convention Center	798 (OC)
211	Arrowhead Pond of Anaheim	799 (OC)

SITE #	SITE NAME	THOMAS BROS. MAP PAGE #
212	Long Beach Convention Center	825 (LA)
213	Los Angeles Memorial Sports Arena	674 (LA)
214	San Diego Convention Center	1289 (SD)
215	Staples Center	634 (LA)
216	Tournament of Roses® Parade	566 (LA)
217	Ringling Bros. and Barnum & Bailey Circus	799 (OC) & 674 (LA)
218	Faery Hunt	592 (LA)
219	Summer Sounds at the Hollywood Bowl	593 (LA)
220	Musical Circus Pasadena Symphony	565 (LA)
222	Walt Disney Music Concert Hall - Toyota Symphonies for Youth	634 (LA)

RADIO STATIONS

BIG BAND/SWING
- 570   KLAC-AM
- 88.1   KLON-FM
- 1260   KSUR-AM

COUNTRY
- 93.9   KZLA-FM

CLASSICAL
- 91.5   KUSC-FM
- 105.1   KMZT-FM

JAZZ AND BLUES
- 88.1   KJAZ-FM

NEWS RADIO AND TRAFFIC
- 94.7   NPR-FM
- 980   KFWB-AM
- 1070   KNX-AM

OLDIES/ROCK CLASSICS
- 93.1   KCBS-FM
- 95.5   KLOS-FM
- 99.9   KOLA-FM
- 101.1   KRTH-FM

POP
- 102.7   KISS-FM
- 104.3   KBIG-FM

TALK RADIO
- 640   KFI-AM

FREEWAY NUMBERS AND NAMES

NUMBERS AND NAMES:

(1) Pacific Coast Highway, PCH

(2) Glendale Freeway/
Angeles Crest Highway

(5) Golden State/Santa Ana/
San Diego Highway

(10) Santa Monica/San
Bernardino/Redlands Highway

(14) Antelope Valley Highway

(15) Barstow/Corona Highway

(22) Garden Grove Highway

(23) Moorpark Highway

(30) Foothill Highway

(39) Huntington Beach Highway

(47) Terminal Island Highway

(55) Newport Highway

(57) Orange Highway

(60) Pomona Highway

(71) Corona Highway

(74) Ortega Highway

(90) Marina Highway

(91) Artesia/
Redondo Beach Highway

(101) Hollywood/Santa Ana/
Ventura Highway

(103) Terminal Island Highway

(105) Century Highway

(110) Harbor/Pasadena Highway

(118) Simi Valley/San Fernando/
Ronald Reagan Highway

(126) Magic Mountain Parkway

(170) Ventura Highway

(134) Hollywood Highway

(210) Foothill Highway

(215) Barstow/San Bernardino/
Riverside/Escondido Highway

(405) San Diego Highway

(605) San Gabriel River Highway

(710) Long Beach Highway

PACKING LIST

- Antibacterial ointment
- Bags of Cheerios (one for your child and one for the birds and fish)
- Ball (blow-up beach balls are handy)
- Band-Aids
- Bibs
- Books
- Camera
- Diapers
- Hat
- Jacket
- Knife (plastic is best - to spread peanut butter, cut up fruit, or cut open a weird seed pod you found on a hike)
- Pediatrician's phone number
- Quarters (for parking, animal food, rides, etc.)
- Sand toys (for the beach)
- Snacks (a lot)
- Sun block
- Sweater
- Swim diapers
- Towel
- Water (a lot)
- Wipes
- Ziploc bags for collecting

EXTRAS FOR TIDE POOLS
- Big snack
- Dry clothes for adults
- Extra towel
- Rubber boots or tennis shoes (ones that can get wet and are good for walking on rocks)
- Two pairs of dry clothes for kids!

EXTRAS FOR SNOW:
- Big snack
- Boots
- Dry clothes for adults
- Mittens
- Sand toys
- Snow suit
- Towel
- Two pairs of dry clothes for kids!

OUR FAVORITE ROAD GAMES

Everyone has a pocketful of road games. These are the ones we like the most:

BINGO Song
Sing the song BINGO but make up your own verses (they don't have to rhyme) like:
There was a girl who really loved cats and Annie was her name-o; A-N-N-I-E, etc.
There was a boy who counted cars and Sammy was his name-o; S-A-M-M-Y, etc.

Find the Vehicle
Find the vehicles on the Picture Guide

Guess the Animal Drawing Game
Draw a part of an animal and see if your children can guess what it is. Add more parts and ask them again. Of course you need two adults (a driver and a drawer) for this game.

Three Favorite Things
This game is best after a visit. Ask your toddlers to name their three favorite things they saw during your visit. Tell your babies and toddlers your three favorite things.

Missing Number:
Count to ten and skip a number. See if your child can find the missing number.

OLDER CHILDREN

Travel Books for Older Children:

• Bates, Colleen Dunn and Susan LaTempa. *The Unofficial Guide to California with Kids.* Frommers, New Jersey,: 2004.

• Fraser, Laura Kath and Pamela Joy Price. *Fun with the Family in Southern California.* The Globe Pequot Press: Guilford, 2005.

• Diamond, Christine and Andrea Moriarty. *Kids Take L.A.* Bookhappy Books: New York, 2000.

• Kegan, Stephanie. *Fun Places to Go with Children in Southern California.* Chronicle Books: San Francisco, 1997,

• Oppenheimer, Lisa. *Around Los Angeles with Kids-68 Great Things to Do Together.* Fodor's Travel Publications: New York, 2002.

• Peterson, Susan. *Fun and Educational Places to Go with Kids in Southern California,* Fun Places Publishing: Lakewood, California, 2001.

• Precious, Lisa. *Premier Parent Los Angeles; A Survival Guide for Parents of Toddlers and Preschoolers.* Passport Books: Chicago, 2000.

• Weir, Kathy. *A Parent's Guide to Los Angeles.* Mars Publishing, Los Angeles, 2001.

ACKNOWLEDGEMENTS AND PHOTO CREDITS

• Page 32. Discovery Center of Natural History Museum of Los Angeles County. Photo by author. Permission to use photograph courtesy of Mary Baerg. Courtesy of the Natural History Museum of Los Angeles County.

• Page 38. Permission granted by Karla Buhlman of Gene Autry Entertainment to reproduce "Gene Autry's Cowboy Code."

• Page 53. Laidlaw Buses in the Pasadena School District Bus Yard. Photo by author. Permission to use photograph courtesy of Scott Walter and Trisha Kyles of the Pasadena Unified School District.

• Page 102. Geese at the Arboretum of Los Angeles County. Photo by author. Permission to use photograph courtesy of Peter Atkins of the Arboretum of Los Angeles County.

• Page 117-118. Children's Nature Institute Walks. Permission to reproduce Children's Nature Institute Walks courtesy of Lizette Castaño of the Docents of The Children's Nature Institute.

• Page 140. Los Angeles Zoo, Photo by author. Permission to use photograph courtesty of.

• Page 154. Blue Cavern Exhibit at the Aquarium of the Pacific. Permission to use photograph courtesy of Mary Vasiltsova of the Aquarium of the Pacific.

• Page 201. The Miniature Ferris Wheel at Adventure City. Photo by author. Permission to use photograph courtesy of Allan Ansdell of Adventure City.

• Page 232. Temecula Valley Balloon and Wine Festival. Photo by author. Permission to use photograph courtesy of Carol Popejoy-Hime of the Temecula Valley Ballon and Wine Festival.

• Page 245. Travel Town Museum. Photo by author. Permission to use photograph courtesy of Tom Breckner of the Travel Town Museum.

• Page 246. Rail Safety Tips. Permission to reproduce Rail Safety Tips courtesy of Warren Morse of the Los Angeles Metropolitan Transportation Authority.

• Page 258-259. Metrolink Maps. Permission to use maps courtesy of Lupe Valdez of Metrolink.

• Page 264. Metro Rail Map. Permission to use courtesy of Warren Morse of the Los Angeles Metropolitan Transportation Authority.

• Page 277. Puppetolio. Photograph courtesy of Steve Meltzer of Puppetolio.

• Some images used in picture guides © 2003 www.clipart.com.

• Freight train clip art by Ken Houghton and www.rrhistorical.com.

INDEX

OUR FAVORITE ADVENTURES

_____

_____

_____

_____

_____

_____

_____

_____

_____

_____

_____

OUR OWN DISCOVERIES

_____

_____

_____

_____

_____

_____

_____

_____

_____

_____

_____

ABOUT THE AUTHOR

JoBea Holt is the mother of twins and is writing books and articles for children about discovering our world. She received her Bachelor of Science degree from the University of California, Berkeley in 1976 and her PhD from Caltech in 1981, and was a scientist with NASA for 25 years. At the Jet Propulsion Laboratory, Dr. Holt's research ranged from the atmosphere of Venus to the arctic forests of Alaska using radar technology from the Pioneer Venus spacecraft, the Space Shuttle and international spaceborne imaging radar systems. During her time with NASA, Dr. Holt created a variety of hands-on educational programs for children using space technology, including KidSat, an earth-imaging digital camera in the window of the Space Shuttle that used NASA communications technology and the internet to allow students in their classrooms to operate the camera and download in the images from space during a mission. In her first non-NASA book, Baby's Day Out in Southern California, she shares with us her experiences and insights about discovering Southern California with babies and toddlers.

SEND US YOUR DISCOVERIES

If you know of a location to include in future editions of this book, or you found an error, please bring it to our attention. Just fill out the bottom half of this sheet and return it to the address listed below. You can also e-mail us at gembooks@aol.com or visit us on the web at www.gemguidesbooks.com.

Thank you for your help.

NAME OF SITE: _____

ADDRESS: _____

_____

_____

PHONE: _____

ADDITIONAL INFORMATION: _____

_____

_____

_____

RETURN TO:

Gem Guides Book Co.
315 Cloverlead Drive, Suite F
Baldwin Park, CA 91706